A Fiction Map

of

Wales

Wales Arts Review's
A Fiction Map of Wales

Edited by John Lavin

with a Foreword by Ali Anwar

The Poetry Foundation
Y Gefydliad Barddoniaeth

First published in 2014 by the H'mm Foundation
All texts © The contributors 2014
'Bolt' by Thomas Morris © Thomas Morris, used with kind permission
of the Wylie Agency (UK) Limited 2014
Artwork © Dean Lewis

Cover design by Dean Lewis © 2014

ISBN: 978-0-9927560-6-2

Typeset and designed by Dafydd Prys
Printed in Wales by Gwasg Gomer

Published by The H'mm Foundation, Grove Extension – Room 426,
Swansea University, Singleton Park, Swansea SA2 8PP

Wales Arts Review acknowledges the financial assistance of the Rhys
Davies Trust.

Wales Arts Review is an online magazine that provides high-quality criticism of the arts in Wales. It was founded in March 2012 – by Gary Raymond, Phil Morris, Dean Lewis and Dylan Moore – and has since become a digital community for writers concerned with questions regarding Welsh culture and its place within the wider world. As well as publishing essays, interviews and regular reviews of performances, books and arts events, *Wales Arts Review* commissions and publishes (in association with The Rhys Davies Trust) new short stories through its 'Fiction Map of Wales' project. A mentoring scheme for young critics was established by *Wales Arts Review* in 2013, supported by a grant from the Arts Council of Wales, and 2014 saw the launch of its search to identify the 'Greatest Welsh Novel' in a series of nominating essays and an online public vote.

Wales Arts Review also acknowledges funding from the Welsh Books Council and Wales Arts International. Thanks to this support it has been able to cover both the arts in Wales and international arts projects and festivals with established Welsh connections.

*

John Lavin has a doctorate in Creative Writing from the University of Wales, Trinity Saint David as well as an MA in The Teaching and Practice of Creative Writing from Cardiff University. He is the Fiction Editor of *Wales Arts Review* and also the Co-Founder, former Editor and current Associate Editor of *The Lampeter Review*.

The Rhys Davies Trust is a registered charity whose objectives are to promote the work of writer Rhys Davies (1901-1978), and to foster Welsh writing in English, especially in the valleys of south Wales. The trust was founded in 1991 by Dr. Meic Stephens, with funds generously provided by the writer's brother Lewis Davies.

The Trust supports such projects as the Rhys Davies Short Story Competition and bodies such as Literature Wales in a variety of initiatives designed to achieve its core aims in the Rhondda and across Wales. The plaques project, which commemorates a selection of Welsh writers in English, the Trust's support for Wales Arts Review's 'Fiction Map of Wales' series, and the republication of some of Rhys Davies's books, are other examples of its activities.

On the death of Lewis Davies, in December 2011, the Trust was left his entire estate and was able to pursue more ambitious schemes, such as the Rhys Davies Conference on the short story, hosted by Swansea University in 2013. In that same year Parthian Books published Meic Stephens' biography Rhys Davies: A Writer's Life, which won in the Creative Non-fiction category at the Wales Book of the Year Awards, 2014.

The Trust's Chairman is Professor Dai Smith, the Secretary is Dr Meic Stephens and its two other trustees are Dr. Sam Adams and Peter Finch. For more information on the trust and its work visit its website - http://www.rhysdaviestrust.org/

*

Rhys Davies (1901-1978) was born at Blaenclydach, near Tonypandy in the Rhondda, where his parents kept a grocer's shop. Leaving school at 14, he worked at a few menial jobs until, at the age of twenty, appalled by the Valley's coarse life, its chapel-culture and his own sexuality, he left for London. He was never to live permanently in Wales again.

He was among the most prolific and accomplished of Welsh prose-writers in English, publishing more than a hundred short stories, twenty novels, three novellas, two topographical books, two plays, and an autobiography.

In 1967 Rhys Davies won the Edgar, a literary prize awarded by the Mystery Writers of America, for his collection of stories, The Chosen One. This honour was swiftly followed by an OBE. In 1971 he was given the Welsh Arts Council's principal prize for his distinguished contribution to the literature of Wales. He died in a London hospital on 21st August 1978.

The appeal of Rhys Davies's work shows no sign of fading. Its humour, inventiveness, attention to detail, skill in creating moments of high drama, its ear for dialogue, and the writer's delight in human nature in all its variety, make his books compelling reading.

Contents

Foreword

Ali Anwar CEO H'mm Foundation

Publishing a book is always a huge responsibility for any publisher, particularly for a newly established one like the H'mm Foundation. We hope this volume will contribute towards promoting and celebrating Rhys Davies's work, one of the most prolific Welsh prose writers of the 20th century. We are indebted to the Rhys Davies Trust for their financial assistance, and delighted with the quality and variety of the contributions to this collection. We are most grateful to all contributors, to John Lavin for editing this volume and Dean Lewis for the artwork.

We have asked the best and most promising Welsh and Wales-based writers we could think of to write a story set somewhere in Wales. The story could be about anything so long as it was geographically Welsh. We deliberately didn't prescribe specific locations to specific writers because we wanted the writers to be as true to their creative instincts as possible. It seemed to us that we might end up with an inferior series if we tried to prescribe too tight a concept. Left to their own devices, the writers would probably write about contemporary Wales with a great deal of success.

And so it has proved – the collection is, I think, extremely revealing about modern day Wales. Not so much in terms of day to day minutiae but in terms of the psychology of the country in the 21st century. In each of these twenty-one stories, all of which are set in Wales, the writer has painted a unique picture of Wales in the post-industrial era.

The other aim of this collection is, of course, to foster new short fiction writing in Wales, which is why we place particular emphasis on the short story form. We also seek to increase the reputation of Rhys Davies, arguably this county's greatest ever short story writer. Davies is unquestionably an author of the first rank but he is also one who does not currently enjoy the same exalted readership and reputation as some of his international peers.

I am a businessman living in Cardiff with my wife Karen and two daughters, Lauren and Kathryn, having arrived from Baghdad, Iraq in 1997. Expecting to spend only a few days in Wales, a place I didn't know, I bought a return ticket – but I still haven't used the return part! My personal story as an 'accidental incomer' is far too long to tell, but yes, like most of the other 'accidental incomers' I fell hugely in love with Wales, its myths and people. I have been happily settled in the south of the country for over thirty-five years.

I started the H'mm Foundation, which is based at the Swansea University campus, with my close friends, the late Gower poet Nigel Jenkins and Wales's best writer Jon Gower. The aim is to build links between the business and the arts communities, and over the past three years the Foundation has been a creative experience for both, a huge source of inspiration for people in business and a source of additional income for writers. Publishing this volume in collaboration with *Wales Arts Review* is one result of this project.

I feel that my good fortune brought me to these shores, although my late mother's last words to me as I left Baghdad were: 'Mind your own business, and be careful with foreigners.'

Introduction

John Lavin

Rhys Davies was and perhaps is *the* Welsh short story writer. In his day he was praised by everyone from John Betjeman to D.H. Lawrence, from Muriel Spark to that master of the form, William Trevor. He won the Edgar Award for the Best Short Story published in the United States in 1966, and was retained on a contract by the *The New Yorker*; something that is indicative of the high esteem with which the literary world as a whole regarded him at that time. And yet, despite his status as arguably Wales' greatest practitioner of short fiction, his works are sadly not as widely read as they once were.

It was partly for this reason and partly out of a desire to encourage and promote new short fiction in Wales, that over the past two years, with the financial help of The Rhys Davies Trust, *Wales Arts Review* has published a series of stories by some of the best known names in Welsh literature, as well as by some of the most promising.

Like the majority of the Davies short stories, these pieces are all set in Wales. But like Davies, who memorably declared 'a curse on flag-waving', these stories are not in any way interested in parochialism, but rather in offering true reflections of society. That they are all set in Wales is not incidental but importantly, it is also not *defining*.

*

When James Joyce set about writing *Dubliners* at the beginning of the twentieth century, the intention was not merely to 'give Dublin to the world' but also to deliver 'a chapter of the moral history' of Ireland. When setting out to put *A Fiction Map of Wales* together, *Wales Arts Review*, while not perhaps having quite such deliberate intent as the great Irish writer, nevertheless did have it in mind to almost *inadvertently* create such an effect. Our reasoning was simply this: if, over the course of twenty-one months, we were to ask the majority of the most significant and promising Welsh writers in English to each contribute a short story that was set in a location in Wales of their own choosing, then how could the face of Modern Wales not reveal itself? Happily everyone we asked agreed.

Unlike Joyce, rather than seek to solely describe the country's capital city, we sought to give as many of the constituent towns and villages that make up the country of Wales 'to the world', as was possible. We did not, as Joyce did with Dublin at that time, see Cardiff as 'the centre of the paralysis' (even if the story that is set there does take place in that city's prison) but simply as one other place on the map (albeit clearly a highly significant one, considering the size of its population). Besides, in contemporary Wales we saw a lot to be positive about and a lot to be proud of too; as Joyce would perhaps have done had he written those Irish stories at a later period in his life (in a letter to his brother Stanislaus he reflected that he had not, in *Dubliners*, given enough time over to the warmth of his native people and to the beauty of their landscape). But, of course, we also saw a lot to worry and alarm, and a lot indeed to *mourn*. The twenty-one individually commissioned pieces collected in *A Fiction Map of Wales* reveal, as they should, a multi-faceted portrait of a by-and-large gentle-hearted nation that has not always been treated as kindly as it might be by its more powerful neighbour. This is perhaps why we think so much of *Dubliners* in this instance. Wales, like Ireland, is a country with a particular love for and indeed a particular gift for the creative arts, and it is a country in which you feel a distinctly palpable need for experience to be retold through art. This volume is important because it does just that. Over the twenty-one stories collected here we see the face of a nation emerge. It is a lived-in face to be sure but one with many stories to tell. One with many new, impassioned futures to *make*.

The stories reveal many things about Wales and, perhaps unsurprisingly, there is a strong emphasis on the repercussions of the closure of the mines and the general de-industrialisation of the country. This book is *very much* a Map of Wales in the post-industrial era.

The opening story, Rachel Trezise's 'The Abergorki Long Veg.

Growing Society', for instance, takes place in a town very like the author's hometown of Treorchy. (Abergorki takes its name, indeed, from Treorchy's first colliery, opened in 1859). Though ostensibly a humorous work dealing with the minutiae of Valleys' life, the piece also focuses, in Trezise's own words:

> quite heavily on what it means to be a man in a post-industrial landscape where male voices, quite literally in the case of the Treorchy Male Voice choir, have been dominant, but… now suffer… from mass unemployment and huge shifts in attitude and culture.

Stevie Davies' 'Tuner of Llangyfelach', meanwhile, examines both the personal history of her characters as well as the social history of South Wales, and finds the two to be inextricably linked. She introduces us to a narrator whose father was 'puzzled that the root of love should turn out so cloven.' As in her devastating recent novel, *Awakening*, Davies is more concerned with the roots of who we are both as individuals and as a society, rather than in the surface level dazzle which perpetuates so much of contemporary fiction. It is a stunning example of the short story teller's art, that medium which her namesake, Rhys Davies, once described as being formed out of 'the lapses into disorderliness of mind and the hidden impulses which provide… tiny, concentrated explosion[s]'.

Stories from the exciting group of young Welsh writers; Thomas Morris, Rhian Elizabeth, Joao Morais and Rhys Milsom; often speak with an unapologetic rawness about the realities of life for their own generation. They show teenage and twenty-something life as it is in the quiet, work-sparse post-industrial villages and towns. In 'Bolt', Morris' protagonist works in a video shop, lives with his ex-girlfriend's mum and has a one-night stand with a middle-aged counsellor. Unlike Sel in Trezise's tale, he is not an emasculated masculine figure but rather one for whom masculinity is an entirely different concept altogether. He is a deeply untraditional male figure and someone who would unquestionably appear profoundly emasculated to a person of Sel's background and generation. Lonely and lost (having moved from Bangor to Caerphilly to escape his violent father), he seeks comfort in middle-aged mother figures, while being happy to reveal facts such as the following:

> The first time I took off Hannah's [his ex-girlfriend] clothes, I was so turned on I came in my pants. She never found out though; I hid it well.

Hardly standard male braggadocio. When the middle-aged psychiatrist he goes home with reveals a penchant for rough sex his response is an endearing combination of perplexity, sadness and plain terror.

Moving away from stories which are so evidently coloured by socio-cultural and socio-economic questions, Cynan Jones' 'Aberarth', is a piece, nevertheless, that is drenched in a past from which the central alcoholic narrator cannot escape. A narrator whose emotional state is mirrored by the erosive landscape around the tiny seaside village which gives the story its title. As ever with Cynan Jones, the work is a startling one, brimming with an austere poetic intensity that seems particularly attuned to the area of West Wales that he calls home. Dic Edwards' 'Distance' meanwhile, set a few miles down the road in Aberaeron and the nearby village of Llanon, also deals with introspection, albeit the introspection of a man torn apart by grief. The main setting of a roadside café by the Llanon petrol station which the narrator thinks resembles the Edward Hopper painting, *Gas*, is used as a medium to discuss not only Edwards' feelings about the artistic process but also his reflections on the human condition.

Carly Holmes' 'Ghost Story' takes us back to Aberarth, and as with Cynan Jones' piece, Holmes seems to have also fallen under the spell of the beautiful Ceredgion landscape. 'Ghost Story' is a spine-tingling tale that does just what it says on the tin but it is also a wonderfully poetic piece that is deeply in touch with the environment within which it takes place.

Francesca Rydderch's 'Love: A Pathology' is also set in Ceredigion, the county that this most thoughtful of writers used to call home.

Needless to say, Rhydderch brings the verdant fields and woods of a west Wales summer to green-bright, blue-pulsing life. These evocations are, however, powerfully contrasted with the central protagonist's memories of urban life in her homeland of Russia, in a subtly nuanced piece that, as its title suggests, has a harder centre than you might at first think.

The Welsh landscape continues to mirror emotions in Georgia Carys Williams' ode to melancholy, 'Swansea Malady', and also in Kate Hamer's Christmas-set 'The Visit', a compellingly honest piece that revolves around the protagonist's return from London to her family home outside Machynlleth. The narrative of this Yuletide visit is the narrator's feelings of emotional isolation from both herself and her parents and yet the story is not one which is devoid of hope, ending as it does with a simple moment of communion.

Family relationships are also in turmoil in acclaimed poet Rhian Edwards' first full-length foray into short fiction. 'Beyond the Perforation' is a bittersweet marriage-counselling comedy that finds the narrator identifying with Bridgend (a location that her American husband desperately wants to leave) and claiming that:

> your hometown is like the black sheep of your family and only blood relatives have the natural right to slag it off. If anyone else tries to trash the place, you turn into a poor man's Braveheart, willing to defend the place to the death with a broken pint glass.

Elsewhere in the collection, the Welsh landscape takes on a more sinister appearance in Jon Gower's almost Tarantino-esque, 'Some Killing on Cydweli Flats'. Although the work is set in an area that Gower describes as being, 'my favourite part of Wales, the Gwendraeth estuary, a place visited only by wild-fowlers, birdwatchers and RAF personnel', the story is a particularly dark one about immigrant vegetable pickers ('cutting turnips for a pound-an-hour-less-than-minimum-wage') coming into unfortunate contact with the criminal underworld.

This a large and varied anthology, taking in dreams of Borges on Twmbarlum Hill (Richard Redman's dizzyingly inventive 'The Plagiarist'); a Welsh Marches poetry reading that doesn't take place (Richard Gwyn's darkly humorous treatise on the life of the artist, 'The Reading'); the tightrope-like relationship between a mother and her teenage son (Linda Ruhemann's poignant, Abergavenny-set 'Fear'); a glamorous film star detoxing in the Brecon Beacons (Gary Raymond's shimmering, elegiac 'How Shall We Sing to Her?'); musophobia in Bethesda in Lloyd Jones' delightfully witty 'The Elephant in the Room: A Case Study'; and an eccentric rug-seller in Tyler Keevil's perceptive, Powys-set meditation on the art of storytelling, 'Fabrications'.

The collection draws to a close with Robert Minhinnick's 'pre-apocalyptic' tale of two beachcombers camping out in the dunes of an environmentally damaged Sker Beach. Set in the not too distant future, 'Long Haul Beach' is, on the one hand, a warning; on the other hand, its message is already horribly close to the truth. Minhinnick, a writer who 'is obsessed by what sand conceals and what it reveals', may be looking at a small stretch of Welsh coastline but he is also telling us a wider story about ourselves and the way we treat each other and our environment. A fitting way to end a collection that has hopefully, to one degree or another, held up a mirror to a nation's psyche. And told some wonderful stories along the way too, of course.

John Lavin
Fiction Editor, *Wales Arts Review*

The Abergorki Long Veg Growing Society

Rachel Trezise

The church hall boasts its customary fête day smell; the mothballsy stink of old clothes from the jumble, stale buttercream from fairy cakes, offset by the faint parmesan stink of the wooden floor. It's here, on Friday nights, that Sel's twin ten-year-old daughters practise ballroom dancing barefoot. The women are fawning over the vicar, plying him with tea and French macaroons. Sel wants to snicker aloud at this cliché but knows the vicar is engrossingly handsome; a young thirty-something with bitumen black hair and big, brown beer-bottle eyes. If he was a woman he would; he knows he would. He drops Dai Tablet's beans on the pasting table set aside for the annual Abergorki long veg growing society show, then goes back to the car for his cucumbers. Cucumbers are Selwyn's thing: gently boomerang-shaped, smooth-skinned, a bright Islamic green. He's won every September for the past five years. The smell of them, acidic and dusty, leaches out of the hatchback as he lifts the door. He heard once their scent is an aphrodisiac. But not for Susan; it'd take an earthquake to rouse her.

As he crosses the courtyard he sees Dai Tablet's white box van approaching, the name of his chemist shop, 'Pascoe's Pharmacy' decaled on its side. Dai pulls up in the parking bay, the stone chippings spluttering under his tyres. 'Am I too late?' he says, clambering out, a package wrapped in newspaper held to his waist. 'Had to deliver an oxygen tank to the old girl on Tylecoch. You know what the one-way system's like on a Saturday.'

'You're alright,' says Sel. 'There's time to set up. What's that?'

Dai pulls the parcel closer to himself. 'Nothing,' he says defensively. Then he changes his tone, grinning nervously. 'It's something new I've been experimenting with in the greenhouse.' He drops the parcel to his side and presses his keys, the van locking behind him. 'Come on,' he hurries towards the church doors, the legs of his khaki corduroys rubbing together. Inside, Doug is setting his produce out on the crêpe tablecloth, carrots and leeks expertly arranged in a balsa wood fruit basket. He's wearing his Cardiff Blues jersey which he knows irks Selwyn no end, lifelong Ponty fan that he is.

'Men?' the vicar says, sidling to the table, as if the concept of male company is wholly alien to him, toned pectorals distinct under his tightly-fitting cassock. 'Would you mind exhibiting a little earlier than planned? The WI are behind schedule.' He checks his watch for effect. 'One of the ladies has gone back for a flan.'

'No problem,' Doug says absently, busy spraying his carrots with a water spritzer.

'Back in three,' the vicar says before turning to receive a bouquet of snapdragons from a child with a sticking plaster on its eyebrow. 'Let's see it, then,' says Sel, eyeing Dai Tablet's bundle. 'Must be pretty snazzy for you to do it away from the allotment, in secret. What is it? Spinach?'

'If you must know—' he drops the parcel on the table, softly unfolding the damp newspaper. 'It's cucumbers, the luxury type, not the Burpless, a different variety to yours.' They're different alright; thirteen inches apiece, sleek and tapered, glossy, spotless. Sel is thunderstruck. 'Good work,' Doug says, leaning over the fruits as if about to perform cunnilingus on them. 'Shut it, Doug,' Sel says shouldering him aside.

'What?' says Doug, affronted. 'There's nothing wrong with a bit of competition, Sel. Complacency comes in otherwise.'

'OK. Shut up.' Sel feels his temperature rising. A prickle moves across his sternum. The vicar's coming back, the black skirt of his cassock lending him a drifting quality – he appears to float through the cattle-like women, causing Sel to check his feet: encased in a pair of big and inappropriate hobnail boots. 'Where are we?' the vicar asks. He rubs his clean hands together, eyeing the produce perfunctorily. 'Beans,' he says, pointing casually at Doug's runners. No fanfare. No pomp.

Doug smiles slyly to himself. 'Thank you, vicar.'

'Cukes, then,' the vicar says.

'*Cucumbers*,' Sel corrects him. 'Cukes are something else entirely, related to the melon family.' The vicar shrugs, unruffled; could not care less about long veg or its given names. 'Cukes,' he repeats himself, gesturing at Dai Tablet's luxuries.

'You're kidding me?' Sel is instantly apoplectic. He wants to step onto the table and stamp the produce down like a wine presser squishing grapes.

'I don't *kid*, Mr Griffiths,' the vicar says, remembering Selwyn's surname.

Selwyn hears himself shrieking abruptly at the vicar, his Adam's apple swollen: 'You can't do this, you jumped up little arsehole.' He chops him once in the midriff, his teenage karate training coming back to him, quick and unstoppable as light. The vicar doesn't flinch. 'Excuse me, ladies,' he says, hurriedly scanning the room. He draws his elbow back, the whipcord of a crossbow. In a second Selwyn's on the floor, cwtched to the table's leg, the coppery taste of blood sloshing around in his mouth.

A countertenor voice is babbling away in the distance, boisterous with a falsetto lilt; talk of sheds, combination locks, ferrets. Selwyn opens his eyes, the lids slow and sticky. His vision is blurred, woolly patches of purple on the lens. He makes out his bare legs, resting on a Terylene sheet, stretching out into infinity. He's tall, he remembers, 6'3. At the seatbelt factory they called him 'the Griffith's tower.'

'I'm telling you, Siâny,' the voice says. 'The sequence is Chantelle's birth date. You remember that don't you?' Selwyn turns to see an overweight man in the hospital bed next to him, long seashell-white hair curling where it meets his rotund shoulders, a mobile phone pressed to his ear. 'Oh, it's you,' Sel says, as if he's known him all his life, though he's never met Georgie Pugh, not properly. He lives a few metres away from Selwyn in an area known colloquially as 'the villas'. The council sold the majority of the seven-bedroom properties off at the height of the housing boom. It's a sought after cul-de-sac now, the prices reaching into the millions, but the Pugh family were too numerous to be re-housed in the flats further down the valley. They remain a comical presence in lucky number 7, infamous throughout Abergorki. Susan calls them 'the Clampetts' after the American sitcom, The Beverly Hillbillies, a phrase the girls have adopted despite never seeing the show. Georgie's been cautioned by the police for the eighth time recently, having continuously allowed his seven-year-old granddaughter to ride his cherry-coloured mobility scooter unattended around the grove.

'Just ask our Jenna for Chantelle's birth date,' Georgie barks into his phone. 'Silly bitch,' he says under his breath as he ends the call. He throws the handset into his bedside drawer. Noticing Selwyn gawping at him he says, 'Iesu Mawr, butty! That's what I'd call a shiner.'

'You should see the other guy,' Sel says thinking for the first time since the incident about the vicar; his felt cassock and hobnail boots, like something from a late night B-movie — the costumes unconvincing. He had a jab on him, fair play. Turn the other cheek, by Christ. Susan'll have Sel's balls in the smoothie-maker for this. He knows she's got a soft spot for the vicar herself, knows it by the way she insists on taking the girls ballroom dancing at the church when clearly they'd prefer the Am-Dram at the Park & Dare.

'Never had you down for a slugger,' Pugh says. He throws his blanket aside, a whorl of show-white hairs on his hot air balloon of a gut. His bare feet hit the linoleum with a slap. 'Must be the stress? The redundancy and what not?' Sel casts his cloudy glare around the other men on the ward; greying creatures packed into their bedclothes like caterpillars in chrysalises; sleeping. Or deaf. 'What do you mean?' he says, his voice a cranky, accusatory whisper.

'Well,' Pugh raises his volume rather than lowering it. 'You must have been on a tidy wage down there. Floor manager, weren't you? And those villas don't pay for themselves. Your missus must be on your back like a stink on a rat out of the Tâf.' Sel hadn't realised that gossip can work both ways, that Georgie could detect, note and repeat his and Susan's misfortunes the way they did the Pugh's. Embarrassingly he'd hit the nail on the head. Susan expected Sel to glide placidly into a new managerial position but he wanted to spend some of his hard-earned goodbye cheque mooching about, perfecting the Burpless, maybe try out some of the leafier stuff. He'd thought that was what Dai Tablet was doing. What idiot would attempt the luxury in the metal- contaminated soil of the valleys? And where the hell did Susan think Sel was going to find a job slap in the middle of a double-dip recession?

'Can you walk?' Pugh asks him.

'I don't know. I haven't tried.'

'Well, try. It's only a touch of concussion.' He smiles, baring toothless red gums. 'Come downstairs with me, have a fag.' He pulls a navy housecoat around his fleshy pink bulk. 'I don't smoke,' Sel tells him.

'Yes, you do, you fibber,' Pugh says. He points with an archer's fore-and-middle finger at his own sunken eyes. 'I've seen you on that decking of yours in my bins, every night, quarter-to-midnight, same time that barmaid from the RAFA gets back and into the shower. Duw, there's a pair of apples on that one, ey?' He lifts a hand-rolled cigarette to his lips and turns, scuffling out of the ward.

Selwyn thinks he might be dreaming when in Georgie's place he glimpses Susan, grappling through the double doors, loaded with the full five-piece set of silver Samsonite luggage they'd purchased for their Mediterranean cruise two summer's ago. On spotting him she drops the hatbox. It hits the floor with a crack and opens, his work ties springing out like joke snakes from a can. 'You!' she says, leaving the luggage at the doors. She approaches his bed, arms swinging. 'I swear you're the stupidest man who ever lived! And pretty soon you'll be the sorriest.'

Sel hasn't had time to formulate a plan, devise an explanation. He studies her sheepishly, his head pushed back into the pillow. He tries to project some semblance of control, composure. 'Just got a bit out of hand, that's all.'

'The vicar?' she says. She stands at the foot of the bed, wringing her hands, her engagement, wedding and eternity rings flashing in and out of view. She's wearing a knee-length summer dress, poppy print on beige, her mousy hair scraped into a messy French roll. She's got a cracking pair of legs on her, Sel's wife.

'What about it?' he says. 'Just because he's a vicar, a man of God. Doesn't mean he *is* God. Five years running I've won that competition. He wouldn't know a good cucumber if you stuffed one up his jacksy.' He sits up a little, energised by his outburst, wondering where it's come from. Maybe they've given him medication. Susan claps her hands over her nose, mortified. 'Don't you even start with that,' she says. It takes Sel a moment to cotton on. 'Once!' he hisses. *One* time he'd suggested experimenting with the produce after hearing about its aphrodisiacal properties. She'd banished him to the attic room for a fortnight. 'Listen,' he says. He takes a deep breath, buying time, wondering what to say next—he has to talk her down. 'There's no need for a scene. No harm done! A couple of black eyes,' he waves, his hand fluttering, as if shooing the injury away. 'It's not like I'm going to press charges on the vicar—'

'You listen!' she says, cutting in. 'They phoned and asked me to bring your things. Here they are.' Man and wife gaze momentarily at the heap of suitcases blocking the gangway. 'All of it,' Susan says. 'I'm filing for divorce. What kind of man cares more about veg than his own two daughter's futures? Not the kind of man I want in my life.'

'You're going to make a play for the vicar?' he asks her. 'Move into the vicarage?'

'Don't be ridiculous!' She pulls at the blouse of her dress. He notices the dark crescent moon sweat patches under her breasts; the strain from the luggage, the stairs. 'A wife is supposed to stand by her husband— ' he knows, even as he's saying it, that he's making a grave mistake. But one of the old men on the opposite side of the ward is awake, a glitter coming into his eyes at the unexpected drama. 'A wife is supposed to have her husband's back. Why do you believe the vicar automatically over me? You don't know him. You don't know what he's like. He could be a kiddy-fiddler for all you know.'

Georgie Pugh is back from his cigarette-break, loitering in the corridor, squinting through the frost-striped window, ogling Susan's calves. 'You disgust me,' she squeals at Sel. She turns on her sandals, heading for the doors. Eyeing him over her shoulder, she says, 'Don't bother coming back to the villas, Selwyn,' a touch of head-mistress trickling into her voice. 'I'm having the locks changed. I might even get the vicar to do it.'

'La-dee-da,' Georgie says, swinging his hips, trying to impersonate Susan and her hard-boiled femininity. It comes off cretinous, grotesque; a bit pantomime dame. A nurse in a lilac tennis-style dress appears, looking from the spilled luggage to Sel and back again, her pretty, plump lips pursed. 'I can hold this in the staffroom for you,' she offers eventually. 'Just for the time being.' She rests her manicured hand on the metal footboard, millimetres away from Sel's gnarled toes. 'The doctor'll be around in the morning anyway,' she simpers. 'Maybe then he'll sign you out.' She looks again at the hodgepodge of ties on the floor. 'I'll call for a porter.'

'Smile, mun,' Pugh says to Sel. He throws his smoking paraphernalia into the bedside drawer. 'Tea trolley'll be around in a minute.'

The tea is scalding. It irritates the emergent ulcers on Selwyn's tongue. After three sips he sets the paper cup on the overbed table, giving up. 'Now's our chance,' Pugh says purring conspiratorially at him from the adjacent bed. 'After they've come for the cups. Before the visiting starts. The nurses change shift. We can sneak down for some fresh air.'

'I told you. I don't smoke.' Selwyn turns away from Pugh to look at his neighbour on the left. The man is in his nineties, features eaten away by age. A catheter tube runs from under the blankets into a bag propped on the bed's frame, half full of a glowing yellow liquid, the exact colour of the energy drink that makes the girl's hyper. Suddenly he can smell the hospital; disinfectant, winter vegetables boiled to mush.

'You're sure now, are you?' Pugh bellows at him.

Georgie's spare dressing gown is short and wide. Sel can wrap it twice around his torso while the hem barely covers his testicles. He holds the material to himself, his arms crossed rigid below his waist.

Georgie leads him along the crazy paving and towards a metal cabin at the edge of the hospital grounds. 'See,' he says, strutting past the hydrangea shrubs lining the boundary. 'Disused office. Where the parking attendant used to be. He's redundant now too. Hospital car parks are free in Wales and good enough for the miserable sod.' He invites Sel into the hut with a swoosh of his arm, his loose flesh shaking. He stoops, rummaging in a plastic bag hidden under the desk, coming up with a flagon of cheap cider. 'Cheers,' he says, loosening the cap, bringing it to his mouth.

'What are you in hospital for?' Sel asks him, shocked at his audacity.

'I dunno. Blood pressure or something.' He shrugs, handing the bottle over to Sel. Selwyn holds it by the neck, the palm of his other hand pressed lightly against its base. 'Have you ever worked a day in your life?' he asks Pugh. Other than long veg, work is the only subject Selwyn talks about with other men, or did, until the redundancy. He hopes Pugh'll tell him about a stint at the glazing factory or a couple of weeks in the slaughterhouse, anything that can bring the conversation around to shift patterns, health and safety.

'Nope!' Georgie says proudly, licking at a cigarette skin. 'Model aeroplanes, I do.'

'You don't want to work?' Selwyn is still hoping for a chance to lament six straight weeks of afternoons in spring 2008.

'Nope!' Georgie says. He lights his roll-up. 'What's the point? No work about for a person of my below-par breeding. She made it that way, Thatcher. I would have gone down the mine, after my grandfather. We were built for that; short.' He holds his hand flat at his flabby chest, as if measuring a child's height. 'Capitalism is a kind of anarchy, mun. Everyone out for what they can get. Maybe you thought you'd got a little bit at your manager's desk on the industrial estate. They do that. They fool you into thinking you can climb some stinking ladder then they kick it from under you. Not for me, boy. I'm not marching to their tune.'

'Fair enough,' Selwyn says. He doesn't want to get into an argument about dignity. Self-respect.

'What are you going to do with all that money, anyway? Go on holiday and come back moaning about the queues at the airport? I can look at the Med on the TV.' Georgie sucks thoughtfully at his tobacco. 'Model aeroplanes,' he says again.

'Cucumbers,' Selwyn says, as if from nowhere. He lifts the cider to his nose and sniffs at it, the bubbles pricking his nostrils. He takes a sip. It's sweeter than he'd expected. 'Guess who thumped me?' he asks Pugh; he'll never guess.

'The vicar,' Georgie says, nonplussed. 'It's all round the hospital, mun. Guess who the vicar is?'

Selwyn shrugs, disconcerted; his business splashed around like spilled milk, stray cats surfacing to feast on it.

'My nephew.' Georgie bears his inflamed gums, grinning. 'By marriage. 'Course, we don't talk to him. An excommunicant so to speak.'

'Why?' Selwyn asks. He's onto something here. 'Why don't you speak to him?'

'You really want to know?'

'I knew it!' Sel slaps his thigh, drunk on mischief. 'He's a paedo, isn't he? I told her.'

Georgie reaches for the bottle, shaking his head. 'Not kids. No. He fucked a dog.'

Selwyn splutters, a slug of cider gone down the wrong way.

'Springer spaniel,' Pugh adds, stone-eyed. 'When he was travelling, around Australia. He took photos, see. Missus found 'em in her mother's house. Nothing like bestiality to set the missus off. Little runt couldn't have picked a worse way to upset his auntie. She can't bear no jokes about sheep-shagging. You know, I've got to agree with her. Why would you fuck a dog? That's what too much travelling does to you, fries the brain.' He looks up from the bottle, gauging Selwyn's reaction. 'Smart woman, my missus. She can't read a word, but duw; she can turn her hand to anything. You should see her on that sewing machine of hers. She shortened the dressing gown you're wearing.'

Susan is visibly tired, drab bags under her eyes, her foot wedged behind the front door. She beholds Selwyn and Georgie, stood on the doorstep, a pair of comedians, like Bert and Ernie. A taxi in the drive, its engine running, the Samsonite luggage piled on the back seat. Selwyn sees a stack of washing, heaped in a black bag in the porch, the girl's Hello Kitty pyjamas poking out of the top. 'What's wrong?' he asks her, pointing them out. 'The bloody machine is on the blink,' she spits, as if it's his fault.

'Well let me in. I can do it.'

Reluctantly she edges the door open. Sel goes straight to the washing machine in the mud room. He stoops at the back of it, driving his hand into its workings, feeling for irregularities. 'Would you do that in your own house?' he hears Susan asking Pugh. He can feel something; nylon, wrapped around the cylinder. He pulls at it while he wonders what Georgie's up to. A glittery pair of tights, one of the girl's, pings out and into his lap, shredded and sodden. He balls them up and carries them to the living room where Georgie is sitting, his feet up on the coffee table. 'The filter pump,' he tells Susan, who's stood, frozen, her hands on her hips. 'Georgie told me something about the vicar,' he says next. 'Something terrible. The vicar's Georgie's nephew.'

'He fucked a dog,' Pugh says, without warning. In the car they'd agreed that Sel would say it. Susan crows, exhausted and disbelieving. 'So what? Why are you telling me?'

'So what? So you know what kind of bloke he is. He rapes pets, gul.'

'You think I'm falling for that?' She's steely, preparing to throw them out.

'Tell you what,' Pugh takes his feet from the table, shabby leather slippers dropping lazily to the Oriental rug. 'Let's go up there, to the vicarage, confront the bugger. We've got a taxi waiting outside.' Susan thinks about it. She looks at the Salvador Dalí-style clock on the mantelpiece above the wood burner, a wedding gift from Selwyn's mother. 'This is a waste of my time,' she says. She looks at Selwyn, puppy-eyed. 'The girls have a competition tonight. I've got to get their dresses pressed.'

'Missus'll press their dresses,' says Pugh. 'Dab hand with the old flatiron.'

Susan wrinkles her nose at the suggestion.

'It's only a couple of streets away,' Selwyn says. 'It won't take five minutes. And if Georgie's lying, if the vicar's right, I'll apologise. If it's what you want, I'll be out of your life.'

She sighs, resigned, wanting Georgie off the settee, away from her Oriental rug.

They ride in the taxi, Susan up front. Selwyn sits on the mid-sized suitcase in the back, Georgie squeezed next to him, stinking of cider. They ease out, all three of them, when the taxi pulls up beside the vicarage's front garden in Cadowen Street, gawping at the fascia like children about to step into a dentist's. A Dahlia bush in the corner is well kept, buxom with pale yellow flowers. The assistant comes to the door, a middle-aged woman in a powder blue trouser suit. 'Kevin!' She calls the vicar by his Christian name, not waiting for introductions. 'Kevin, come out here.'

'Sorry to trouble you,' Susan says, timorous, regretful.

'What is this?' The vicar's wearing a black shirt over blue jeans, a chink of white dog collar gleaming between his clavicles. He steps out, squinting against the low autumn sun, liquorice hair flat, damp from the shower. 'Get away from here!' he shouts at Pugh.

'There's a way to speak to your uncle,' Sel says.

Pugh steps up to the vicar, snorting, his nostrils opening and closing like a bull's. He draws his fat head back, then releases it, nutting the vicar square in the neck, the crack like a Rich Tea biscuit snapping. The vicar flops to his knees, a hot worm of blood spurting up the doorframe. The assistant slumps, her hands flickering uselessly about the young man's shoulders. 'For reporting Chantelle to the law,' Georgie says. 'That'll learn you! Where's the harm in a little girl riding a scooter?' He brushes his hands, as if of blood, though they're perfectly clean. To Susan he says: 'Spiteful, mun. Just spiteful.' Susan covers her mouth with both hands, talking into her palms.

Georgie laughs, a tremolo chuckle, then turns and runs, his rolypoly body jouncing down the garden path.

Bolt

Thomas Morris

I'm filling my satchel with Butterkist popcorn and soon-to-be-gone-off Dairy Milk when she comes into the store. She looks at my bag, puts a hand over her eyes, and says in a costume-drama voice, 'I've seen nothing, Andy. Continue as you are.' She walks a steady pace through the New Releases aisle, the sound of her heels muffled by the red carpet. She used to come in with her husband, but I haven't seen him in months.

The shelves are almost bare, and all week the regulars have commiserated me, expressed their regrets at the situation. Sometimes I'll say in pretend anger, 'I'm mad as hell and I'm not gonna take it anymore!' And sometimes I'll say not much at all, just nod and accept their apologies and money.

But I'm not desperate yet. Rent at Hannah's mother's is low, less than low – it's just bills and some contribution to food that she often won't even accept. I think it's partly guilt at the way her daughter treated me, but I reckon she also enjoys the company. And we do get on – she's like Hannah without the neurotic stuff.

The woman makes a funny trotting noise with her mouth as she walks through the Ex-Rentals aisle, then looks at me and laughs. Aside from the closure, the horse has been the talk of the day. There was a wedding up by the castle, and the couple had booked a horse-drawn cart. Martin, the town's only homeless man, told me about it earlier.

'I seen it!' he said, like some sea captain describing a mermaid sighting. 'The guys unhooked the horse to fix a wheel on the cart and – bang! – she was gone, just like that. It ran through the town, on its own – cartless! Women were screaming, and children cheered wildly! But when it reached a red light by the shopping centre, it just stopped. It saw the red light and wouldn't move. And before the lights turned green, the owners had caught up with it and reined the bugger back up!'

'But why did it stop at the lights?' I said.

'I dunno,' Martin said. 'You'd have to ask the horse.'

The woman pulls to a sudden halt at the Classics section, with her elbows resting at her side, her arms out in front, her hands bent like hooves. She's the town's only psychiatrist and she's pretending to be a horse.

'Is this one any good, Andy?' she says, holding up a video. Hannah used to have sessions with her when she was younger, and told me she found her "creepy". But I've always liked the psychiatrist. She looks good for her age – late forties, I'd guess – and the store always smells nice after she leaves.

'What is it?' I say.

'*The Apartment.*'

'Ah. Romance at its most anti-romantic – that is the Billy Wilder stamp of genius, and this Academy Award winner from 1960 is no exception.'

She looks down at the video.

'That's just the blurb, Andy,' she says. 'Is it any good?'

'I haven't seen it,' I say. 'I just know all the synopses.'

'So now you confess.'

'Yeah. Like a man on death row.'

She puts the video down, then realises it's the wrong shelf. She goes to put it back, but I tell her not to bother.

'You can't beat VHS, can you?' she says. She sweeps a hand through her brown-grey hair, and bracelets jangle on her wrist.

'Oh you can,' I say. 'The amount of time I've wasted in front of a video player waiting for the bloody thing to rewind –'

My phone vibrates before I finish my speech. There's a message from Hannah's mum: dinner's in the microwave, I can heat it up when I get in.

Back at the till, I take some chocolate from my satchel. It's late in the evening and my sugar levels are low. Hannah's mother has taught me all about this – the need for regular eating, and the importance of listening to my body. She's good like that; she takes an interest.

'How you feeling about it all then?' the psychiatrist says, trotting over to me.

I lift my head above the counter, and put a hand to my mouth to hide the chomping.

'Sad to be leaving,' I say. 'But it's a good chance to do something else, you know. I might go travelling for a bit.'

'Where you thinking Andy?'

It feels nice to hear her say my name. But I've seen enough mental-hospital films to know it's all part of the psychiatrist's toolkit.

'Well?'

I gesture at my mouth to show I need to finish chewing before I speak. It'd be nice to say her name to her too, but I don't know what it is. She did tell me once, but I can't remember it. My boss doesn't know her name either, and she's been coming in for too long for us to ask her straight out.

I swallow the last melted lump of Dairy Milk and I can feel the chocolate coating my teeth.

'Australia,' I say. 'Did you ever see *Picnic at Hanging Rock*?' I think her name might be Andrea, but I can't be sure – she's always used her husband's membership card.

'Don't bother,' she says. 'I lived in Melbourne for three years. It's full of racists and the sun goes down at six. Winter or summer, it's dark when you finish work.'

'It looks amazing though,' I say. 'All that space and freedom. And –'

'You should go to Berlin,' she says. 'It's a great city. And the people there actually value their freedom, you know? They fought for it.'

I think of *Goodbye Lenin!*, of old men with hammers at the wall, of hands touching through the gaps where bricks had been, of the boy's mother sleeping through it all.

'But I don't speak German,' I say.

'Yeah, well,' she says, 'neither do they.'

I nod, like a pupil receiving instruction.

'What are you doing tonight then?' she says. She raises her left foot and caresses the back of her right calf with it. If I were a woman, would I wear heels to a video store?

'Tonight? I say. 'Nothing.' I run my tongue across my teeth and they feel grainy with the chocolate.

'Your last night and you're doing nothing?'

'Correct.'

'*Verrry* interesting,' she says, all Transylvanian.

Since Hannah left I've barely been out. All the people I know around here are *her* friends, and now we're not together they don't particularly want to see me. Besides, most of the good ones have left the town too. So if I'm not working, I just stay in the house and watch *Wallander* with Hannah's mum.

The woman continues her way round the store, picking up videos and putting them down.

'Everything's a pound,' I call out to her.

'I saw the signs,' she says.

The strip-light flickers. It clicks and clanks like there's a bee trapped in there. I'd change the bulb but there's really no point.

Hannah once told me that at each session the psychiatrist tried to make her cry. She told her that Hannah's family didn't speak about their issues, about the divorce, and that's why Hannah had the problems she had. According to Hannah, the crying didn't help though. She'd just leave more upset than when she arrived.

I walk through the shop, straightening the videos.

'Where's the boss then, Andy?' the psychiatrist says when I get to her aisle. 'Isn't she here for the big goodbye?'

'It was her mate's wedding earlier,' I say. 'She's at the party now. We have to come back in on Sunday anyway – to pack everything up – so we'll get to say goodbye then.'

'I meant a big goodbye to valued customers like me, Andy. Am *I* not valued?'

'Very much so,' I say. Tom Hanks on the cover of *Big* stares out at me, as if he knows I've been stealing chocolate. 'But I'm the only one here, I'm afraid.'

She smiles.

'I suppose you'll have to do, Andy. Anyway, don't mind me. You must be closing up in a bit?'

'No worries,' I say. 'Take your time.'

She picks up *The Apartment* again.

'What do you think then? Fancy watching it?'

'In here?' I say.

'No, no. At my place.'

I think of the meat and vegetables going cold in the microwave, the gravy congealing.

'Ah, come on,' she says. 'Come keep an old woman company.'

Outside, autumn lurks like a mugger. You can feel the change in the air, on your cheeks. My boss told me that before it was a video shop the place used to be a garage. The car-park is where the forecourt used to be. And there's something about this bottom part of town that feels like a garage, like somewhere that people are only passing through.

When I pull down the shutters, and padlock the bolt for the last time, I get the same feeling I used to have the night before a new school year. The feeling that'd make me lay my uniform out on my bedroom floor, down to the socks and shoes, and then lie in bed not-sleeping.

Sitting beneath the ATM, lit by Dominos Pizza, Martin holds a sign saying, 'Need money for a penis reduction. Live free or die trying!' I unzip my bag and hand him four bags of Minstrels and a party-share-sized bottle of Coke.

'I turn up for five years and this is all I get?' he says, and he readjusts his Man Utd bobble hat.

'It's more than I'm getting,' I say.

'What you gonna do now then?' he says.

'Go home,' I say.

The psychiatrist walks towards her car. With his teeth, Martin tears open a packet of Minstrels. He looks beyond me, to the car park.

'I meant now as in tomorrow,' he says. 'Like next week, what you gonna do?'

'I dunno,' I say.

He lifts the pack to his mouth and tips the Minstrels in.

'You should get another job, mun.'

'Good advice,' I say, and watch him chew.

He looks past me again, to the psychiatrist standing by the car. I turn around and look at her. Her hand is resting on top of the door.

'You best be off,' he whispers. 'Rule number seven: never be late for the shrink.'

She drives us up through town, past the castle, past the old furniture shop and past the closed-down post-office. The car smells minty from the little green tree that hangs on the rear-view mirror. In the headlights, I can see horse shit on the road, flattened with tyre tracks. When we get up near the train station, a group of girls with heels the size of Coke cans run across us, ignoring the lights. The psychiatrist pulls up sharply and beeps. One of the girls slaps the bonnet.

'Motherfucker,' she shouts at us, and then she slowly crosses the road, staring at us the whole time.

'Nice,' says the psychiatrist. 'A healthy attitude to anger.'

'I bet the horse would have stopped,' I say.

'You reckon?' she says.

'Aye,' I say. 'He sounds like he had a *healthy* respect for authority.'

'Bollocks,' she says. 'There's no such thing.'

We drive past St Martin's church, down St Martin's road, and then up Caerphilly mountain.

'You hungry?' she says.

'Yeah,' I say.

'I never cook,' she says. 'What do you think about getting a burger?'

The Snack Bar is a wooden shack at the top of the mountain. On the menu it says, 'Established in 1957 – We Are Older Than Motown And *Coronation Street*'. The psychiatrist orders us both a Mountain Monster Burger, and the guy tells us it will take five minutes. I bring out my wallet, but the psychiatrist insists on paying The burger man laughs.

'Just let your mam treat you,' he says. He has a big face, and his pores are visible even though it's dark. We don't correct him, and he keeps on smiling.

'Where've you come from tonight then?' he asks. I say Caerphilly, and he starts going on about the horse.

'They came up here for their wedding photos, they did,' he says, pressing the burgers down with metal tongs. 'They came here on their first date so they wanted photos of themselves with a burger.'

'That sounds very romantic,' the psychiatrist says. I see her voice in front of us, a warm breath in cold air. And the oil in the pan spits and spats.

'Aye,' says the burger man. 'Well, they came up here and told me about the horse running off like that. It's mad innit? I can't believe it stopped at the lights.'

We agree that it's mad, and the burger man tells us how he's actually an actor and a writer, that this job is just something he does to pay the rent. He gives us a flyer to a play he's written and starring in. There's a picture of him wearing a silver suit, a ball of flames behind him, and the words 'Trial and Error' arched around his head in Comic Sans.

'What's it about?' the psychiatrist asks, squinting at the flyer in the burger shack's light.

'It's about a guy who's not very good at having relationships,' he says, and he takes a handful of onion slices from a tupperware box and tosses them into the pan. 'But it's very humoristic though. It's a comedy. Do you reckon you can come see it?'

I tell him I'll definitely try, and we take a seat at the one of the tables. Down below us the streetlights chart the housing estates, and Caerphilly twinkles in the night.

'I like your coat,' the psychiatrist says.

'Thanks,' I say. 'My ex's mum bought it for me.'

The psychiatrist smiles, then looks past me, over to the town. She's got a concentrating look going on, as if she's remembering something. Hannah used to be the same. We'd be having a conversation and then she'd tune out and stare off at the corner of the ceiling.

'Caerphilly looks alright, doesn't it?' I say, looking behind me.

'Yeah. It's a paradox though.'

'What is?'

'The fact that it only looks nice when you're away from it.'

I nod and try to pick out the castle down there among the lights. There's a sound of shoes over pebbles then – the man bringing us our burgers.

'Cracking, innit?' he says, looking over the town.

'It is,' I say.

'I reckon I've got the best view in all of south Wales,' he says, and he sets a plastic ketchup bottle down on our table. 'Anyway, have a good un.'

I eat my burger greedily, glad to have something warming my hands. She nibbles hers slowly, like she's not even that hungry. And she keeps watching me, too. So after a few too many big bites, I go, 'Well, thank you, I really needed this.'

'You're welcome,' she says slowly, and she puts her food down. She taps a finger on her cheek, then. 'You've some sauce on your face.'

'Yeah?' I say. 'Well, it's the new style now. All the kids are doing it.'

*

Her hallway smells recently hoovered. She flips a switch and the place still feels dark. She lights incense in the living room and brings out red wine and purple tumblers from the kitchen.

'Do you want some?' she says.

'Why not,' I say, settling down on the orange couch.

'I'll turn the heating on now,' she says. 'The place will be like Spain in no time.'

We toast to new beginnings, though I don't know what new thing I'm actually beginning, and we both take sips.

On the wall above the telly there's a photo of a naked man and woman grappling each other.

'Can I use your toilet?' I say.

'Depends what you want it for.'

'Mostly toilet things.'

'Then yes,' she says. 'It's the second door on the left there.'

Like her, the bathroom smells nice. There's pictures of flowers on the wall, and there's potpourri or something on the cistern. I go to wee but nothing comes out. This happens a lot. I'll go to the bathroom to escape awkwardness or take time out, but when I get there I'll forget this and try to piss.

I sit down on the toilet and send Hannah a sad face for a text:
☹

She hasn't replied to my last few.

The film is funnier than I thought it'd be. But it's really sad too. When Shirley MacLaine overdoses on sleeping tablets I can't watch. It seems too real.

'Here's a question,' I say, during a lull.

'Thanks for the warning,' she says, picking at her sleeve.

'Do you know what the two most popular phrases in US films are?'

'Let me think,' she says, and she tilts her head as if that'll help. 'Ummmmmmm. No.'

'*Let's get out of here* and *Try and get some sleep now*,' I say.

'Interesting,' she says.

When Shirley MacLaine says to Jack Lemmon 'Shut up and deal', we're both in tears. The psychiatrist wipes her eyes with her sleeve and goes to the kitchen. She comes back in with another bottle of wine, pours us large measures, then starts talking about Simon, her first husband. She says the marriage was *emotionally demanding*. I don't know what to say, so I edge the conversation back to her job. She tells me how draining she finds it. I ask her to diagnose me, and she laughs.

'I'm not very good at guessing personality types, Andy. That's not how counselling works. You seem a very nice boy though. And that's a professional judgment, by the way.'

'I'm twenty-three,' I say.

'Yes, like I said: a boy.'

I look down at her carpet. It's green.

'Whatever happened to that girl you were with?' she says. 'I haven't seen her in ages.' She dips her hand deep into the popcorn to retrieve whatever's left. She puts some to her lips.

'Moved to London,' I say.

'Ah, an ambitious one then. Ambitious people always end up in the cities. Well, until they have a breakdown and come back. Are you two still together?'

'Not exactly.'

'Oh?'

'We're on a break.'

In reality, Hannah broke up with me three months ago and I spend my nights sending her aggressive, depressing emails, getting to bed around the same time as the moon.

I've popcorn kernels stuck between my teeth and I dig a sneaky fingernail in to wedge them out.

'Do you resent her?' she asks.

I still have my finger in my mouth. I move it from the caverns of the molars to the wisdom tooth that's coming through at the back.

'Why would I?' I say, drying my finger on my work trousers.

'You moved all the way down from Bangor and then she went and left you for London. And now you're still here, working in the video store.'

'Well, not-working in the video store,' I say.

'Oh yeah, sorry,' she says. 'You know what I mean though.'

She folds the empty bag of popcorn in half, and then in half again, and so on and on until it's a little red triangle. She picks it up and moves it in the air, like it's a boat sailing through a rocky sea.

'Yeah,' I say. 'But there's no work around here for her. She had to move.'

I reach over the arm of the couch, to my satchel, and take out another bag of popcorn.

Hannah and I started going out in the final year of university. When we finished our finals we both moved home. But after my father got jealous of all the time me and my step-Mum spent together – that's when I had to leave. I didn't tell Hannah about any of this, though. I just came to Caerphilly to visit and never left. That was a year ago now, and I haven't heard from my father since.

'So you don't feel let down?' the psychiatrist says.

'Maybe a little.' I think of Dad coming at me with the hammer.

'That's the hallmark of maturity,' the psychiatrist says.

'What is?'

'Ambivalence.'

'I'm not ambivalent,' I say. 'I miss her.'

'No, no, I mean... to be able to see the good and the bad, to be double-minded.'

'Ah. Well yes,' I say, 'I am frightfully mature for my age.'

For some reason, she finds this very funny. I don't know why, but it makes her laugh. I generally know when I've said a good line – indeed, I have many – but that one really didn't deserve this reaction. She settles back on the couch, lies down, and rests her feet on my lap.

'You don't mind, do you?' she says.

'It's your house,' I say. 'You can put your feet wherever you want. I mean, this couch is probably, like, your office. Actually, do psychiatrists have offices?'

'They generally do,' she says. In her tights, her feet look webbed. 'But I'm a counsellor – and that's a different thing.'

'You're not a psychiatrist?'

'Nope. I started the training, but God, it was just too much work. Everyone round here thinks I'm a psychiatrist though. I used to tell them I'm not, but I've just given up now.'

'I see,' I say. 'Do you ever work from here though?'

'I've learned not to bring work home with me,' she says. 'You know, after Simon, I started seeing this counsellor from Cardiff and we'd do it in her living room. But she'd always fall asleep halfway through.'

I don't know if she's speaking about counselling or sex with a counsellor.

I say, '*And how did that make you feel?*'

She gives me a look. She's registered my comment but doesn't find it funny.

'It was strange, all right. I'd ask her was it me, but she'd say no, go on. I stopped going the third time it happened.'

'Weird,' I say.

'Yeah, but I felt guilty about not getting in touch. It's never nice when someone stops seeing you without letting you know. But that's what I did. I couldn't face calling her about it.'

'Why did she fall asleep all the time?'

'Well, here's the thing,' she says. 'I was feeling really bad about it all. And even though she was the one being unprofessional, I couldn't help feel as if I was being unprofessional by not getting in touch. I started having dreams about seeing her in post offices and airport departure lounges and all those other obvious symbolic places. And then one day I was walking around Cardiff – and I was actually thinking about her, wondering how she was getting on – and then I saw her across the road on Queen Street. So I went over and I told her I was sorry I'd stopped going, but I just felt uncomfortable about her falling asleep.'

'What did she say?' I say. I think of my mother asleep. The weight of her arm draped over the side of the couch; the way the light came in through the window.

'Well, we went and got some coffee, and she apologised about it all. She told me she'd been going through a bad time. Her husband had been violent. She said she really shouldn't have been doing the counselling herself, but she needed the money to get out. She said she'd worked through a lot of it with her own counsellor and now she was feeling much better about it all. She was glad to meet me though, because she felt guilty about the way things had gone.'

I picture the chain: counsellor → counsellor → counsellor.

'Let me top you up there,' she says and refills my glass.

I don't tell her about my mother. Instead, I tell her about the night I found a man in a suit, lying on the side of the road, and how I thought he was dead. I called an ambulance and waited beside him in the dark for twenty minutes. But when the paramedics did their stuff, he woke up and told them to leave him alone. He said he'd just been having a nap.

Her bedroom is smaller than I expected. The place is spotless, like a show home, and her body is in really good shape for a woman her age. Hannah is so insecure about her body that all the sex happened in the dark. But the psychiatrist is confident – she removed her top and bra whilst we were in the doorway. And as expected, she smells wonderful.

As she moves down on me, I reach for my mobile on the bedside table. I call Hannah and set it to speakerphone. She won't answer, but when she listens to her voicemail she'll at least know how I'm spending my time.

I'm getting into it when I realise I've been very selfish so far. So I push the psychiatrist off and start doing all the things a guy should do. I don't think I'm very good at sex stuff, but she seems to enjoy it. Licking her, I think of licking batteries, and the jolt of the current running through my tongue. But before I know what's happening, we've changed positions, and she's straddling my waist and asking me to spank her.

Not really knowing what I'm doing, I awkwardly slap her on the bum. She groans, and I can tell the groan is exaggerated, deliberately encouraging. And there's something about her encouragement that I find off-putting. I spank her a few more times, and then she gets down on her knees.

'Hit me in the face,' she says.

I feel myself seize.

'You can do it as hard as you like,' she says, her head leaning towards me.

'I don't want to hit you in the face,' I say. 'Why would I want to hit you in the face?'

'Just a slap then,' she says, 'go on. It'll only take a second.'

She closes her eyes and swallows something that isn't there. The tendons in her neck are thick, but the skin looks thin, as if it's stretched too tightly around her bones. I study her face. Her mascara has smudged, and a thick black track bleeds across her temple. I raise my hand. Her eyes are still closed, but she bites her lip now. I've never hit anyone before, not properly. And with my hand in the air, I don't know what I'm going to do. I keep it there, aloft, for a moment, two moments, and then, in the end, I just finger-flick her on the nose.

'Come on,' I say. 'Let's just do it.'

So we settle on sex the usual way – no funny business – and when we're done, she cosies up to me and rests her head on my shoulder.

'How you doing?' I say.

She makes a noise, a sighing noise. 'You've no idea.'

I'm thinking of Hannah, of our first time in my college room, and how it feels like a very long time ago; how it seems like a line has just been drawn between then and now.

'No idea what?' I say.

'I dunno,' she says. 'I'm just too old for this.'

'You're not old,' I say, running my hand over her leg.

I can feel the jut of her chin on my chest as she looks up at me.

'Am I meant to believe you actually think that?'

'Yeah,' I say.

The first time I took off Hannah's clothes, I was so turned on I came in my pants. She never found out though; I hid it well.

'You're very kind,' she says. 'Seriously though, I'm fifty-six. I could be your mother.'

I laugh, and then I think of Mum. A blemish of something, something hot, creeps up my neck.

'And how are you doing?' she says.

'Yeah fine,' I say.

'Good good,' she says, and she reaches over and turns off the lamp.

I'm still thinking of Mum, and *The Apartment*, and Shirley MacLaine passed out on the bed.

'I was only six at the time,' I say.

'Shh,' she says, putting a finger to my lips. She whispers gently, stroking my neck. 'Shh, try and get some sleep now.'

When I wake up I've three missed calls from Hannah's mum, and two texts from Hannah. The first one says, '**When are you moving out of my house?**' and the second has no words, only question marks:

????

The psychiatrist is fully dressed, standing in the doorway, and I'm under the covers, still naked. I can feel an erection stirring. Through the curtains there's a peek of morning light.

'How you feeling?' she says.

'Naked.'

'And your head?'

'Murky,' I say, scratching my arm. 'How about you?'

'I'm alright,' she says. 'Not too bad. The benefits of being a *high-functioning alcoholic*, I suppose. Any plans for the day, then?'

I think about it.

'Nay,' I say.

'*Neighhhh*!' – she's back on the horse game again. 'Fancy a picnic later?'

'That'd be nice,' I say. 'Yeah, why not?'

She gives me a shirt of her ex-husband's to wear, and makes me scrambled egg on toast. We're in the kitchen, and every now and then she gives me a hug or a kiss on the back of the head. While I'm drinking a cup of tea, she massages my shoulders and tells me I have a lot of tension in my body.

'You've been very stressed,' she says. 'The shop closing down must be very hard for you.'

'I don't know,' I say, forking some egg into my mouth. 'Maybe.'

'That's gone now though,' she says. 'You can start again now.'

*

It's bright and cold out – as if the sun is just an inch too far away – and we're sitting at a picnic table across from the castle. The psychiatrist takes crisps from a giant bag we bought at Tesco, and eats two or three at a time.

'Here comes trouble,' she says when two ducks waddle up. She throws them a slice of Hovis each, and the bread lands on some freshly-fallen leaves.

'Tell me a secret, little duckies,' she says. The ducks just nibble at the bread, chomping till it's all gone.

'Looks like they don't want to talk,' I say.

A little boy, in a coat like Paddington Bear's, walks past with his mother. He points at the ducks and goes *quack*!

'Now that's how you talk to ducks,' the psychiatrist says. She pierces the top of her Capri-Sun with the straw. 'Quality duck-talk.'

I take a slice of bread then cut some brie. I run my finger along the edge of the plastic knife and lick off the bits of cheese. The label on my shirt is starting to itch, so I smooth it down a little.

'It'll be cold tonight,' I say.

'How so?'

'Clear skies,' I say, gesturing with my brie sandwich. I take a bite and keep talking. 'Clear skies means no cloud coverage. And that means nothing to keep in the heat.'

'Sounds like the thought processes of a depressive,' she says.

'It's science,' I say.

'Well, mother nature must have had post-natal depression,' she says, and I snort with a laugh.

'Do you think you'll ever move back home then?' she says. There's an army of ducks around us now, all looking to be fed.

'Back to Bangor?' I say. I blow my nose into my hand, then rub it on the bench. 'I doubt it.'

'Well, what do you want to do?' she says. 'You've been out of uni a year now.'

'I know,' I say, watching the little boy throw bread to the ducks in the moat. I picture the bread going soggy, sinking in the water. 'I just don't know. I can't even remember what I wanted to do.'

I take out my phone and there's another message from Hannah's mother: **R U OK?**

'Let's get these buggers,' the psychiatrist says, and she hands me a wad of bread from the bag. 'Okay, step one: remove the dough from the middle and roll it up like a ball, like this.' She scrunches up the bread in her hand until it looks like a fist or a knotty heart.

I copy her and place the frame-crust down on the picnic table.

'No, no, pick that back up,' she says. 'That's the important part.' And then she takes her frame of bread and looks at the duck.

'Let's see if we can get this square bit around one of the ducks' necks,' she says. 'Like those games you get in fairgrounds, you know? And when it starts nibbling at the bread, that's when we'll throw the dough-ball.'

We do it for five minutes but it doesn't work. Throwing bread around a duck's neck is harder than it sounds.

'It's getting cold,' she says. 'Do you want to head back?

'Aye,' I say, though the temperature feels the same to me.

We go back to hers, she brings out her duvet, and we settle on the couch to watch more films. We watch *Sunset Boulevard* and then

Vanilla Sky. Through the kitchen window, I can see the day is already over, the night is inky-black. Ten minutes into *Goodbye Lenin!* we start having sex, and she keeps asking me to fuck her harder. I tell her to calm down, that I'm going as hard as I can. When we're done, we both sit up and she tells me that her first husband killed himself by running into traffic, that the second husband had an affair. He left her two months ago, she says. I tell her I'm sorry – I don't know what else to say. She asks me to tell her what happened to my mother, but I don't want to talk about it.

'You need to,' she says.

'I don't,' I say.

'It's okay if you want to cry,' she says.

'I don't,' I say.

The film has stopped and we watch the screen go blue. The tape reaches the end of the reel, and it begins to rewind, begins to wind back to the start.

'Just popping to the toilet,' I say, getting up.

I go to her bedroom and get changed into my own clothes, into the VideoZone uniform. When I come back in, she's on the couch, flicking through the TV channels. She's wearing her cardigan, buttons undone, a glimpse of breast still visible.

'Shall we get in pizza?' she says.

'I should probably get going,' I say.

She picks up the remote control, then puts it back down on the arm of the couch.

'Okay,' she says.

She offers me a lift but I tell her I'm fine to walk. She sees me to the door and kisses me on the forehead, tells me to be safe. It's misty out, and the ground is starting to stiffen with frost. I go along Mountain Road, the lights of the town disappearing as I move further down the mountain. Then I walk across St Martin's Road, past the church, all the while being careful not to slip. And though it's dark, the town's awake with people now. There's a queue of guys outside The Kings, as bouncers laugh and let in groups of girls who must only be sixteen. *Come on*, the guys say, *it's fucking freezing*. A couple argue outside

Chicken Land. The man wants to get a taxi into Cardiff, and the woman wants food. She's sat on the floor, her back against the window, refusing to move until she gets a burger. The man tells the taxi driver to wait, tells him this'll only take a minute. I walk through them, through the mist that's so low, and I keep going until I'm past Tesco and Martin, a blanket over him, eating a sandwich. I walk past the castle and the shopping centre and take a right at the lights, towards Hannah's house, back to Hannah's mum.

Tuner of Llangyfelach

Stevie Davies

The piano's held together, I explain over the phone, with elastic bands and string: well, in a manner of speaking. It's an heirloom: been in my brother's garage for years and in a ruined farmhouse before that. I've no idea if such a wreck can be salvaged – but perhaps he might just look it over?

Bang on time, Owen Rhys stands at the door with his toolkit, a boyish-looking, old-fashioned guy in corduroy, fortyish, his abundant hair side-parted – softly-spoken and courteous. Leaving him to take stock of the patient, I settle in the attic study. Even here, you can hear the piano's falsity and confusion.

- Tia, calls the tuner, – Never say die.

- Really? You can do something with it?

- Certainly. But – what's the history of this piano? Because – this'll sound odd – I may recognise the instrument. I'm almost sure the person who last tuned it was my dad.

Down on his knees, Owen studies the instrument's dusty back. – Ah. Here we are. Perhaps. Can you see?

I crouch beside him. What am I supposed to be seeing? The wood's a chaos of score-marks. I put it down to Mother Nature running amok while the piano slept. Slept for years, decades, and lost – in the wake of fratricidal family conflict – its mind. The family's unappeasable jealousies built and boiled through time, for reasons no one now recalls. We youngsters, university-educated, got out. I fixed on New Zealand. It's our antipode, I told myself: should be safe enough there. Decades later I've returned, to salvage an inheritance.

There's a mark, apparently, which I'm implored to confirm, the sign, the tuner says, and his voice cracks, of his lovely dad. – Here look. 'O.R. LLAN. RECREAT'. Latin for 'Owen Rhys of Llangyfelach restored this.' See? Can you see it? Clear as day.

When he straightens up, there are alarming tears in the tuner's eyes and he accepts a cup of tea.

- I was apprenticed to Dad, he tells me. – He indentured me, binding me for five years. He signed, I signed. It wasn't a legally enforceable document, just a pact between the two of us. It's so moving to see this piano. If it's the one. Yes, it is, you saw his mark. Our firm has been restoring pianos for a century and there's a pride to it, you know, folk trust us. A rival company had just set up – Kleinkind's – it worried dad, not least because Kleinkind saturated the market with cheap Chinese pianos, a thousand pounds a go. Rubbish pianos.

- But Chinese instruments are the best in the world, aren't they, Owen?

Whatever's so special about my piano, I wonder, that has him searching into those underground places of the heart – wells where old tears collect, their salt a barren solace?

- Aye, Tia, *nowadays* Chinese pianos are second to none. Different story then. These were all duds. The first we really knew was when we were called out to a piano in Treforys. Dad got to work when – pow! a string snapped – great bang, like a bomb going off. Another string – pow! It lashed him in the face, under the eye, he had the scar the rest of his life.

- Dad told the owner, – Can't do anything with this, boy. You've been sold a pup. Complain, take it back. It's lethal.

- It pained him to see people palmed off with junk. And he saw more and more of it. He made a pretext to visit Kleinkind's workshop. It was attached to a warehouse. Like a hangar it was – relic of the old steel works, down where the enterprise park is now – packed wall-to-wall with these clones, as far as the eye could see. Honest-to-God, it was like the terracotta army in the emperor's tomb. You had to see it to believe it. And Dad said it was a vision of the future, of apocalyptic decline. Chapel he was, see. What Kleinkind did was, when customers complained, he just swapped their rubbish piano for a new rubbish piano. Once the three-year guarantee was up, end of.

- I suppose your father confronted him?

Is my piano somehow under suspicion? It couldn't logically be. Mine's inherited. I love it anyway. Even if it has to be eviscerated and I'm left with an empty shell. I remove the mugs as a hint that tuning should commence. But Owen follows me into the kitchen and insists on drying up, still talking. My neighbour but two is a talker like this. When I see her coming I hide in the garage. Nobody's spared.

And yet I like the guy. The gentleness of him, the dark, kindled eyes. The sense of family pieties: who else do I know – aside from myself – who loved their father so profoundly that the rest of life bore the mark of sorrow? And perhaps he intuits this kinship. Although of course mine was a quarreller like the rest of the Francises – emotional, hot-tempered, puzzled that the root of love should turn out so cloven. I see in my mind's eye his baffled eyes – and I have to turn away inwardly, softly closing the door on him.

- Kleinkind was a charmer, Owen goes on. – No getting away from that. Where do you hang the tea-towel, Tia? Gentlemanly chap, mind – impeccable manners. Instead of defending himself when Dad accused him, he parried with a question: how many working men in the Valleys can afford quality instruments for their kiddies, would you guess, Mr Rhys? *Quality*? It was the first time in my life I heard Dad raise his voice. After that he was on a mission, I don't think he was ever quite himself again – or, yes, perhaps just, briefly, once. I'll come to that. He'd tune people's pianos for next to nothing. Thing was, he felt he'd seen the End. But he reasoned that he could in some way arrest this process of ... untuning. Piano entropy. Dad was the boy with his thumb in the dyke. He even undertook to restore rogue imports – more or less rebuilding from scratch. I do believe these pianos killed him. Mam was very bitter.

- But you're not saying, are you, that my piano is –

- Good God no. Venerable instrument is this, Tia. Sorry, I'll stop my chopsing and get down to work. Funny old world though, isn't it? Let's gauge the timbre first.

Owen begins to play: Bach's *Das Wohltemporierter Klavier*. I realise at once that he's no mean player, despite the reverberations that roar round the instrument's body and explode out in frenzy.

- You may well flinch! Each piano's different, see. Timbre's determined by the harmonics – different harmonics for the same pitch. A little inharmoniousness lends richness to the tone. You didn't know that? Well, your instrument's a challenge – but, Tia, it'll be worth it to you, I promise, if it takes all day. I've got a packed lunch in the van.

- Eat with me. Of course, Owen. I've made soup.

*

- You see, he says, breaking open a warm crusty roll and smothering it in melting butter, – Dad was pious, that's true. Straight-dealing – modest to a fault. But he had a zany sense of humour and plenty of hwyl. He'd dance Mam all round the house, singing at the top of his voice. All that went out the window, once he started trying to resurrect pianos. He'd been a tender father – hands-on they'd call it nowadays. One of the old Gower swimmers: he'd swim way out at Pwlldu with me on his back. I never felt afraid. And no matter what comes later, Tia, if you've enjoyed such childhood security, nothing mars it. Even when the rage infected him and he quarrelled with the deacons. And started boasting that nothing was beyond his powers. The real man was still there, behind the rage.

- You see, he'd undertaken a labour impossible for one craftsman, stacking the odds against himself. Me he saw as a fellow-crusader and successor in the battle against these profane imports. Not easy for an adolescent lad. I had a sober sense of filial duty – but I'd drag my heels and roll my eyes. Dad sued Kleinkind – and lost. And Kleinkind threatened to sue us. That case never came to court. I must admit I was ashamed of Dad, muttering to himself, his face all mottled. He signed the pianos he'd restored so he could make account of himself at the end of time.

- One day we were called to a farm towards Kilvey.

I take a mouthful of water. I know where this is going. Owen has led me to Cae Twmpyn Farm; to my grandmother and her barricades. The livestock sold off and the pyre of fifty pound notes. To the moment when her children came to blows at the farm gate and Uncle John nearly lost an eye and Auntie Gwen went charging like a bull across the cobbles at my mam. To the beginning of the end.

- Yes, I say. – I know the area.

*

We park outside Cae Twmpyn, the tuner and I, in his van which smells of linseed oil and menthol. The farm was once a tenancy of the Kilvey manor, its mediaeval curtilage defended by towering walls. We grandchildren knew every field by a corruption of its ancient name: they'd been worked by our family for centuries. Owen and I pass the mounds after which the farm was named: twin tumps, a hundred yards apart, where once a Bronze Age cinerary urn was excavated containing fragments of human burial. When the longed-for snow came we'd toboggan down the slopes. On the south-west side the ground slants down to the cliffs above the sea, a grey shining triangle between headlands, with a little beach when the tide's out. Nobody farms there now. There's a caravan site on the lower field.

As we enter the grounds I breast the memory of Gran's barricades. How picturesque ruined houses look when they weather into the earth. Grass carpets her rooms, her walls are yellow and orange with lichen and fireweed thrusts up seven feet tall.

- Yours was the last piano Dad ever restored, Owen says as we perch on a broken wall. – And he died three weeks later. The farmhouse even then looked distinctly seedy. A birch had rooted by the chimney, I remember, and tiles were slipping. When we knocked, no one answered.

So we went round the back and tapped on the windows. Eventually an elderly lady appeared. Pale blue eyes, piercing. Rather formidable. I remember her clear as day, I'll explain why in a minute. Indoors it was, well, a mess. The old lady said she was living a student's life and couldn't be bothered to clean. I thought she was a bit – you know. Dad set me to sweep the room, which I did with a poor grace. He snarled that for all he cared I could go and work for Kleinkind in his junk yard if I took that attitude. I said nothing but my expression must have riled him because he told me to get out of his sight and ask the old lady if she wanted any jobs doing.

- So did you?

- I did. And she said, – Yes, young man, I wish to go for a swim.

- A *swim*?

- In the sea. I thought at first she was having me on. Eventually back I traipsed to Dad. Scarlet-faced. *She wants me to go swimming with her.* Well, that tickled him. He burst out laughing and his old, soft self was back – as if it had just been biding time. Mind you, I was hardly in a mood to appreciate that. I drew myself up to my full five foot four and told him it wasn't in my contract that I had to go swimming with old grannies. And I wouldn't, he couldn't make me. He laughed harder and said, *Tell her we'll all go together when this is finished.*

- And did you, Owen?

- Mortifying it was. Yet now it seems a blessed interval. Your gran was quite a woman, Tia, and no mistake. She was an original. Whatever was she like in her heyday if this was how she was at eighty? The embarrassment! – didn't know where to look. My dad and your gran swam out, way beyond my limit. I saw them basking out there, floating on their backs, water like a millpond, chatting away presumably. And later he played to her. Chopin.

What Owen has tendered me feels like breaking news. I cwtch it up in my heart. I can't stop smiling. I want to cry. I remember playing the recorder to my gran and how all the asperity left her as she listened. Driving back, we're both silent, side by side, like shy cousins many times removed. Yes, like distant kin, whose stories mesh at one seam only.

I wish Dad could have heard this. His tales were of bewildered rejection. Of loving too much and being short-changed. Of a taciturn dad with fists. Of a mother who signed off from being a mam once her husband was underground. Greedy bloodsuckers, she called her adult children. After she'd burned her savings, Gran slapped her hands together, as if to say: *Good riddance.* From now on she was just going to be herself. She reverted to her maiden name. Dad described his sister rooting in the bin amongst the ashes of a fortune in twenty- and fifty-pound notes.

My Uncle Bryn took steps to get Gran committed. Nothing doing. She'd got the local doctor in her pocket, so Bryn said. And the social workers were impressed by her intellectual grasp. They said she talked to them about her OU studies and feminism and played for them on her piano. And oh, a lovely cup of coffee she do make, they said, as if that clinched the matter. The family solicitor leaned back in his chair and informed Bryn that it wasn't arson to burn a fortune, though it might be construed as eccentric or subversive. On the other hand, people poured fortunes down the drain every day in bad investments or high living.

- Your mother has left a will, he said. – There'll be enough for her funeral. And just the one small bequest. I cannot divulge that to you.

Meanwhile at Cae Twmpyn the farmhouse descended into senility. Nature ran wild in there. Convolvulus vines overwhelmed the piano, covering it with their white trumpets. Insidious tendrils lifted the lid, clasping the hammers and strings, soundboard and bridges. Year by year as the bindweed rotted, it left a scurf of dry brown dust that began to fill up the cavity. Moths laid eggs on the bindweed and larvae pupated on the keys. Snails festooned the inlay with slime that dried to a map of roadways.

Until the day came to call it home from the dead.

Aberarth

Cynan Jones

The coast from Aberarth to Aberystwyth is an erosional coast, the rocky shore platforms wear down slowly allowing waves to attack the base of the cliffs, causing cliff failure.

West of Wales Shoreline Management Plan 2; Section 4. Coastal Area C

*

In the recent nights lying awake things have poured from him; but now it changes, and the world's just folding into the hole in him, like water into a dunked cup.

He can't sleep, lies there with this feeling of being empty, of filling up.

For a while the drink took him but that's worn off, leaving him awake, like being left wide open at the side of a road. As if the drink had passed on, dropped him off – something he'd hitched a ride with for a while.

There was nothing to hold together now.

He lies there, undrunk but not ill yet with that weird night-time clarity when the alcohol is on the turn. That moment of brief calm, like the cancelling motion at the change of tides. Thoughts pouring in and over.

For months he had been trying to change things, had resolved during the day to go home and be different. To take home some surprise. Just something simple, like ice cream. A sign that he would turn things round. But the key in the door was this thing and he couldn't. It was this habit.

There's a hish-hush of a car now and then, the still new sounds of his rented bedsit. He hears the people in the room below change channels on the television, the sound travelling out through the boarded fireplace. And on the unit he hears the crab. Intimate little noises.

He'd started drinking in the afternoon, that patient way. There was all this time with the early finish, leaving slow heavy hours to get through. It was like time had become granular, and the drink went into it and made it fluid again, dissolved it to something he could handle. He just wanted to get through the hours back to the safe place of work. He had the comfort at work of a child going into its bedroom.

As people came in to the pub he wanted to get away. Everyone knew everybody here. But somehow all his momentum had gone. Really, he felt like he was waiting for a lift from someone who hadn't turned up. He was glad he was not a verbal drunk. He just let it happen. Kept filling up the empty cup, drinking like remembering a skill he'd learnt. He drank through the hours rhythmically. Time just blurred.

When he left it was dark and the fresh air hit him, knocking him off balance a little, the sudden spin of his head like having a lungful of foul smell. He just walked down to the harbour sucking in air, everything off kilter, feeling that horrible pointless drunkenness. Then he watched the tide come in for he didn't know how long, lifting the boats, their rigging clanking on the masts as they left the mud and went up slowly with the water, correcting themselves like a drunk getting up from a low, soft chair.

He lies there now, remembering that. The slow water. He thinks of his pots, down on the bed, wondering if anything is in them, the water over them slow and oily, swallowing them, as if they themselves were creatures being engulfed. He is the frightened and trapped animal in them, there in the dark.

Up on the unit the crab scrapes and clicks, the tub lurid somehow in the light that comes through the window from the nearby streetlamp. Every now and then the a car passes, makes a hissing noise, like water coming over rocks.

'Why the hell did I bring it back?' he thinks. 'I don't even have a pot.'

Just the small bagful of stuff grabbed when he told her he would go. His clothes still in a black bin bag, starting to smell of plastic. A darts trophy. A picture of Gemma. A silver cake slice that was Mum's that he will not let her have.

He feels a building sense of oddness, thinking of the pots beneath the water, gathering things, the tide pulling over them, the cold dark sheet of it. He is so close to drinking again, just to help him sleep. For the few hours it might give him.

He lies there. Clarity. He worries about the strange thing that happened to his head the other day, the way it seemed as if he was being lifted away from himself. Just the stress, he says. Like whispering to a child at night. He feels like he is travelling on an empty railway carriage.

The headache begins, mildly blinding light from an oncoming car. He lies there quietly, waits for morning, thinks of water.

I don't know why I did it, even, he thinks. I'm not even a drinker.

*

He goes through the corridors with the same faked smile as the other visitors, makes polite nods to people, everyone as horrified as each other, feeling guilty, happiness put on like a paper hat on Christmas day, (has to be done, pull your cracker).

Usually he times it to visit before lunch or supper so he can leave when the food arrives – leave her with something; but today he is earlier. Even so, there's a pervading smell of soft food. He feels sick. Acid sick.

In a loud voice somewhere a nurse is talking to a patient – a resident they call them. They have comic names, old clichéd names. There is an unnatural warmth to the place. Somewhere the television is on very loud.

When he looks at the place from outside he can't get rid of this image: of the old people in their chairs and wheelchairs bobbing up and down in a warm stew, like soft vegetables in a soup.

'Hello Mum.'

She's sitting in the chair by the bed staring at the window but she's too low to see anything but the grey sky and she's disinterested in the pitiful magazine that lies open on her lap, half hidden by the shawl that's fallen from her.

He sees a wishy-washy watercolour of a woman in love, the fancy handwriting of a story title.

It is strange and gutting to see her. The darkened glasses hide the only part of her he really recognises still.

Out of the window, he sees across the fields to the beach, sees the council building overlooking the coast.

'Mum,' he says, crouching by the chair and taking her incredible hand. And she looks at him and smiles. Her big, even smile. That and her eyes is all that's left of her. In her room, the hard smell of geraniums. They smell of aluminium.

'Let's sit you up,' he says, as forty years ago she said to him. He knows, with futility, that she has been like this for hours. Slumped, unattended. Just smiling that big smile back to the nurses who have popped their head in, cheery voices, asked if she's all right. It's the ones who make the fuss that get attention, like babies or kids in school.

'I'm sorry I didn't come for a few days, Mum,' he says, wonders if she noticed. He just wants to spill it all out, why.

He sits her up and asks if she wants a cuppa but she just smiles and he sits there holding her hand. He nearly starts talking to her. About everything. Starts talking, not stopping, with his words going into her and being soaked up, soaked away, the pain, anger and confusion he's holding in.

It would be okay because she won't respond. It would be like nursery rhymes to her; the sing-song sounds of fairy tales to a child who can't yet talk. But he sits there in silence, staring at the photographs of himself, his ex-wife and Gemma. Gemma as a baby. Him as a child with his brother and sister.

They come 'when they can', but they live away, work, have families of their own; they have distanced themselves. He does not regret staying here, but it is hard sometimes to be the one who has to see the worse things, deal with her confusion, her body dying bit by bit, organ by organ rescued by another pill.

He knows she simply wants to die. But it will not come.

Sometimes he will see things he should not have to see. If she is in bed, or not dressed fully, seated in the low chair in her nightie, swaddled with blankets and shawls. He will have to help her with things it should never be his place to, that will horrify and recur to him, that gives him a dread of going to see her now.

At the beginning, sometimes, she was not even in her own underwear and he spent hours sewing knots of colour thread into the labels of her clothes with big clumsy hands so the nurses could not make mistakes.

He rubs his face, smells the saltwater on his hands. Has a great want to take her outside.

*

He drives down to the Yacht Club and parks the car overlooking the shore. Some of the boats have not yet gone back into the harbour, are up on blocks and stilts around him.

The tide is pulling out, leaving a wet line on the rocks.

It is a grey sea, and the breeze licks up a few white crests.

It is not right, he thinks. It is not right here. This is not where it is from.

He looks down at the crab in the tub, cramped, unable to stretch itself. As if it has grown to fit the box in an effort to break out. There is something primal and ancient about it. The sense of something that will be around for a very long time.

Behind the bungalows on the shorefront, he can just see the roof of the old people's home.

I cannot leave it here, he thinks.

*

He gets out of the car and goes onto the beach. The right beach. The beach the crab came from.

The shale cliffs further down the shore, the constant peaceful hiss of a waterfall. The two carcasses of floating mines, rusted now and gutted; the pools that arc in the humanised shape of the old fish traps.

He has the odd awakeness of no sleep, a hard grey headache. From the whisky, his stomach feels up in his chest somewhere. When he moves, his headache shifts, like something loose in the boot of a car.

He can see up the beach the cliffbank has come down. The big shape of it, squared boulders of earth; the strange smooth leg of mud smoothed by the high water like a sucked sweet.

Lying on the ground, the slipped cliff looks like it has been down like that always. There is a look of relief to it, a look of being settled.

It feels to him that it was a long time since he was here, though it was only yesterday.

The crab bunched in the corner of the pot, trying to stay out of the sun after the water had receded. His mother slumped in the chair. A grown man crying, staring at the clothes spilling out of plastic sacks.

After this I'll stay down, he thinks. Walk round the point. I'll stay here for a while.

Steadily an oystercatcher goes over the water and he looks down at the crab in the tub. Then he takes it to the water.

It's okay now, you're down, he says. You're down.

Love: A Pathology

Francesca Rhydderch

When Anya saw the girl on the bus, she didn't say anything to her about the letter. She was used to typing out bad news for people, learning every detail of their suddenly diminished life expectancy before they found out about it for themselves. It was what she was paid to do.

The secretary before her had perhaps wanted to be helpful, leaving all those medical diagrams taped to the wall above the desk. There was a heart that looked like a rack of lamb trussed up by spidery ventricles to each side, and two coloured sketches of someone called Betty Boop. In the picture on the left Betty wore a suspender belt with a red heart on it, and painted-on eyelashes that went all round her saucer eyes. In the right-hand version she had empty eye sockets, a huge cranium and a tiny skeleton. When Anya asked her boss who Betty Boop was he'd said she was a character in a classic – *old* – cartoon. It was just there for fun. *Boop-boop-de-boop* he said, then laughed when Anya didn't.

Anya took the posters down and bought a second-hand glossary of medical terms in a charity shop to keep on her desk, and after a while the sparse trickle of words and phrases started to thicken into sentences that scared the life out of her. She tried to distract herself by poring over their phonetic pronunciations, repeating them like a mantra, just as her mother used to mutter her way through her morning and evening prayers as she stirred tea leaves into the pot, not believing any more, but not quite disbelieving enough to abandon them. *What follows after tea?* she joked to Anya as she sat in her school uniform staring at the table sleepily, and then, when Anya shrugged her shoulders, being a teenager, refusing to play along: *The resurrection of the dead, you silly girl!* Anya remembered the way the gilt cup holder had caught the light, and her mother smiling at her own joke.

It was a stupid old Russian joke, Anya thought. She still didn't find it funny. It made her feel ill. It was enough to make her cry, to think of her mother laughing, saying, *You silly girl! It's just a joke.*

*

Anya was planning on leaving early that day, but she had noticed the girl in the waiting room. She reminded Anya of herself when she was young: with long, dark hair, and a nervy look on her face. Anya had left her file until last, not wanting to know what was in it, by which time it was nearly four-thirty and she had to hurry through the letter like all the rest if she was to catch the five-fifteen.

Outside, it was raining hard. When she had first arrived in this country, delivered from one grey airport to another, the first thing Anya had noticed was the glistening rain that fell on the fur jacket her mother had given her as a going-away present, weighing it down. And it had been warm, compared with what she was used to. She'd put the fur at the back of the wardrobe, and bought anoraks and windcheaters better suited to the damp Welsh coast. She'd thought about selling it from time to time, but she hadn't, not until Malcolm lost his job. Instead, she'd gathered her new coats about her, blanketing her homesickness with layers of fleece and gore-tex.

The driver tore her ticket off the machine and she walked down the middle of the bus, signalling hello to the man from the library and exchanging glances with the girl. She went to her usual seat, and looked out of the window at the hedgerows rising and falling as the bus left the edge of town, taking the road south.

Her mother had said she would regret it, leaving everything she knew behind, especially her, Anya's only mother. Her mother who had given her everything. Who washed the net curtains every week and put cheerful pot plants outside the flat's front door in the concrete hallway. Who scrubbed the graffiti off the lift doors herself if she had to. Who always did her best, especially for her daughter, who was going to become an English teacher, she was sure of it. *You will be top of the class*, she had said, peering at the dried-out tea leaves at the bottom of Anya's glass. *You will use your languages. You will make money!* All these predictions had turned out to be true, although Anya's mother had been given to believe by the tea leaves that Anya would be rich, a teacher in a good Moscow school; that they would move to another flat and she would be kept comfortable by her daughter for whom she had slaved – *slaved* – to keep and feed. She locked the door of the flat at night because of the yobs who hollered up and down the stairwells, and sometimes during the day too, when she went shopping, with a clear conscience. *You're better off doing your homework instead of hanging around with those hoodlums!* she said. Anya got through her homework as well as she could in spite of the boys' howls from the lift shaft. *Good*, her mother nodded, checking it over when she came home from Sennaya Ploschad with a full basket (although she couldn't read English – all she could see was that the handwriting was neat). *Very good! Now wash your hands.* No matter how often Anya washed her hands, and she washed them often then, too often, like her mother, they still smelled of cabbage and *smetana*.

*

The smell that the men brought onto the bus with them was something else, something like shrimp paste. They got on at the bus stop outside a Chinese takeaway, herding each other down the aisle, tripping over their own feet, filling up the empty seats wherever they could find a space.

'They're drunk,' Anya said out loud, surprised. It was still early.

She thought the girl might turn round, say something, or smile, at least, but she didn't move. She was wearing small white earphones and tapping one foot lightly and rhythmically in time with whatever it was she was listening to. The group had concentrated itself around her. They smiled at her, holding onto the metal poles to stop themselves sliding off their seats.

'Alright?' one of them said to the girl. Anya knew him. Malcolm used to work with him.

The girl nodded and looked out of the window.

Anya could see him thinking about trying again, then he glanced round and saw her.

'Hiya, Ans,' he shouted down the bus, so that the rest of them all turned to stare as well. 'You alright?'

'I'm well, thank you, Jack,' she said. Her voice sounded so quiet, compared with his. She cleared her throat. 'And you?'

He got up and came over, almost falling into her lap as the bus took a corner.

'Can't complain,' he said, sitting down. He took a cigarette out of his pocket, put it to his mouth ready to light. The girl gave him a look and he put it away again. 'How's Malc keeping?'

'Good,' Anya said. She could smell the factory on him, that mixture of raw meat and something sanitised, the spray they used to hose down the abattoir at the end of the day, almost sweet. It reminded her of the early days of her marriage, when Malcolm would rush home from his shift, and they would go to bed straightaway and then get up again to make supper. He didn't eat meat himself, he said, stroking her shoulder. Did she cook vegetarian food? he asked. *Of course*, she'd said. *Anything but cabbage!* He laughed. *You're so funny*, he said, and she smiled because no one else ever said that to her.

'What's he up to, these days, old Malcs?' said Jack.

'This and that.' It was a phrase she'd learned from Malcolm since he was made redundant. 'How about you? What's all this?'

She looked over at the rest of the group, who were shouting across the aisle to each other so loudly that even the girl must be able to hear, despite her headphones. The lad sitting across the way from Jack was eyeing the girl.

'Leaving do. Emyr here's been given his marching orders,' Jack said, reaching for his cigarette again. 'Last in, first out.'

That was how it had been with Malcolm. She nodded, looking at Emyr, sitting there like a boy who'd been taken to the headmaster for doing something wrong, his teacher's hand on his shoulder. Only Jack's hand was like the joints of meat he sliced into chunks all day: huge and unrefined, marbled with veins in unexpected places.

Jack drew on his cigarette, leaning over her to open a window so the driver wouldn't notice the smoke. He was starting to look like his father, with his flat cap and his slowly wizening face. Anya could tell from the way Emyr glanced over at Jack's reddened, chafed cheeks, the bits of dried skin round his lips, the flesh that hung from his turkey's neck, and his smoker's gasping reach for breath, that he himself would never be like that. He would never get old.

'It's not just Emyr neither,' Jack belched. 'They're saying there'll be more next time.'

'Why?'

'They reckon the boss is going to be done for trading horsemeat. Might get shut down.'

'And has he?'

'There's a lot of stuff we been cutting up we got no idea what it is. Could be anything.'

He took another drag on his cigarette. Anya coughed, and he put it out under his shoe.

Dust and mud had dried on the bus windows so you could hardly see out. They were on a long flat stretch of road with the sea on one side and hills on the other. Villages made up of chip shops and semi-detached villas close to the road came and went, the darkening spaces in-between becoming more drawn out each time.

'Where you from, then?' Emyr said to the girl, out of nowhere.

The girl took her time to answer. She looked Emyr up and down. She probably didn't have to work hard to catch a boy's attention, Anya thought. Anya had never had much of a chance that way, although one of the boys in the stairwell used to look at her. She'd always been with her mother so she'd never dared look back, but she still remembered how much she'd wanted to. Although her mother let her go down in the early mornings to collect the post from the mailbox in the lobby, before anyone else was up. Her mother didn't know that she had a penfriend in England. Her teacher had arranged one for all the class. Anya's penfriend was called Connie. She had blonde hair and cystic fibrosis. Sometimes her parents wrote her letters for her, when Connie was under the weather. Anya used to be sick with disappointment if she saw the parents' writing on the envelope.

'Down the road,' the girl said. Her voice was deeper than Anya had expected, and louder, too, as she talked over whatever it was her earphones were pumping out.

'By the caravan park?' said the boy.

The girl thought for a moment.

'Just after that,' she said.

'Where?' he persisted.

Anya leaned forward, waiting for the answer.

'Up from the village,' said the girl.

'How far up?' Anya asked. 'That's where I live. Up there.'

The girl turned round, and looked at Anya as if she was noticing her for the first time. There was something transparent about her eyes, as if she wasn't all that interested in other people's feelings. She must dye her hair, Anya thought; it didn't look natural. Anya had never touched hers, even when it started to become streaked with grey. Her mother said she should, when Anya sent her pictures. *You are getting to be so old!* she said. *You'd look much better if you went to the hairdresser's now and again.*

'Yes,' the girl said. 'Up there.'

Emyr watched the girl, his eyes glazed over by beer. He was someone who could be easily deceived, Anya thought. He looked angry at the idea that he was being taken in.

'Nice tits,' he said to the girl. 'Are they real?'

She had barely taken the headphones out of her ears when he started to throw up, mouthfuls of vomit that landed at her feet.

The driver parked up by the nearest field and threw the men off the bus.

'What you doing?' Jack said, as they staggered down into a ditch, the automatic doors already closing behind them. 'We're miles from the Ffarmers.'

'Not my problem,' the driver said.

'How we supposed to get home?'

'Get a taxi.'

It had stopped raining, but the sky was heavy with more. In the field they flailed around in wet barley that came up to their waists, trying not to lose each other, so that the next day passing commuters would wonder at the shapes they'd made among the rows of wickered spikelets, flattening them under their weight. Only Jack and Emyr seemed to know what to do. As the bus pulled back out onto the road Anya saw Emyr climbing up onto Jack's shoulders, holding his mobile as high as he could, trying to get a signal.

*

When Anya had said she was going to England on an exchange, her mother had liked the idea of it at first. It had suggested she would be getting something, or someone, in return. But Anya had come to Wales, not England, and never come back, and no one had come to take her place. She'd written a letter to explain. Her mother hadn't answered for a long time. Finally, she sent a postcard: *No better than a mail-order bride!* she wrote. Malcolm had laughed and said Anya was more perfect than any woman he could have sent for by mail order. He had blushed, because he wasn't used to saying such things. Anya had put her mother's postcard on the mantelpiece, behind the clock. She wrote back by airmail at Christmas. She hoped the vandals on the stairs weren't causing too much trouble. She wished her mother a happy new year.

Anya stood up. So did the girl.

'Are you getting off at this stop?' Anya said to her. Normally she was the only one. Their house was up a deserted, bumpy track on the outskirts of the village.

The girl nodded. Anya thought she should say something about seeing the girl at the hospital earlier today. Maybe she should ask her what she'd been doing there, to get the conversation going. Then they could come on to the letter. Anya could tell her she knew what was in it.

The bus was out of sight already. Anya looked over her shoulder before she made her way up the lane. The girl was winding up her earphones and putting them in her handbag. Anya started walking up the hill, more quickly than usual.

Beyond the caravan park the sun was veiled by thinning clouds. Tall hedges to each side of the lane were garlanded with cow parsley, white saucers of delicate petals balancing on thin stems. As Anya got higher up the track she saw pink bearded iris and bluebells coming through the undergrowth. She breathed in the summer smells, still juicy and damp after the downpour. She was surrounded by acres of wildness and quiet, apart from the rooks clattering in the sycamore tree at the top of the hill. The deep, dank greenness all around her was already sprouting up above her shoulders, forcing its way out of the soil. She could feel life breathing through the earth, carrying her with it.

She wished they'd had children. Malcolm had always wanted children.

As she got closer to the house she knew she would see the television screen flickering in the window and hear canned laughter. When he came to the door she would know from his flushed face that he had dozed off while he was waiting for her. *What's for supper?* he would ask straightaway, and she would feel bad for leaving him alone all day.

She wanted to talk to her mother. After they'd eaten she would phone her mother. Perhaps she would find a cheap ticket online, go and see her before it was too late.

She put her hand to her chest. Her heart was burning itself out of breath. The pain frightened her. She tried to breathe deeply but that just made it worse. She slowed down, although she was still afraid of the dead quiet of the lane behind her. She thought of her mother saying her evening prayers, her old knees pressing into the rug by the bed. She glanced down the hill again.

When Malcolm opened the door she could tell he'd been worrying, wondering where she was.

'How did it go?' he said.

She hadn't phoned through with the results. She'd promised she would but she knew that once she said it out loud the two-dimensional heart from her poster at work would leap off the paper, pumping out of time, keeping her awake at night, and the cartoon pin-up skeleton would come out with *Boop-boop-de-boop*, and if she fell asleep she would dream about flicking through a glossary trying to find the word – what was it again? – the word for whatever it was that was wrong with her.

And she pulled it out of her bag, this last letter she had typed today with her name and address on the envelope, and passed it to him. He read it and took her to sit down in the easy chair. He made tea for her on the stove the way her mother did because he knew she liked it, and she drank it quickly, even though it was too thick, with the leaves not properly strained. She was thirsty and there was that catch at her throat again. As she drank she looked up at the window and she saw a shadow that made her think of the girl, her fine, dark hair feathering out behind her, crossing over the yard to the sycamore tree in the twilight.

The Visit

João Morais

Right after the ID check and the dog sniff and the pat-down, the big screw with the chest like a slab of sirloin goes through the rules again. No touching. No hugging. No kissing.

We leaves the waiting room and walks through to the visiting hall. Each con waits at a separate table. They're all wearing orange bibs to show that they were the ones who got caught. Everyone finds the brother or the boyfriend or the spar they were looking for and no-one gives a fuck about what the big screw just said.

Maylins always likes to play it cool. When he offers his fist for a spud I bats him away and makes him stand up. I hugs him like I'm trying to get lost in his cleavage.

When we lets go, the couple on the table next to us are still going at it. He's got a red Liverpool shirt on under his orange bib, and she's wearing a black strapless top and two gold eyebrow hoops. She hovers slightly above him as they tear into each other's gums. They're necking so hard that she looks like a gannet trying to retch some fish guts into his mouth.

We sits down. I clocks Maylins for the first time in three months. You can really notice the size he's put on. He'd chafe his shoulders trying to get through most doors now. And even his wrists look as thick as my thighs.

– Fair play. You're lookin hench, I says. – You're gettin on for bein the biggest Welsh guy I knows. If you pumps up any more, we'll have to start callin you Aled Schwarzenegger.

Maylins looks pleased, and lets out a bit of a smile.

– It's all the bread, he says. – We gets three meals a day, but they always fills up a serving table with loaves and loaves of bread. I just makes sure I has a loaf with every meal. You knows what it's like, bro. There ain't nothin else to do here apart from watch telly or work out.

You likes this banter, cos you knows what you're gonna have to say when you stops with the wisecracks. – Yeah man, I says. – You're a big boy now. You looks like this guy I saw in a porno once.

But your spar don't like that one, and the nervousness in your voice must be showing by now.

– I ain't clocking you like that. I ain't been on arsetraffic.com, I carries on. – There was two birds in it.

And Maylins looks at you again like you really shouldn't be talking about porn no more.

– Behave yourself, bro. I doesn't get to spend hours lookin at that sorta stuff like you.

– Well if you needs to keep your mind off things, you should write more letters.

He feels the back of his head, where his hair is shortest. – People lies with words. They makes up all sorts of stories. If you got something you wants to say, you has to say it to my face. Chantelle comes round once a week anyway, and sometimes I gets a visit from my Mumma and all.

And as he leans back, all you can think is it might be easy enough to lie when you're hiding behind some words, but it's easier to get away with it when you're face to face and you can hide behind a mask.

– So what you got to say en bro, he carries on. – I best not have wasted a visitin slot if you're just gonna whine on about porn and letters.

He smiles, and you thinks to yourself that in twenty minutes time he's gonna wish that's all we been talking about.

– Right then. I'll start right at the beginning, I says. – It all kicked off about this time last week.

You goes proper deep into your swede to tell the story. You sets the scene, exactly as it happened, and gives him a running real-time commentary.

You tells your spar how you'd not long woken up that afternoon. Mumma is downstairs and you're just weighing up some contraband in case you has to go on a mission. There's a knock at the door so you goes down and answers it. Straight away you wishes you hadn't cos there waiting on the street is Evo Lynch. And seeing that scum with the teardop under his eye and the scars around his neck don't half make you have to brace your knees. But even if you had ignored the knock, Mumma's always got the telly on extra loud when she tidies up so he probably woulda heard the screaming domestic on the chat show she's half-watching anyway.

So you carries on and tells your spar that he got the right idea, renting a different place every coupla months after each crop finishes and fucking off before the bills come in, cos then no twonkey knows where you lives. Stick in the same house all your life and word gets round, standard.

So you tells your spar how it went down.

– Sapnin brer, Evo says. – Long time, long time.

You looks at him but the last thing you wants is him casing out your joint to find stuff to come back for later.

You're thinking: – Gotta keep my face straight.

You're saying: – Safe, bro. Standard.

And he wastes no time at all. – Brer, I needs a favour, I does. I'm late and I got to get up Pentrebane on the double.

You're thinking: – I hope you can't smell all the contraband I got weighing out in here.

You're saying: – Gone Ely in five, bro. Go see this bird.

Which is almost true, cos Stacey had been texting you earlier, and wanted you to come and chill. And you were half thinking about it cos you got a few hours to waste. It was a Tuesday and Kyle wouldn't be there. And she must still be keen cos she's still sending you messages even though you ain't seen her in a few weeks cos you got a new bird on the go.

You hopes with that he'll get the message and fuck off, but he looks over your shoulder and opens a nostril to get a better sniff. You hopes his beak has picked up the cut grass out the back garden, cos behind you at the end of the kitchen the door is wide open. If he's smelling the other grass up in your bedroom, you and the old dear are in trouble.

But instead he says, – Standard, brer. If you're gone Ely anyway, you can drop me off at my boy's school. It ain't far. Top end of Pentrebane. Right by the top shops. Practically on your way.

You're thinking: – Nice one for offering up some petrol money.

You're saying: – Let's go en, bro. Best be off now if we wants to make it before your kid leaves school.

You steps out the house without even telling the old bat wha gwaan. You hopes later on when you goes to see your new bird that she don't realise you're wearing six month-old trainers.

We gets in the car, and takes a right onto Cowbridge Road. We bombs it down to the Ely roundabout, flying past all the pubs, charity shops and kebab houses on the way. It's busy on the pavement. You got your eyes on the birds, especially the ones in the tight tops. But Evo's got his eyes on both the birds and the guys, especially the blokes in hoodys and baseball caps.

After bombing past the Ely roundabout and taking the second turning into Fairwater, Evo's swede slowly turns to look at you. His eyes are burning through your temple, and you misses second gear twice and almost stalls the engine.

You're thinking: – We're in suburban land, bro. There's loads of nice bungalows and semis here for you to clock and it's the type of place where they leaves their kitchen doors open all night.

You're saying: – Chill, bro. We'll be there in five, standard. We're almost at the Pentrebane hill now. Have a smoke in the glove compartment. No need to worry.

But he just keeps staring at you, and every time your pulse pumps it feels like he's scooping out a little bit more from your noggin.

– I needs a spliff I does, he says. – I gets nervous when I sees my son, brer. My boy don't know yet how bad of a father I really am.

You're thinking: – Fuck, All I got is those turbo ones for when I goes to see the new bird later.

You're saying: – Standard, bro. There's one in the fag pack in the glove compartment.

So he sparks up the magic wand and has a few puffs. He smells the smoke coming off the cherry, which fills the car up with the bitterness that crack, weed and tobacco brings. You knows he recognises the smell cos he practically takes the rest down in one lungful.

His head starts going up and down like he's agreeing with

something. – I knows what you're thinking, he says. – You thinks I'm a bad father for smokin then going to pick up my boy.

You makes an effort to steady the tone of your voice, and not to be too enthusiastic in your answer.

– No, bro. I bet you're a good father, standard.

– I learnt bad habits, see. Me and my ex didn't mean to have my son. Then I basically did what my old man did to me. When I was a nipper, he looked my Mumma bang in the face and said he'd be back at closin time. She never saw him again. And I ain't much better either.

We drives without chatting for the half-mile climb up Gorse Place, and turns past the flats onto Beechley Drive, the last part of the hill and the first point of Pentrebane.

As you parks outside the chippy at the top shops, you goes to take off your seatbelt but Evo stops you. He puts his hood on and pulls all the strings, so all that is showing on his face is the mole to the right of his beak. He pulls your hood over your own noggin, then flumps it into the steering wheel. We stays like that for a second or two, then he lets go. Before you gets the chance to ask him very politely What The Fuck, you looks past all the Mummas going to wait for their nippers and you sees a familiar arse about thirty feet away. It's one of those nice plum bums you could never forget. It could only be Chantelle. Even though her hair is scraped back and she ain't done her face yet, she's still looking beautiful. She's wearing a tight pair of grey jeggings and some tan sheepskin boots. It looks like she's dressing to impress someone later on.

She looks round but don't clock us, and walks into the chippy. – I really can't be arsed, Evo says. – That girl ain't nothin but trouble.

You ain't sure if it's the sight of Chantelle or the magic ingredient in the wand he just had, but Evo's sweating so hard he looks like he's basted himself up for a jailbreak.

– I dunno why you doesn't wanna say hi, you says. – She's safe, she is. Mint and all.

His smile is all cracked and yellow. – Someone got a crush, he says.

You're thinking: – How do I put this.

You're saying: – Come on, bro. She's special, that one. She's the type of bird who don't give two fucks. Everyone fancies her. She's one in a mill, standard.

And he looks out the window and says it himself. – One in a mill.

You're thinking: – Some people needs to be told in black and white.

You're saying: – You knows what I means, bro. She's so fit you'd pay good money to suck the last dick that fucked her.

He takes his hood down.

– If you knows what I does, brer of mine, you wouldn't be sayin that to me.

The way his face is set makes him look like the front end of a Chinese Dragon.

– Well no, spar, you says back, even though you knows you gotta change the subject pronto. – I dunno what's going on in your swede.

You're back in the visiting room again with Maylins. The couple to our left are still going at it, forcing their tongues down each other's throats. You wonders if they carries on like this whether you'll catch a bit of tit out the corner of your eye. You has to stop a minute to take a big gulp of air, cos you got to the bit where you can't look at Maylins in the face while you tells the rest of the story.

You breathes in and out and takes your spar back to that afternoon last week.

You're in the car with Evo, and Chantelle is putting a bag of chips on the passenger seat of her car across the road. You can't help but follow her arse as she bends down. – Put it this way, Evo says. He breathes out smoke and you can feel the spots forming on your forehead already. – We got a special type of relationship, me and Chantelle. She might be trouble, but I got feelins for my girl there, and my girl there got feelins for me. So the more you talks about her like that, the more I feels like I wants to pick your nose with my big toe.

With that, Evo gets out the car and walks down the street to pick his nipper out of school.

You stops the story again and looks at Maylins. He's gone all shoulders and no neck. You've added fifteen years to his face already.

The guy to your left has his hands around the back of his Mrs's swede. She's leaning over the table, her gut just about sitting down on the surface. You realises that they haven't talked all session. Just tongued like they might not ever see each other again.

You tells your spar the rest quick-time, before he got a chance to think. Evo comes out, and his kid is running in front of him in his red and white school uniform. He's all streaked with mud and grass stains. You tells your spar how you ain't sure what was bigger, the little nipper or the bag on his back.

When the kid gets closer, you realises that you recognises the crew cut and the gaps where the milk teeth have fallen out. Then you realises that you are in a bad situation. It's like one of those horrible moments where you're half way through a piss and the toilet seat lid falls down.

Before you gets a chance to put your own hood up, the nipper is looking through the passenger seat window. – Oh look, he says. – It's the big scaredy-cat.

Evo clips him on the crown. The nipper looks up at his old man. – SHURRUP Kyle, Evo says. – I thought your Mumma taught you manners.

And the kid goes quiet and says, – But that's what Mumma calls him. She told me he was a big scaredy-cat and he ran away.

Nothing more is said until Kyle is buckled up in the back and Evo is all in your face like an August wasp. The belt strap cuts across Kyle's neck.

– So then, Kyle, he says as he turns to face his son. – I guess I doesn't have to tell you my man's name then, if you knows it already.

And the kid drops you like you was two stone on a crash diet. – This is Mumma's special friend, he says. – He comes round and he brings pizzas and they even lets me have my own one, but I doesn't like it when he comes round cos I has to go to bed early.

Evo looks over. His face barely moves as he talks.

– It's only been three months, he says.

– It ain't like that, you says. – I didn't know Stace was your kid's Mumma. She never told me, she didn't want me to know. And nothing's happening, it's all over. I got a new bird on the go now, I swears down.

You starts the engine, reverses, and before Evo got a chance to function you're through Pentrebane and heading back down Fairwater.

You knows that if the nipper weren't in the back singing happy songs to himself then Evo would have stomped you so hard his knee would be in your throat.

As you gets to the shops down Fairwater Green, you realises that Evo's been looking at you the whole time.

– Pull over. I think I needs a can to cool off, he says.

You stops the car on the side of the road and Evo offers out a palm. You slaps it with a tenner before he has to ask. He gets out and goes into the shop.

You're thinking: – It ain't far on a bus to Riverside.

You're saying: – Kyle, go ask your Dada for some sweets. Go on, son.

As soon as the little nipper is in the shop, your engine is back on, and you're headed back towards the Ely roundabout. You doesn't look in the rear view mirror until you gone round two bends.

You stops your story there. When you gets your head back into the prison hall, you realises that your spar ain't really been listening for the last few minutes. There's no way of telling if he's cool about it or if he's swimming up an Egyptian river.

– I ain't made none of that up, I says. – Sorry you has to find out like this, bro.

You looks at your hands and you looks at his face, and you can't tell who's more nervous.

– But she was here last week, he says. – There was none of this. Everything was normal.

And all you can think is that the only reason why things were normal is cos Chantelle bottled it.

But before you has to say anything else, the guy and his Mrs to your left starts shouting. The big screw from the waiting room has his arms around her, and he's pulling her out of her seat. The guy stands up, but another meaty screw blows a whistle, and the guy sits down. On a tannoy, everyone is told to stay sat and still. The guy puts his hands on the table, then pulls his fingers in, scratching the table as he goes. You sees him swallow and almost choke, and you knows that he is probably gonna spend the next forty-eight hours in solitary with nothing for company except a bucket.

– That ain't the way to do it, I whispers to Maylins. – If you really needs some brown, don't get your Mrs to bring it in. Get someone you knows to chuck it over the wall.

But Maylins ain't really clocking what's going on.

No one in the room says a word. When the big screw comes back, he ain't got the guy's Mrs no more, and he's carrying a pair of handcuffs. – Don't worry, son, he says. – We're gonna rip that right back out of you.

Back outside in the real world, the sun is out but there ain't no heat. I walks through the car park and gets in my car. The driver's side is already open. I gets in and turns to look at my new bird. Her hair is scraped back but she got her face on, cos she knew she was seeing me today. She gives me a peck on the cheek.

– Did you tell him? Chantelle says.

– Yes.

– Did you tell him everything?

– Yes.

Maylins heard nothing but the truth. But what he might not have heard is how after you fucked off from Evo and his nipper you went straight round Chantelle's house and started to curse her out and asked her how many dicks she got on the go at the same time. And then how she said stop being a dick yourself, I got feelins for him and he got feelins for me cos he's my fuckin cousin and I ain't no cousin fucker. Now you best go and pick him and Kyle back up before he bricks your living room window.

Chantelle smiles as I puts the car into gear and drives off. Just like Maylins, she don't have to hear it all. He don't like sending letters and she won't be hearing from him anyhow. And as I smiles back at her, all I can think of is how lucky I am that I got my mask on.

Some Killing on Cydweli Flats

Jon Gower

A scarecrow wind scythed over Pinged and Llandyry and swept away towards the old washeries, over the acres of sad earth. Here they planted the vegetables in rows so straight they grew in serried ranks, a turnip army ready to march on Llanelli.

That wind. It was a dead wind. A grey wind. A wounding wind sharp enough to flail the skin off your hands. Take off your very face if you weren't careful. Leave you looking like a swede. Really.

With the sea ready to claim the flat lands of the east, eager to inundate Lincolnshire and leave the Wash awash, some agents, working for powers such as Waitrose and Sainsbury's had bought up substantial tracts of land around the Gwendraeth rivers, and along the banks of other estuaries. The markets needed their vegetables. The housewife and househusband must be served. Here, in the grey loams of the Cydweli Flats, they grew the produce they desired, to be plastic-wrapped for their fresh marriages.

They grubbed up acres of sea lavender and purslane, or otherwise blitzed the saltmarshes with selective herbicides, followed by a campaign of dumping lorry loads of nitrates on the razed earth, before finally turning the soil over with ruthless machines designed to work under big skies. Then, and only then were the marshes ready for planting.

That wind. It keened over the fields of cauliflowers, sprouts and potatoes and, because this was bleak midwinter, it seemed to blow in straight from Russia, hauling chill from the Urals and rendering the Carmarthenshire earth as hard as permafrost. In the middle distance, over toward Trimsaran and Crwbin, the only remaining stand of blackthorn hereabouts – now that so many hedges had been razed or uprooted – cowered under the effect of the wind, hunchbacked by the insistent, persistent onslaught.

As the vegetable pickers drudged through the hours of backbreak work the wind seemed to mourn those who had died in the area: Victorian dockers of mangolds, coracle men with a flair for catching sewin and cockle pickers made tubercular by the gouts of rain, the endless seeping drizzle.

Today's employers didn't give the men any protective clothing, so they made do, with sou'westers and a lot of assorted rubber wear. One man even wore flippers, and not for a laugh, either. On waterlogged days the veg fields could turn into quagmires, suck at your boots like jellyfish.

Lennie Evans, one of the young men cutting turnips for a pound-an-hour-less-than-minimum-wage was thinking with every cut green head that he shouldn't be doing this. He really shouldn't be a human robot standing under sheeting rain. He had four A-levels and three fifths of a degree in medicine and the last time he'd spent this much time slicing he'd been removing a spleen with a threadwire saw in an anatomy practical. His tutor'd said his handiwork was good enough to let him practice on a live patient if he liked. But Doctor Friss was only joking. Or half-joking at least.

But things had come to a pretty underpass. His life had been completely turned around as a consequence of a foolish mistake when he spent a night, just a single night with a woman who got pregnant and it was only then that she told him that her father happened to be someone you really shouldn't mess with, which was shorthand for a dastardly criminal in the Barry Island mafia who had a penchant for designer knives and trying out carving lessons on gripped human flesh. It all led to Len having to leave town and what was worse *his parents* having to leave town and change identities to boot. After all, this was a very well connected sociopathic gangster who really could hunt you down wherever you were cowering. But these root veg and beet fields were off his radar. Nobody in his right mind would want to live out here.

So Len was a former medical student now plucking veg from hard ground for the daily Waitrose run, in the company of half a dozen drifters and grifters. Malc the Alc, a Scot with a leathery face, whose name said it all. The Dutchman Gerbrand, never said boo to a goose but worked like a Trojan. Dave Pearce, another drop-out who'd been doing philosophy and did seem wise for his years. Then there was Mark, a sullen junkie whose life was divided equally between work and junk and Tommy, who had a wife and seven kids somewhere in the Midlands. And finally Trinder, a total malcontent they'd all be glad to get shot of, as he moaned more than the wind.

They all had their work cut out. Twenty thousand root vegetables, padlocked under frost-ice, which had to be wrested from the ground, trimmed, washed and then shrink-wrapped at the farm before a driver would collect them to take them down to a central distribution centre somewhere near Magor on the M4.

Twenty thousand vegetables. Not that Len had time to ponder too much about numbers. He had other things to worry about. Such as the near-dead man they'd found in one of the old aircraft hangars just a few hours ago.

They had gone there to eat lunch, in what passed for warmth, even though it was like cold storage in there. They didn't get as far as unwrapping the sandwiches.

He was dangling. The man hung in the air, his arms suspended by two lengths of rope, each as thick as naval hawser and he'd been there long enough for his hands to whiten through lack of blood flow. They looked like two white tulips, limp, slowly desiccating.

But he was alive.

The man's voice was dry, desperate, sparking tinily like radio static. In a strained voice, but in a curious accent, the man offered Len and his mates a small fortune if they could just cut him free and get him to a hospital. He gargled out a figure of twenty thousand pounds and they knew they could probably get him to go higher. Bidding for your own life – it was always a buyer's market.

It was hard for them to place the accent even thought the pain-wracked face suggested he was Romanian or Bulgarian, one of the new wave of immigrants anyway. He was weak, had lost a perilous lot of blood. The ground beneath him was like a sticky blotched carpet and Lennie was horrified to see some of the red stuff adhering to his wellingtons.

They took their positions to help.

The trouble is something awful happened as they were cutting him loose when the dour Dutch boy Gerbrand's turnip-knife slipped, went in without fuss or ado between the man's ribs and he just seemed to deflate before them, the air leaving his body as a cold mist around the mouth, matching the bated breath of the onlookers and the bystanders in the dumb show in the cold aluminium shed, watching the man leave this life without so much as a by-your-leave or proper whimper.

They had come into the hangar as free men. Now they were burdened by what they knew, witnesses or in some cases accomplices to a death, a manslaughter and the slaughtered man lay there on the ground in front of them, his eyes glazing like mackerel.

So what happened next happened to all of them: they were all so totally, overwhelmingly implicated. Trinder said they were up shit creek without a paddle, and he had a point for once.

They knew they had to get rid of the body. No doubt about that but the soil outside was completely frozen. You'd need jackhammers, or the sort of trenching drills they use when setting telegraph poles. All they had were spades and it would take them until February to cut a hole big enough for the body.

It was Len who had the idea...

The beet boiler, set up in one corner of the hangar, was a large aluminium box, big enough to accommodate a car the size of a Mini set on a plinth of old railway sleepers. The conveyor belt rattled the beets along from the processing lines, looking like misshapen bowling balls, and they would drop into the scalding water to be boiled until they were soft.

'What if we drop him in there for an hour or so? There won't be much left of him by tea-time?' suggested Lennie, pragmatically.

They conferred and after ten minutes of ghoulish debate Malc the Alc strode over to the far wall and threw the electricity switch and started to boil the water. While that happened the men stripped the clothes from the corpse – he looked far more of a corpse with every passing moment, as the death mask set rigid. They placed the clothes in a barrel which was used for burning palette tags and set them on fire, stoking the flames with anything burnable they could find in the shed, so they added piles of wrapping paper, stuff that advertised 'Two for One Deals', 'Finest Quality', 'Shop Early For Christmas'.

By the time they'd done that the water was beginning to steam and so they put the body on the conveyor and it started trundling him along, lifting him slowly toward the lip of the tank. There was something, well, sacred looking about him, the rope burns like stigmata, the flaccid belly innocent as a baby's, the sense of life being unutterably over for the stranger heading for the boil.

Lenny then had his second brainwave of the day; one that would ensure their secret was safe, that there would be no weak link in the chain.

Next to the beat-up old kettle in the far corner of the hangar there were seven mugs, one for each of the gang. Lenny's proclaimed 'Welcome to LA' in day-glo letters while there were four that were giveaways from doctors' surgeries brandishing logos for 'Xanthal,' 'Nembutose' and Rantiril, 'The laxative for the discerning bowel.' Lenny always laughed when he saw that, never grew tired of its hopelessness. Then there was a plain green mug that belonged to Ger and a chipped enamel one that Malc was strangely protective of until they found out that his mother used to keep her teeth in it and thus had sentimental value. He put them on all a makeshift tray made from a cardboard box and carried them over to the crew.

He placed the tray and the mugs on the floor in a manner which was nothing less than ceremonial. The others watched him like hawks, nervous and attentive at one and the same time.

Then he picked up the first of the mugs, his own, and took it over to the boiler. He stood there for a few seconds, a priest taking stock before the sacrament, before he turned the little brass tap that allowed you to take a sample of the liquids therein. He filled his mug an eighth full and did the same with all the others.

The men looked on horrified, their faces whitewashed with horror, as if they were wearing masks in a Noh play.

Lenny handed out the mugs and then took the first supremely significant drink, downing it in one and doing his level best to make it look as if he were doing nothing more than drinking Vimto. The others held their cups as if they contained rattlesnake juice, or the blood of the unborn, or a pint of the Devil's own piss but one by one they drank the contents down, knowing there was some well nigh unbelievable logic in this demonic communion. Draughts to salve their conscience? Maybe not. Drinks to bind them together forever, in a pact of silence as tight as tensile steel? Perhaps.

They stood there dumb and transfixed by the moment, the taste hard to get rid of, as it was more than just taste. It was a memory they couldn't excise, a portent of what prison food would taste like if they weren't careful, now that they'd entered fatefully into in a pact of silence, like so many Trappist monks.

And that might have been that. Seven workers had been bound together by an impossible guilty secret, a stain on their collective souls as bright as beetroot. Except there was a scurry in the corner of the hangar, where an outsize rat, big as a small domestic cat, slinked behind some old silage sacks. A metallic glint attracted Lennie's attention and when he looked more closely he saw a chain and that chain connected to an attaché case, like the sort of thing you'd see attached to the wrist of a diamond mule in a Bond movie. He picked up the case and put it on a straw bale to take a better look.

'You'd better put it back where you found it.' It was Gerbrand, whose voice was unfamiliar to them all, and gained some authority from that fact. Trinder said whatever it was it belonged to someone else and they were all going to die painful deaths, which wasn't useful.

But curiosity needs to kill the cat.

Lennie picked up a sharp-edged tool from a pile of metal detritus and snapped open the lock with surprising ease.

They'd all seen scenes like this one in films, where the lid of a case opens up to reveal tightly-packed blocks of currency. Michael Caine's usually somewhere about, or George Clooney and there's a soundtrack that's a shimmer of violins.

They looked at it aghast before feeling the need to count it and when they unpeeled one of the blocks and found it was a major amount of money in itself, fifty pounds short of fifty thousand pounds and that fifty was probably a miscount so they realized that they had stumbled upon an honest to goodness fortune even though there was probably little that was honest behind it. Then the Dutch boy spoke again and this time his voice had the timbre of the oracle at Delphi.

'I saw a helicopter.'

They waited for amplification, which came very slowly, phrase by phrase.

'It came in off the sea and landed just outside this place.'

Another pause, a long one.

'Then I saw a man with a chain attached to his wrist coming out of the helicopter and the chain was attached to the case.'

'This case?' asked Lennie, his voice a little high-pitched, a bit heliumed-up with anxiety.

'Yes. This case. This case was attached to his wrist by a length of chain. He then came out of here without it.'

Another pause, painfully long. Their eyes egged him on to continue.

'And then he ran to the helicopter, jumped on board and it took off again in the direction of the sea.'

The information bludgeoned them into silence. It was a while before they could breathe properly, let alone speak.

Lennie was the one to sum it up, the scale of their dilemma.

'So there'll be someone coming to pick it up. Maybe the dead guy was the one who came to pick it up and they tried to find out where it was hidden.'

'They?' queried Malc the Alc.

'It would take more than one person to hang a man from ropes in the air, Malcolm. That's self-evident.' Lennie was taking charge, minute by minute.

Malc looked crestfallen, his eyes puppy eyes, maybe for the first time in his life.

'So they'll be back...'

'Or maybe they haven't gone away. Maybe they're watching this place, waiting for Mr Dead's accomplice to show up,' offered Trinder almost chirpily. No wonder they all loathed him.

'Is it time for us to start shitting ourselves?' suggested Dave Pearce, at his helpful best. You could just tell he was a philosophy graduate. The way he cut to the heart of the matter. Made you think.

'I think we should take a vote,' offered Lennie, adding that by his reckoning each one of them would have at least four hundred thousand pounds before apologizing that he wasn't that good at maths. But he was near the mark, he maintained.

'Anyway,' he added, 'there's a lot of money there, and so there's a lot of money divided by six.'

'They'll slit out throats,' said Gebrand, who was getting almost chatty.

'If they can find us,' said Malc.

'Oh, they'll find us all right,' chipped in Mark who was already imagining grade A smack that he wouldn't have to buy off the skanky dealers he normally visited in their rat holes. Opiates had made him depressive. It figures.

When it came down to it they voted to take the money and run. Or rather, hide.

And for four long days nothing happened. In fact by the fourth day most of them had started to dream about what they'd end up doing when they weren't on the veg and their thoughts turned positively tropical, with sun-kissed beaches and pina coladas and lots of lying around and not a Brussels fucking sprout within a million miles. In their dreamy reveries they drank a lot and stayed warm all day and never had to bend over with a knife in their hands to cut a stubborn stalk ever again.

They thought these thoughts in silence, in a nervous stubborn silence, which weighed down on them as if they had breeze blocks on their shoulders.

Then on the fifth day, when they were all strung out in a long line picking cauli, they heard the drone of a far-off helicopter which then grew louder as it buzzed in low over St Ishmaels and Salmon Scar. Within minutes it was right overhead, which made them all nervous beyond, so it was with a huge sigh of relief that they watched it pass over and keep heading east although it didn't pass far enough east, but rather veered and banked and abruptly landed on the old earthwork known as the Bank O' Lords.

The doors of the helicopter opened and a dozen men in black silk suits, each man wearing a black balaclava mask, ran out. The swords they carried, or rather the scimitars they carried, glistened in the late afternoon sun. The men didn't stop to appreciate the exotic spectacle, tearing the hell away across the vegetable rows, stumbling over the cut stalks which acted like trip wires, like stumbling blocks. Lennie saw the Dutch boy get beheaded even as he managed to reach a little boat tied up on the biggest creek feeding into the Gwendraeth Fawr. He saw a severed hand lying on a bed of sea purslane, the fingers clenching and unclenching uselessly before turning rigid. He saw smears of red against the purplish greens of the marsh grasses, like a painting of butchery.

Lennie managed to get its outboard engine racing and he had the forethought to leave his jacket draped over the back of the boat when he slid into the water, watching the craft head straight out to sea. And by some miracle, some ridiculous miracle, the men didn't actually see him slink into the muddy water, and by the time they saw the boat and ran back to the chopper to send it skywards to chase after the boat, Lennie had managed to crawl his way into the buckthorn growth, which was a place that tore at your skin, a terrible place of savage thorns which could spear your eyeballs. But just as he felt the threat of the sharp-spined plants so too did he feel their protective safety as he pushed himself further in, knowing there were bloody acres of the stuff. Unless they had thermal imaging equipment he was safe, and the good thing was that the buckthorn groves – if you could call them that – abutted the dried up concrete culvert where they'd left the case. The whole thing almost made a religious man of him, but not quite.

Lennie still thinks of that day, not that often it has to be said because who would want to cultivate the stuff of nightmares, truth be told? To remember drinking a man's vital juices mixed with beetroot. To recall a severed hand, palping the very moments of death.

It's a warm wind that blows over the beach on Antigua and the birds are more colourful than any postage stamp. Sometimes, when he dozes like this, even as the afternoon sun turns from satsuma slowly through to pearl, the men in their bandanas run in from dark corners, across the Gwendraeth marshlands and Cydweli Flats. They give chase, vibrant with imprecations and alive with their lunging sabres and he hears that scarecrow wind as it shivers the leaves. He may then shudder himself awake, or choose to fall into deeper sleep and leave them far behind.

One thing's for certain in his Caribbean home. He will never ever eat a root vegetable again in his life and the very words Brussels sprouts give him the hives.

For him, now, life is all papaya and he likes it that way.

Yes, all papaya and ghost crabs nibbling the flesh of his heels as he paddles in the waves: a shirr of blue water as it laps against his toes.

Yes, life is good now.

As the sun settles into the sea. And as the day's heat, blow-lamped over the mangrove line, must now surely dissipate, allowing the cooling zephyr of the night to blow right on through.

Our Cardboard Binoculars

Rhian Elizabeth

I'd lost count of how many people my father had been. For a long time I knew who he was. His name was Tom Jones and he wrote this song for my mother called 'With These Hands' and when we didn't see him, which was all the time because he was busy flying around the world in his private jet making women take their knickers off with just his eyes, she would play that record so we could hear him instead. When I asked her why I'd never seen him, she would say to me…

'Because your father was a bastard, Jackson Jones.'

Then one day when she was in work I found the record around the back of the settee and would you believe it, there he was on the cover. I finally had a face to go with the voice.

Tom Jones. My father.

It was a bit weird really, because he wasn't like me at all – not what I expected. Me and my father, we had the same surname, but we looked so different. Tom Jones had curly black hair and mine was blond, and his eyes were dark and mine were green and when I thought about it, none of the girls in my class at school had ever thrown their knickers at me. This one girl, called Laura Evans, she had once thrown her HB pencil at me, and the tip got caught in the skin on the bridge of my nose and dangled there for a good ten seconds and made me bleed and I've still got the scar, but there were never any knickers, not one single pair.

So when I got a bit older and I learned how to use the Yellow Pages and so I went through it looking for Tom Jones and trust me, when you live in Wales, there are a fuck load of Tom Joneses to get through. But I managed to narrow my search down a bit. There were twenty-seven Tom Joneses in Cwmdu, the village where we live, and I rang them all one by one, twisting the white cord around each of my fingers asking them, my name is Jackson Jones and are you my father? Some of them were quite rude to me. They hung up on me the phone and one Tom

Jones, he even told me to piss off. I was shocked to find out when I got even older that Tom Jones was this famous Welsh singer who had sold millions of records and that one part was true though, lots of women had thrown their knickers at him... but he definitely wasn't my father.

My father was lots of other men. I got to meet those. They had faces and cars and everything. One of them took me and my mother on holiday in a caravan but none of them stayed around for very long. It made me a bit angry, so I decided there was only one thing for it. I had to kill every man in Wales. If not every man in Wales then at least every man in Cwmdu. It was actually Morgan Davies' idea. Morgan Davies was my best friend and we lived on the same street, twenty-six doors apart. He didn't know his father either and he said that we needed to teach them both a lesson for leaving us because leaving your kids isn't a nice thing to do. It sort of made sense.

He wasn't dressed like a murderer when he knocked for me on Friday night. I say Friday night but it was really Saturday morning, three am. He was dressed like normal Morgan Davies, baggy denim jeans and a black Adidas hoodie sagging down over the top, brown sauce stain on the chest that had been there forever, as if his mother had bought it from the shop like that. He was wearing gloves, too, these girly ones that I remembered him wearing last winter when it snowed and I told him then he looked like a poof, like I told him again on Friday night. They were glowing under the street light. It was like he'd dipped his hands in some radioactive paint or something. They buzzed a bright pink colour and he had a pair for me in his pocket as well, yellow ones that were just as bright and poofy.

'I'm not wearing those,' I told him.

But he said I had to. We didn't want to get any of the stuff on our hands, did we? So I put them on and I looked really, really stupid. Morgan Davies had gone and made us a pair of binoculars each- two cardboard toilet roll tubes stuck together with Sellotape. He hadn't bothered to colour them in with a black felt or anything to make them seem real, so we looked like the stupidest criminals ever... a couple of kids playing cops and robbers in poofy gloves. Well, two robbers and no cops.

The main road was dead quiet when we walked down it. We'd left our mothers in our houses fast asleep in bed and there was literally no one around, no people and no cars, just a swarm of buzzing gnats that were taking part in some kind of late night disco under the street lights we passed. The middle of summer and still warm despite being so late and I won't lie, I was sweating walking up that road. Morgan Davies said he could feel a storm coming on but I didn't believe him. He was always saying stuff like that, like he was some kind of mystical native Indian chief who could talk to the wind and the trees and the elements.

We were sweating and talking quiet and heading for Park Street and when we got there we hid behind a big yellow metal skip in the road. We put our cardboard binoculars up to our eyes but there was nothing to see. There were no lights on behind any of the curtains of the windows on that terraced street. And the windows that mattered the most, the windows of old man Jenkins' house, they were black, too. As black as the sky that had no stars in it. Old man Jenkins – in his nineties and always in the local paper, proudly cradling something in his crumpled arms, a marrow like it's a massive, fat green fish he's reeled out of the soil in his back garden. His garden was the reason we were in that street so late. Morgan Davies jumped the wall first and I went over after him. It wasn't a high wall so it was easy enough.

I couldn't make out my feet below me and Morgan Davies, he was just a shadow leading us down old man Jenkins' flat garden path. All I could see was his hands. They were like two pink apparitions or spirits hovering and moving in mid-air and my own hands also burned like nuclear ghosts. But Morgan Davies had a torch in his hoodie pocket and when we got inside old man Jenkins' greenhouse he shone it around the pots and plants and soil and bulging green shoots and flowers, the rays bouncing around the glass walls like laser beams. He started searching and moving things about – watering cans swimming with dirty, leafy water, and heavy tubs of earth and mud caked tools that were messily arranged on wooden shelves. The scraping of metal hurt my ears and I was sure old man Jenkins would wake up, but Morgan Davies said nah, he was as deaf as a post.

I felt like I was standing deep in the heart of a rainforest. Some plants were taller than me. Thin and green they snaked and twisted and twirled from the shelves until they touched the glass roof. I was sure that if that roof wasn't there to stop them they would have climbed all the way up to the sky itself. It was warm as anything in there and I was sweating even worse than I was on the walk up. My hands under my gloves were getting greasy and clammy and the smell of wet dirt and roots and leaves, of earth, that kind of outdoor smell, made me feel sick. Morgan Davies pulled a tomato, plump and red and perfectly round like a snooker ball, off one of the leaves and when he popped it in his mouth with his teeth, I heard it squelch and split. I didn't know how he could eat. My heart was beating so loud I thought even deaf as a post old man Jenkins would hear it up in his bedroom. I was really glad when Morgan Davies found what he was looking for. The yellow beam of his torch illuminated a red topped bottle with a skull and crossbones label on the front. He picked it up with his pink gloved hands and shook it at me.

'Old man Jenkins uses this stuff to stop the cats getting to his vegetables. Remember all those posters people put up?'

I thought about my posters then, the posters I made when I was looking for my father. I stuck them up around the village and Morgan Davies helped me. There wasn't a lamppost left untouched on the streets of Cwmdu. I printed them off on the computer myself. A4 paper and big, bold Comic Sans font. And I remember exactly what the posters said.

They said…

'Hi, Dad. It's me. My name is Jackson Jones. You had me 14 years ago and I'm not that angry. If you want to find me you can find me on Cwmdu Road, number 76'.

So you can't go saying I didn't give him a chance. The Yellow Pages, and the posters. It's not like I wanted to kill my father, but like Morgan Davies said, over and over again… leaving your kids isn't a nice thing to do.

But in old man Jenkins' greenhouse Morgan Davies wasn't on about those posters anyway. He was on about the posters of all those missing cats. They were on lampposts too, and in the shop window on the main road. Some of them were proper professional posters like I had made on my computer but a lot of them were just notices scribbled on postcards and pieces of paper. Every week there seemed to be a new missing cat in the village. The notices would say stuff like…much loved family pet lost since 3 weeks… reward of £200 if found. Ones like that.

And then they started to find all these dead cats all over the place. They were in the gutters and on the pavements, like bin bags blown in a storm. Fur and blood and flopping tongues and popped out eyeballs, and cat brains and eye juice. They found some cats in the lake and people started to talk and they were saying that it was old man Jenkins' who had done it, to try to destroy the evidence.

'Jenkins puts this poison down on his garden,' Morgan Davies said in the greenhouse, 'and the poor little cats come and lick it up like it's tasty, sweet milk, just like our fathers will.'

Morgan Davies grinned then, and he looked a bit creepy in the eerie light of his torch. He thought it up all by himself. He didn't need any help from me. In fact, I had no input whatsoever in our murder plan. His mother worked in the bakery on the main road and before he came out of his house that Friday night, he had taken her keys off the hook in the kitchen. We were going to break in and use old man Jenkins' poison to poison all the men in the village because if our fathers lived in the village, they were sure to eat there. Everyone else did. The bakery was famous for its delicious cakes and corned beef pasties, and freshly baked bread that had won awards for being the nicest in Wales. And Saturday mornings were the busiest mornings of the week, busy with people queuing up for sliced cobs and chocolate éclairs and packs of four corned beef pasties for a pound. I'd eaten many an éclair there myself and I won't lie, they were lush. Morgan Davies had the keys in his hoodie pocket which was massive enough to fit his torch and binoculars in as well, and now the bottle of old man Jenkins' cat and father killer was stuffed in there, too.

We left the greenhouse and the garden. Back down the dead roads. Morgan Davies opened the door of the bakery, the keys like a jangling tambourine in his fluffy pink fist, and no alarm sounded. No alarm, I thought, because what criminal would steal cakes and loaves of bread? Proper criminals with proper binoculars stole tellies and money and mobile phones.

The massive display counter inside was empty. It was a glass abyss of nothingness but by the morning when my father, and Morgan Davies' father, got to the front of the queue, it would be crammed full of beautiful cakes, cakes with strawberries neatly placed on top of cream and pastry, and chocolate éclairs, and baguettes with mouths flopping with lettuce and cheese and chicken mayo filling, and those crusty loaves which tasted so prize-winningly good. They would be spoiled for choice, our fathers would, and they would take a while to decide what they wanted but when they did, when they sunk their teeth into their pasties and their cakes, they would choke to death, eyeballs popping out like them cats', and they would deserve it, because leaving your kids isn't a nice thing to do.

Morgan Davies knew where the kitchen was. It was round the back through some long, plastic curtains that tickled my face when I went through them. I just followed him and his gloves and his torch beam again. The kitchen was spacious and cool, not claustrophobic and hot like the greenhouse rainforest. It was dead dark and quiet in there, except for the drip, drip of a tap that echoed into the metal of the sink below. It smelled of freshly baked bread. The brown and white cobs were lined up on a counter, Morgan Davies shone his light on them. They were wrapped up ready for the morning rush and on the wall was a box labelled latex gloves and one, blue and limp, spewed out like a dead cockerel's head but Morgan Davies was all set with his pink ones. I watched him take things out of the fridge. He wasn't being careful to be quiet. He peeled back the Clingfilm on plastic tubs which were full of sandwich filling and he shook old man Jenkins' poison over them like he was a baker seasoning them with salt and pepper. Nothing was safe in the kitchen. He sprinkled everything he saw. The bread and the pasties and the cakes and the sausage rolls, and then he dared me to do it, too. He said to me...

'What would your father like to eat the most?'

I had no idea. I didn't even know his name. I just knew how much I loved those chocolate éclairs and I saw them there in the fridge all chocolaty and tasty looking. So Morgan Davies slid the tray out for me. The yellow light of the fridge lit up the whole kitchen much better than his torch did. He passed me old man Jenkins' bottle of poison and so I did it. My luminous hands were shaking like mental. I tried to stop them because I didn't want to embarrass myself in front of Morgan Davies who was cool as anything, as cool as the kitchen fridge itself, but I couldn't help it. I hadn't even met my father and there I was, about to kill him. We both shook that bottle around until there was nothing left in it. Morgan Davies locked the bakery up behind us with his mother's tambourine keys and we walked down to the lake which was less than a minute away. I kept looking behind me but the sleepy streets of Cwmdu were comatose.

Morgan Davies threw old man Jenkins' bottle into the lake when we got there. He launched it so high and so far with a swing of his arm like a discus thrower that I didn't see it land but I heard it splash into the blackness of the water. I imagined it bobbing like one of them dead cats had bobbed when old man Jenkins threw them in. And then we threw our gloves in but we could see them land, what with them being so bright and all. They didn't sink, they floated, like four radiant lily pads on top of the lake. Morgan Davies said they would be at the bottom by the morning and even if they weren't, no one would think anything strange about it anyway, to see two pairs of poofy gloves perched on the lake like that because there was loads of things at the bottom of that lake and on top and stuck between the rocks and the weeds. Car tyres and dead cats, and empty Coke bottles and beer cans and crisp packets and stuff like that. If anything, our gloves just made the lake look pretty.

That's when the rain came. The sound of the thunder in the sky jolted us both as we stared at the lake and the island in the middle of it, and the geese that were sleeping in the bushes not bothered one bit by the grumbling sky, with white feathers that glowed as bright as our gloves. We dropped our cardboard binoculars to the ground and we ran back home. We shot up the streets and across the roads like two burning comets. We ran so fast I think we got to the start of our street before the rain drops that left the clouds like Morgan Davies knew they would had hit the pavements. But they did hit the pavements, alright. The clouds were like a net heavy with water balloons and they dropped right on us in the street and exploded on top of the parked cars with big splashes of water and one by one they set off their alarms. We had to get inside before people on our street, especially our mothers, started waking up.

'What about our cardboard binoculars?' I asked Morgan Davies before he went.

He had been careful to wear poofy gloves for finger prints and for the spilling poison, but we had been lazy about our binoculars. He said he would go back to get them in the morning and he would throw them in the lake, too, and then I watched him run through the puddles twenty six doors down and disappear into his house.

We killed seventeen people according to the local paper. Some of the customers at the bakery had been lucky to get away with just their stomachs pumped at the hospital. The story took up the whole of the front page, not like old man Jenkins who only ever made the inside pages with his marrows. Old man Jenkins didn't die. He didn't go to the bakery that Saturday morning. Ten of the dead were men and seven of them were women, that's including Morgan Davies' mother.

Now I'm making some new posters up on my computer in Comic Sans. I read the names of the men who died in the paper and none of them were Jones so I'm giving my father another chance. When I press the print button I'm thinking about those dead cats and those posters, and while I wait for mine to shoot out of the printer mouth I go downstairs and choose one of my mother's records from around the back of the settee. I turn the volume right down on her record player, so that she doesn't wake up. I don't put on 'With These Hands' though. Instead my father sings to me, ever so quietly, something different and something a bit more cheerful… 'What's new pussy cat woah oh oh oh oh oh'. And I know he's not my real father, but I wish he was because any father who has girls throw their knickers at them instead of their HB pencils, seems like quite a cool father to have.

Ghost Story

Carly Holmes

She was the only girl I've ever known who could make walking boots and a duffle coat look sexy. I was in love before I even got out of the car, before I'd even met her properly. Curls like kinked copper piping, eyes the same colour as rain-soaked oak. She stood in the lane and smiled as if she wanted nothing more than to spend this autumn day in the woods with a city boy, a friend of a friend, and help him with his thesis on haunted houses. I could have spent the rest of my life just sitting there, gripping the steering wheel, watching her smile at me, but I figured I had thirty seconds, tops, before she started to get nervous.

I slid out of the car and hefted my backpack onto my shoulder, trying to stand tall and relaxed as if I did this country living lark every day. My new walking boots were already starting to scrape the skin from my right heel and I knew I'd be limping before we got further than the first stile. My mate in Cardiff, the one who'd hooked me up with this beautiful creature, had lent me thick wool socks and told me they needed to be worn outside the jeans, pulled all the way to the knee. When I whined that they made me look like a twat he told me that the deerstalker hat with the price tag still dangling made me look like a twat. The socks just made me look slightly froggish.

'Megan?' I asked as I bent to stop one of the socks from shuffling back down my shin. 'Hi, I'm Matt. Thanks so much for saying you'll help.'

She gave me her hand. 'It's a pleasure; my gran loves visitors. We'll go straight in now, before lunch. You won't want to be there when she gets stuck into the cawl.'

We walked to the houses grouped along the lane. 'Old fisherman's cottages,' she said. 'They're all the same here in Aberarth, they turn their backs to the sea. And this one's hers. Boots off, I'm afraid. She doesn't like to vacuum that often.' She grinned at me. 'And you might be more comfortable if you wore the socks under your jeans.'

I sat in the tiny front room, testing my Dictaphone, while the kettle and Megan whistled in the kitchen. Her gran eyed me expectantly from an armchair.

'What's that thing?' she asked.

I showed her the Dictaphone and clicked a few of the buttons. 'It'll record everything you say and then I can write it up later.'

She seemed impressed. She nodded a couple of times and stared at the wall for a while, mouth pursed. 'Not going to give me cancer, is it?'

'No, Mrs Howells, it's safe.' I held it out to her. 'Do you want a closer look?'

She flapped a hand at me and tugged her blanket further up her chest. 'You keep hold of it. No reason why I should have to have it.'

The return of Megan had me fumbling pen and papers to the carpet. I think she knew the effect she had on me but she was graceful about it and let me help her with the tea while she picked up my notes. Her gran sat and watched us through narrowed eyes as milky pale and faded as sea glass. 'Crumbs!' she barked as I took a piece of cake. Megan softened the command by winking at me as she leaned forward with a plate.

Once centre-stage, Mrs Howells set aside her suspicions of my character and modern technology and shuffled forward in her chair so that she could tap my wrist with her spoon whenever the fancy took her.

'It's way up in the valley,' she said. 'Up where the Arth is still more stream than river. She'll take you,' a nod towards Megan, 'though I don't like her going and I've told her so. There're a lot of ruined cottages up there, scattered through the woods. Most of them were crumbled down to nothing by the time I was born but that one was still lived in. My mother took me there every Sunday with a basket of bread and some potatoes. Christian charity, she said, but I knew it was because she was scared.' The quick, precise flick of her spoon against my wrist bone made me jump.

'You see, she was a witch. The woman who lived in the cottage. Nobody ever said as much but we all knew it. Once a month she'd come down to the village and stand in the lane, not looking at us, not speaking, just waiting. We'd all, each household, fill her sack with what food we had and then she'd go. She touched my mother once, laid a hand on her stomach when she was pregnant with me and blessed the bump. Four miscarriages before that but she carried me straight through and delivered me with barely a drop of blood spilt. But what you can give you can also take away, that's what my mother thought, and that's why she made the extra offerings. Just. In. Case.' Three more taps of her spoon. I had to stifle a grin and knew that Megan was smiling behind her mug.

'And then one day she had a child with her. A girl, not much more than a toddler and weak as a newborn. There was something wrong with her, you know, in the head. Constantly dribbling. She'd walk in circles if she were put down. Nobody could believe the witch had had her the usual way, no man would dare go near her, so the little one must have been dumped in the woods like people dump kittens they don't want. Either that or she stole her.

'Anyway, things carried on as they were and no questions asked. Blankets and firewood and vegetables in the winter, apples and fish in the summer. We all rubbed along and the child seemed healthy enough. Didn't like us though. I never saw her smile, not once. My mother made me give her a bag of my old toys one Christmas and she tipped them out onto the ground in front of me and stood on each one, grinding them under her shoes. I cried all the way home.'

She settled back in her chair and raised her eyebrows at Megan, who stood up and gathered the mugs. 'More tea?'

I nodded and murmured a thank you but was so engrossed in her grandmother's story I forgot to look up to watch Meg leave the room, and by the time I remembered she'd disappeared back into the kitchen. Mrs Howells thinned her lips and folded her arms, staring at me. We waited in silence until Megan returned and only then did she unfold her arms and carry on.

'Yes, she was an odd one, that girl. She used to spend her time sitting in the upstairs window of the cottage and gawking at the world around her. There can't have been much of a view, it was all trees, but she'd sit and stare and point the way you or I would if we were dropped onto the busiest street in London. Who knows, maybe she saw things in the trees the likes of us couldn't see?

'When the witch died the girl couldn't have been more than half grown, eleven at most. We should have done something then, someone should have, it's not right to leave a little girl up in the woods all by herself. But, you see, we didn't want her. None of us wanted her. So we never talked about it. Left the odd bag of potatoes by the door, that kind of thing, and pretended that she didn't exist. She made it easy for us, she never came to the village in the daytime, though there were some who said they saw her now and then after dark, digging through the allotments.'

She nodded at the memory and reached for her tea. 'Any more cake, Meg? I can't remember exactly when she died but it was a few years later. Some childhood illness she should have left behind with her pigtails, but I suppose she was a late bloomer for that kind of thing, what with being so backward. A few people said that they'd stopped seeing her at the window but none of us wanted to know so nobody knocked on the door. Nobody went in to check.

'A couple of tourists found her a few months later. Walkers, they were, and they raised a right fuss afterwards, trying to get the police interested. Made us feel like criminals. She'd been dead a while. Curled on the floor beneath the window in the upstairs room she was, fingers hooked round the edge of the sill. As if she'd tried to drag herself up for one last look out. Poor girl.'

I took another piece of cake. 'Did you ever find out where she came from? Did any relatives come forward?'

She glared at me. 'I haven't finished yet, young man. You can ask your questions later. You wanted to hear a haunted house story and I'm just getting to that part.'

She acknowledged my mouthed apology with a slight movement of her head and cleared her throat.

'So there we were, all very sorry for the poor girl but really, it wasn't as if we'd done anything wrong. She was taken away and buried in the churchyard on the top of the hill. You couldn't pay for a view like that these days. Meg can take you up to see the grave, I'm sure, if you can handle the walk.' The doubtful glance she gave me spoke volumes about her confidence in my ability to handle a walk even half that distance.

'After she was buried we didn't give her any more thought, if I'm honest. It was over and done with. There were a few hardnosed types, mentioning no names, who went up to the cottage to see if there was anything worth taking, and a few ghouls who wanted to see where she'd died, but the rest of us left well alone. And then the troubles began.'

My Dictaphone suddenly let out a high-pitched squeak and I echoed it with my own chirrup of alarm. Megan chuckled quietly from her corner and her gran threw back her head and bellowed her delight.

'Got you scared, have I?' she asked, as I fiddled with the tiny machine. 'Like a ghost story, do you?'

I tried to laugh. 'Love them. I'm a big kid when it comes to a good ghosting and the scarier the better. Please, carry on.' I was desperate to press my hands to my hot cheeks but didn't want to draw any more attention to myself.

'So,' she continued, still smiling, 'during that autumn, a few months after she'd died, we had an outbreak of whooping cough in the village. It claimed nine young lives in a few weeks. They had to shut the village school; there was no one to fill it. In the winter we lost five souls at sea. Old Evans and his three lads first, in one fell swoop, all gone. There wasn't even a storm. Poor Aggie, his widow, she was never the same.

'By the next spring we were all of us wearing black in one form or another. I lost both parents to their hearts and the lady who lived next door broke her leg and got an infection that carried her off. There were whispers that the witch had put a curse on us for neglecting her child, and some folk even started leaving offerings up at the cottage. I got married and fell pregnant and barely left the house once I started showing, the looks I got. Everyone expected me to lose it, you see. But I didn't. Her mother.' She pointed at Megan.

'And then people started hearing things up in the woods. A courting couple came running down the lane one day, showing a lot more flesh than was decent and whiter in the face than my bed sheets. And you can trust me on this, young man, my bed sheets are the whitest things you'll ever see. They said they'd been sheltering from the rain in the cottage when they heard someone moving around upstairs. Before they could get their clothes back on footsteps came running down the stairs into the next room. The inner door burst wide open, ripped off its hinges. They didn't stop screaming until they were half a mile away and too out of breath to scream any more. Stopped their kissing and cuddling it did, though, which pleased the girl's mother no end because the boy was a bad sort and no good for her.

'Then young Tomos was found hanging from a tree next to the cottage. He'd failed his school exams and couldn't cope with the shame, so the story goes, but I'd seen him that morning and he told me that he was going to be allowed to take them again in a year. He wasn't cheerful but he didn't seem about to kill himself either. So, what do you think of that?'

I nodded and sucked on the end of my pen. 'Great, Mrs Howells. Not your usual haunted house story but it's definitely got me spooked.' My cheeks had died down enough by now for me to risk a joke at my own expense.

She bridled and raised her spoon. 'Not a proper haunted house? Tell me what you were expecting then. Go on. Not a proper haunted house! What would you say if I told you I've seen things with my own eyes?' She didn't let me answer. 'Now, I don't like to talk about this and I don't believe in ghosts like you see on the telly. Headless horsemen and the rest. But I do believe in bad spirits, and bad energy. I do now, anyway.' She shifted forward and lowered her voice.

'It was a couple of years later and there'd been a few more incidents. The hunt that went through the woods every Boxing Day came to a sticky end, horses bolting and bones snapped all round. A little boy went missing from Aberystwyth and was found wandering in the woods, covered in bite marks. Human bite marks. He wouldn't tell a soul how he got there. There was nothing that couldn't be explained away by ordinary men and their ordinary wickedness, but still. I'd taken to walking through the woods myself, to blow the cobwebs away. I was having some trouble with my husband and liked to get out of the house when I could. But I never went near the cottage. As soon as I could see it through the trees I skirted off the path and kept my distance.

'The day it happened I was alone and happy enough. I'd walked for a while and stopped below the cottage, on the riverbank, to cool my feet. I couldn't see it through the overgrown trees and barely remembered why I was avoiding it anymore. It was a warm afternoon and I was almost asleep when I heard something hit the ground behind me, so I turned to see. It was a wooden horse, about the size of your fist, and just like the one I used to have when I was little. I remember I was pleased and thought I could take it home for my girls. Then I saw something else, a few feet away. A tin pig, the kind you paint and add to a farmyard set. I stood with it in my hands and looked at it and I knew exactly where its ear would have a slight nick. You see, it wasn't just like the one I'd had when I was a girl, it was the one. The one I'd given to the witch's child all those years before.

'Well, my heart started beating fast then and I looked up at the cottage. I was still a way away but even so I could see there was someone standing in the doorway, just standing there, watching me. I forgot I was a wife and mother then, a grown woman, and I turned to run.' She swallowed loudly. 'And that's when I was grabbed from behind. Arms around my waist, and tight so I thought they'd split my ribs wide open. Someone pulled and dragged me towards the cottage. Words in my ear, wet words hard as pebbles. Now you! Now you! I screamed and kicked and heard shouting in the distance. It was a couple from the village. Incomers they were. I'd been as unwelcoming as the rest when they'd moved in but I was glad to see them then and never heard a bad word said about them after.

'By the time they reached me I was alone and scratched up, in a state. They had to half carry me back to the village. I was terrified I'd be pulled back to the cottage so I clung to them all the way home.'

Her hands were shaking. When I cleared the fear from my throat she flinched and pushed them beneath her blanket, and I pretended I hadn't seen.

'So, that's my story. I've never been back to those woods since and I wouldn't again, not even if you paid me. I don't like Meg going but she's as stubborn as her mother.'

Meg shifted in her chair and glanced at me. 'Nearly time for lunch. I'll heat up the cawl.'

I followed her into the kitchen. 'What a great story. She really believes it, doesn't she? Do you think she'll mind if I ask her a few questions?'

Meg moved close to reach a saucepan down from the shelf behind me. 'I think she's had enough for today. She's still there, in her head. I don't want to leave her scared.' She touched my shoulder, quickly. 'I've heard it before, anyway, so I can probably fill in any gaps for you. We should go in a minute. It's a long walk.'

I stood by the window and waited as she heated the cawl and switched the television on, leaning over her grandmother with a murmured comment and kissing the top of her head. Mrs Howells accepted the tray placed on her lap with a nod. 'Thanks, cariad.' Her hands were steady now and her attention seemingly on the lunchtime news bulletin. Megan had been right about not wanting to be in the room when she started eating though. Any appetite I'd had crashed into the wall along with the bits of half chewed carrot that exploded from her mouth.

As I squatted on the doorstep and wrestled my feet into my walking boots, she called to me from her armchair. 'You look after my granddaughter, do you hear me? Don't think of coming back without her.'

I craned my head around the frame and gave her my most reassuring smile. 'Don't worry, I'll keep her safe.'

Megan stepped past me and pulled the door closed, but not before I heard her grandmother's response. 'Patronising little city boy. He'll start running as soon as a cow moos at him, I know his type.'

True to my word, and stung by this slur on my manhood, I tried to help Megan over the first two stiles. We tussled, legs at extraordinary angles, until she laughed and pushed me gently away. 'I can manage, really. Save your energy for the uphill bits. And for the cows.' She winked at me and I imagined leaning forward, kissing her. I bent and fiddled with my boot.

The path narrowed through gorse and thorn, winding up the side of the hill. The village was soon no more than a grey slide of rooftops and chimneystacks. I was too out of breath to speak, too focused on not panting, but Megan seemed to float in front of me, twisting to point at the view as it fell away behind us, pushing her hair back with an impatient hand.

'You don't mind taking me?' I asked when the path had levelled out a little and I felt less sick. 'After what your gran said? It doesn't scare you?'

She stopped and pulled a bottle of water from her backpack. 'Don't be silly. I don't believe in ghosts and I've played in those woods since I was tiny. I know my gran thinks something happened to her there, but she was quite fragile back then.'

She offered the water and looked away from me, down over the gnarl of treetops towards the flat grey of the sea. We'd climbed a fair way and cleared the woods but they stretched ahead and beneath us, in the distance. I guessed that was where we were going, to rejoin the river and follow its rush to the cottage.

'My granddad used to beat her,' Meg said, still staring down at the sea. 'It got so she was too scared to be at home and too scared to stay away in case it made him angrier. She had breakdowns and even went into hospital for a while. You wouldn't think it to see her now, so strong, but she used to jump at the buzzing of a bee in the garden. She thought it was him all of the time. She thought he was just behind her, even when he was in the next village, working. He became her entire world.'

We carried on walking, but slower now. 'Did she go to the police?' I asked.

Megan shook her head. 'I don't think she even tried. You just put up with it back then. No, he died. Heart attack. My mum was still a girl but just as relieved. She had her fair share of bruises too. She says they wore pink at the funeral and tap danced behind his coffin.'

She did a quick jig, clumsy in her thick layers, and laughed as she stumbled and I caught her arm to steady her. 'All downhill from here,' she said, gesturing towards the valley ahead of us. 'And that's where the fun begins. There's no real path any more so we'll have to do a bit of clambering once we get into the woods. Take a good long look at the sky while you still can, Matt. The trees are so dense at the bottom, where the river is, you won't even know the sun's shining.'

'We need breadcrumbs,' I told her as she strode ahead. 'To lead us back out.'

'Oh, I can get us back out,' she assured me. 'If they let us go.' And she grinned.

That fear again, just a tickle between my shoulder blades but as addictive as anything I'd ever known. I loved it.

I followed Megan down through a sheep scattered field to where the trees elbowed each other. She slipped under the fence and faded away, lost against the dim backdrop. As I scrambled after, skidding to my knees, I called out to her to wait. The pale angles of her face gleamed supernaturally pale as she turned to me. 'Are you okay?'

I resisted the urge to take her hand. 'I couldn't see you properly. It's like the light's being squashed by all these trees.'

She nodded and peered at her watch. I wondered if she had plans for the evening. 'It's going to be steep for a while now,' she said. 'Be careful and if you start to slip just sit down.'

After the third skid had landed me on my back I decided it would be easier to just stay seated and slide the rest of the way. I didn't know how Megan kept her footing. She glanced round a couple of times to check on me but we didn't speak until we were at the very base of the valley, enclosed on all sides. I could hear the river toiling somewhere out of sight. It was several degrees colder and my jeans were heavy with mud. I tried not to shiver.

Megan pulled me to my feet. 'Not far now. If we can get to the riverbank we can follow it to the cottage.' She started to force her way through the undergrowth, swearing quietly as brambles scratched at her legs. 'They caught a monkey in these woods a few years ago, you know. It had escaped from a private collection and didn't know how to survive by itself, out in the wild. A couple of kids saw it first and ran home to tell their parents, then two of the local farmers took their shotguns and went after it. Not much of a hunt, by all accounts. The poor little thing ran straight up to them. All it wanted was to be looked after. They took it into the pub afterwards, all puffed up like they'd done something clever. The little dead body dangled by its tail for everyone to see.' She grimaced. 'It trusted them to keep it safe and they killed it. Probably laughed as they pulled the trigger.'

We were at the riverbank now. I tipped my head back and could just make out tiny patches of sky between the thick layers of tree canopy above me. They looked a long way away. The movement made me dizzy and the leaf mould I was up to my knees in made me sneeze. Something had gone from the day. I was struggling to recapture that sense of anticipation and fun I'd felt before we entered the woods. If her sober monkey story was anything to go by, Megan's mood was dipping too. I didn't really have anything to lose.

'Maybe we can go for a drink afterwards,' I said. 'If you want to?'

She smiled at me and reached to brush something from my shoulder. 'That would be nice. You can tell me a ghost story over a pint.'

Before I could decide whether she was flirting she'd turned away and started walking upriver. I suppose I should have taken the lead and trampled the worst of the brambles, helped her over the fallen logs, but I was content to stay behind and enjoy the way her jeans tightened across her thighs as she kicked a path clear for us. I allowed myself a tiny daydream or two.

When she stopped I was so engrossed in my own thoughts I barely registered the sudden stillness until I'd cannoned into her and almost knocked her off her feet. We were both warmed from the walk, cheeks pinked by exertion. She clutched at my arms to keep herself upright and pointed over my shoulder. 'There it is.'

And there it was. So tangled in ivy I would have missed it if I'd been by myself. Half of the roof was gone and the other half looked as if it was hanging by cobwebs alone. There was no door to keep the elements out, no glass in the window frames. They punctured the stone walls, blank and black, like eye sockets. I started to walk over, fumbling in my backpack for my camera, clicking off a couple of shots, and then something moved in the upstairs window. A quick, pale blur of something. I squeaked and took a step back, and behind me Megan laughed.

'It's a dove, look.' She clapped her hands and the bird launched itself from the sill, flapping wildly as it tore away. 'But I know what you thought. Just for a second it could have been a face. That's the window the girl used to sit at, before she died.'

She stepped past me and walked up to the doorway, pouting and draping herself against the frame like a model on a photo shoot. 'Do you want a picture of me?'

I thought I might as well fire off a few rounds, seeing as she was asking.

'And what about one from the window? I could sit up there and look out, the way she did.'

She ducked inside the cottage. I could hear her stumbling around.

'Be careful,' I shouted. 'The whole lot might come down on you. It doesn't look safe.'

She shouted something back, something unintelligible but reassuring, and I relaxed and scuffed around outside while I waited for her to reappear. Blocks of stone lay scattered, presumably loosened from the cottage walls by harsh winters. I prodded one with my toe. It was a chunky blue-grey, shot through with seams of milky quartz. Beautiful enough to take home and lay on my mantelpiece as a souvenir. I bent to pick it up.

Beneath it, something pink lay half buried in the earth. Pig pink. I held it in my hand and turned it over, wiping it clean on the front of my jacket. Its rusted face leered up at me. There was a slight nick to the ear. I shuddered with my whole body then, felt the shudder kink the hairs on my head and crease the skin across my feet. I dropped the toy and stepped back, looking to see if Megan was at the window. I thought I could hear her somewhere inside the cottage, I could definitely hear someone, but there was no answer when I called out.

This was usually the best bit for me, when the thrill teetered over into fear and that fear threatened to gallop away with my adult self and turn me back to a child. Monsters and werewolves flickering on the edges of my vision. But I suddenly wanted Megan outside, with me, where I could see her and know she was okay. Then I could let myself enjoy it, the getting spooked and the afterglow of safety when the grown man in me reasserted himself.

'Meg,' I shouted, 'just come down. I'm getting cold.'

My eyes were starting to water. 'Megan, answer me.'

When she appeared at the window, popping up in a flurry of hair and limbs to fill that dark space, I actually screamed, and then we both laughed and I couldn't stop.

'Did you think I was her?' she called. 'It smells really bad in here. No ghosts though.'

She hooked one hand around the frame and leaned out. 'Get one of me like this.'

I looked at her through the camera lens. 'Get back in first. If you fall and break your neck your gran will make mincemeat of me.' I adjusted the focus and watched as she hauled herself back inside the cottage, crossing her arms on the sill and smiling down at me.

'Better, Mr Health and Safety?'

I grinned at her. 'Much better.' I raised the camera again.

Then she turned her head quickly as if she'd heard something in the room behind her. When she looked back at me her face was almost mask-like with surprise. I started to say something but she jerked with a sudden, vicious convulsion and her mouth opened wide. Loose masonry from the window scattered down to my feet.

I tried to laugh, still half convinced that she was joking around. 'Meg?'

Her lips clamped shut, teeth grinding, and then opened again, wide. But she didn't speak.

Over her shoulder a face appeared, chin resting on the curve of her neck. If we'd been anywhere else it would have looked like a gesture of affection, the two heads so close. But here, it was something else. 'Meg?' I said.

We stared at each other. Something twitched at her waist and I knew then that she couldn't move, couldn't speak, because of the arms encircling her ribcage. 'Meg?'

The face, the other face, turned to me. Young, pockmarked, and grinning as if she'd only just learnt how and now would never stop. That grin stretched her skin so that the corners of her mouth were torn and bloody and I could see the meaty length of her tongue. She looked at me and whispered something into Meg's ear, and Meg shut her eyes. They were glassy with tears when she opened them again. Her hands clung to the sill, fingers white and rigid, and then something snapped with a crisp rip and she sagged and let go. I thought of twigs crunching underfoot but knew it was one of her ribs.

I still believe I might have done something then, gone inside and got her out, but as we looked at each other, the three of us, I heard footsteps making their way down the stairs, somewhere in the dark cottage, and I knew the three of us would soon be the four of us. My body hijacked any conscious intention and threw me backwards, away from the footsteps and the grinning face, and from Meg.

She was still staring at me, tears on her cheeks, when I dropped my rucksack and ran back to the river. Up to my waist in it and plunging downstream, legs and arms thrashing, screaming Meg's name. But I didn't look back.

I don't know how long it took me to reach the beach and I don't know how long I lay there on the sand, monstrous in my seaweed wrappings. I was half drowned and hypothermic. The police brought Meg out of the woods, splintered through with broken bones. They worked hard to get me to admit to having killed her, to being high on drugs. They didn't believe me when I told them about the witch.

When they finally gave me my camera back I sat for hours with the photographs, just looking at her. There were two that the police had missed. In both of them, the witch stood in the doorway of the cottage and watched me not watching her. Her child leaned from the upstairs window and grinned, not at me, but past me, at Meg. I burnt those ones.

But the photographs of Megan, twirling, posing, pouting, I'll keep them forever. She really was the most beautiful girl I've ever known.

The Elephant in the Room: A Case Study

Lloyd Jones

Events at a meeting of the Welsh Academy of Psychiatry, November 13, 2012.

I am pretty certain that all of you sitting here today will have heard of writer's block, defined by one of my colleagues as an inability to begin or continue writing for reasons other than lack of basic skill or commitment.

Samuel Taylor Coleridge, F. Scott Fitzgerald and J.K. Rowling are among many authors who have succumbed to this debilitating condition at one time or another.

But I want to discuss another type of 'block'. I want to tell you about an emotional barrier, which may have far-reaching consequences for the psychiatrist and his patient. The condition is little known in the world outside our profession, and is seldom discussed in academic papers or journals. I will describe it simply as psychiatrist's block. The over-used phrase 'elephant in the room' is especially relevant in this case. I must admit that it has taken me considerable personal bravery to stand before you today, to discuss phobias in general, but if I can help just one person then my actions will have been worthwhile.

First, I would like to deal with some historical case studies involving psychiatry and animals, in keeping with the title of my talk.

Where better to start than with Freud's Rat Man, a patient suffering from an obsessive compulsive disorder. One of his symptoms involved a fantasy in which both his fiancée and his father were gnawed alive by rats contained in a pot tied to their buttocks.

The patient, a highly intelligent lawyer, was cured of his obsession but, with the pathos and irony typical of our profession, he was killed as soon as he felt better – in the Great War.

The vast majority of psychiatrists have never had to deal with such a fascinating case. Their lives would have been far more interesting if they had. Are modern people more boring, or were previous generations more neurotic? And what could have possibly caused the patient's obsession with rats and buttocks? Freud had all the answers, as usual. Punishment for childhood masturbation, disguised homosexual fantasies – yes, Vienna was the place to be all those years ago, at the dawn of psychiatry. Sadly, all the Rat Men were spirited away by the Pied Piper of mental health many years ago.

At this point I would like to mention another example of animals roaming around the field of psychiatry.

Take Alice, that sweet little girl who went a-wandering in Wonderland, and who gave the dormouse such a hard time. Yes, that innocent little girl who felt obliged to mention her cat Dinah over and over again, as if wishing to torture the poor mouse. Whose neurosis was in question? Did the real life Alice fear mice, and if so, was she getting her revenge on the written page? Or was Lewis Carroll having a swipe at Alice's governess, the shrewish Miss Pritchett, who could be seen as his rival? Herr Doctor Freud, where are you when we need you?

And since we're living in an age of wall-to-wall celebrities, most of them barking mad, let's study some famous people, people with fear etched all over their faces.

Michael Jackson was scared stiff of dogs.

Adolf Hitler was terrified of cats. So was Genghis Khan, so was Benito Mussolini, and so was Napoleon Bonaparte. Scared of cats? You're cut out to be a mad, despotic tyrant.

Now here's the biggy. Walt Disney, yes Walt Disney, a man made famous by a mouse, was scared of...er...mice.

So those of you with unreasonable fears and deep-seated phobias, take heart. You're in good – and very bad – company.

But that's enough frivolity. Let's get back to brass tacks, because I want to tell you about three cases in which people have been treated successfully for a deep fear of mice. Incidentally, I'd like to remind you that a group of mice is called a mischief.

Patient A was a Hell's Angel from the notorious Welsh chapter, the Blue Pistons. He conformed to all the stereotypes associated with the

Hell's Angels movement: he was large, hairy, violent and smelly. Treating him was like going for a walk with the Incredible Hulk down a dark alleyway in the tenth week of a binmen's strike. I was obliged to open all the windows before he arrived for his weekly treatment, and I also took the precaution of having a panic button installed. One cannot be too careful, though in the eventuality he turned out to be as tame as a hamster. This is the testimony of Patient A, as I recorded it on a digital voice recorder.

Me and the boys decided to go for a ride one Easter. Bit of a laugh, holiday like. So we hit the road without a map as per usual and ended up in the Lake District. Pure chance, but I'd always wanted to go there, me mum used to read me them Peter Rabbit stories, god bless her. Eventually we found a campsite prepared to take us and we only just managed to get the tents up before dark. It was very cold that night but we had plenty of booze so it didn't matter much. We had a good session and I woke up early because of the cold, went outside and the ground was white. Lovely to look at, but an old biker like me gets worried about his machine so I kicked her over just in case.

Woke them up I did, so being a gent I boiled some water and made the lads in my tent a brew. We'd left a bottle of milk leaning against a fence post but when I tried to pour some into the mugs nothing came out. I thought the milk had frozen so I pokes me finger in to get some action. You won't believe what'd happened, a little mousy had climbed in there when we was sleepin' and it'd only gone and drowned, poor mite. His little face reminded me of an Angel from Somerset we tossed in a river at one of them festivals and played about with for a bit, pushed him down with some paddles. Nearly drowned the poor bugger, pardon my French guv. Anyway, I couldn't get any milk out while mousy was acting as a stopper so I pushed him down with a twig so the milk could get out. Didn't seem to make any difference to the tea, the boys didn't notice. I told them afterwards and they thought it was a laugh. In fact it seemed to get mentioned every Easter after that, death by milk instead of death by crucifixion, and one of the girls always gave me a white chocolate mouse with a little red ribbon round its neck, in fact that's how me and Maggie got together in the first place. She moved in with me the third Easter after it happened. Got me red wings now guv but you wouldn't want to know how a man gets his red wings.

So there we have the testimony of Patient A. However, it wasn't the campsite incident which kicked off his mouse phobia. Nothing so simple, unfortunately. No, his musophobia had started quite suddenly when his girl, Maggie, ran off with another biker a few years later. Poor Patient A was so traumatized – actually, he was a bit of a wuss – he'd developed a nervous reaction to chocolate mice whenever he saw one in a shop. And what started as a chocolate mouse aversion developed into a full scale fear of the real thing. He intimated at one point that a huge mouse with a red scarf around its neck had appeared to him during a bad acid trip, and maybe that had done some unpleasant things to his mind, already somewhat unbalanced.

I decided to play it safe with Patient A, for obvious reasons. You don't want a seven-foot gorilla having a psychotic incident in your treatment room.

He started a conventional course of treatment, involving desensitization, in which a cage containing a live mouse was moved towards him slowly across the room over many months. All seemed to be going well; he had been ready to hold the mouse in his hand at our final meeting just before Easter 2001, when sadly fate intervened and he met a violent death in a feud involving shotguns and a lot of blood somewhere in the woods above Colwyn Heights. By all accounts he suffered a painful end. I am told that a slate mouse has been carved on his gravestone, and that every Easter a little red ribbon is tied around its neck. Being a sentimental soul I like to think that Maggie goes there every year to pay her respects. May his soul rest in peace.

Patient B, who came to me in the winter of 1995, was a presentable young man who had entered university as an arts student. After the customary year in a hall of residence he had teamed up with a fellow student and they had rented a house on a hill above the old slate-quarrying town of Bethesda in North Wales. I believe he was taking a joint honours degree in Welsh and English, though he seemed to spend most of his time studying the local barmaids. Seldom did he arrive at my room in the Students' Union building without an accompanying waft of alcohol.

This is the story of Patient B, in his own word, as I wrote it down in my diary. I quote:

It was bedtime in Bethesda on a stormy night in December. I must have been doing some college work for a change, because I was relatively clean and sober. I had sat with my housemate, Jim, also a student, in front of a big fire being drawn up through the chimney in noisy gasps. A great storm was raging down the Ogwen Valley and we were enjoying its screams and tantrums, since we were snug and cosy. Jim offered to make us a mug of hot chocolate and we spent a pleasant hour listening to nature and marveling at its power.

Just then a couple of tiny black mice appeared from nowhere and started to play around our feet. We had never seen them before, indeed we had no idea that we were sharing our little cottage with them, so we sat stock still while they scuttled around our feet. I was not scared of mice at that stage, and I remained totally unphased. We were intrigued and amused by the mice's antics. They almost danced at times, or scuttled here and there in quick darts. We could see their whiskers quivering and their tails snaking from side to side. Throughout this little circus display they remained completely unaware of our presence. So we sat in our worn old armchairs, in front of a hot fire, listening to the wind in the chimney and watching our miniature performers.

And then something extraordinary happened. One of the mice crept up my left ankle, and after nosing around it worked its way into my sock and seemingly went to sleep there. In no time at all the other had followed it and had also gone to sleep. I lifted my trouser leg and saw two little bubbles playing doggo, or should that be mouso, inside my regulation black stocking. Jim and I exchanged glances and grinned. The mice had been a surprise, but this feat of theirs truly astonished us. I felt like David Attenborough somewhere in the jungle, in the company of a really rare species. But since it was well past bedtime I had to do something, so I gently dislodged the mice from their temporary hammock by pulling away the top of my sock, and they rolled down to the floor, looking like two little kids playing rolly-polly in the snow. We went to our beds, and did no more about it, though we had a chat the following day as to whether or not we should buy a mousetrap. We decided to leave things as they were, and to act only if the mice became a pest. In the event we never saw them again. Perhaps they were storm mice, appearing only once in a while, when the valley was experiencing a tempest. Indeed, I remember writing a short story in which our two little rodents, dormant over long periods of history, became active only when the wind whistled at a particular pitch on the rocky panpipes of the Black Ladders.

And so ends the rather fanciful account of Patient B. Again, it was a secondary issue which had created a fear of mice in this patient. It seems that he was a bit of a climber, and one day, not so long after the storm mice appeared, he was up on the Black Ladders – a notorious accident spot in the Carneddau range nearby – when he experienced a frightening vision. He was leading a two-man climb up a severe pitch when he attempted a particularly difficult jughold above him to the left. As his fingers fumbled for the hold he had the distinct sensation of feeling fur or whiskers brushing against his hand. Looking up, he saw a huge mouse peering down at him, its dark eyes gleaming with malice. He let out a scream and nearly lost his grip on the rock. Fortunately he was able to knock in a belay and descend to the ledge where his companion was waiting for him, full of anxiety. Patient B was too embarrassed to tell the truth and he invented an excuse, but he refused to go on and they abandoned the climb. Subsequently he developed a superstitious aversion to all rodents, black storm mice in particular.

Again, I utilised a desensitizing technique, though slightly different in his case, since Patient B had a well developed sense of humour and I felt that his condition could be alleviated with levity. So I asked my mother, a keen knitter, to create two black mice for him. She had a Kafkaesque disposition, which suited the occasion, and she produced two absurd, cartoonish mice, each with eight legs like a spider and other surreal attributes. These were hung in a woollen cobweb in the corner of the room where the storm mice had appeared, and I encouraged Patient B to approach his new friends, getting closer and closer every day. This worked wonderfully. Patient B overcame his fear and went on to become a legendary climber. It was he who first conquered the appropriately named Mouse of Horror pitch on Cemetery Gates in the Ogwen Valley. Indeed, he and his equally famous climbing partner are still known as Gorgon and Zola.

Patient C was completely different. She was a bright young girl of seven, almost precocious, who lived with her teacher parents in a lovely house in its own secluded grounds on the outskirts of Colwyn Bay.

Our patient had been texting one of her friends in her bedroom one evening when her eye was caught by a sudden movement in the corner of the room. On looking up she saw a mouse, which executed a little dance and then washed its face with its paws before disappearing beneath her computer table.

This girl had been only slightly disturbed and had tried to use her intelligence to calm herself, making jokes about her computer mouse, etc. *What does a mouse do in the daytime?* she asked me at our first meeting, and when I said I didn't know, she laughed and said *mousework*.

But she was sleeping badly and her schoolwork was suffering. So I hit on a plan.

I advised Alice's parents to buy a humane rodent catcher, the sort which traps the animal without killing it. Next, I approached a homeless man who could be seen daily in the centre of town, playing a tin whistle rather badly, and made him a proposition. In return for a small sum of money he agreed to play along with my ruse.

When, eventually, the mouse was caught in our plastic trap the parents called me as arranged. When I went to the house all three of them were standing in the driveway, waiting. With the mouse between us on a garden table, I outlined my plan. I said:

Alice, this mouse deserves to live. It has its own life, its own part to play in the cosmic story. So I propose that we let it go. But obviously we wouldn't want to let it free in the house, or the garden, since it would probably head straight back to the warmth and comfort of your snug little bedroom. So this is what I think we should do. Together, we'll head for a nice little park on the other side of town and release it into the wild, somewhere nice where your mousy can make a new life for itself.

Naturally, this plan went down a storm, so while the family went to get togged up I made a quick call to the homeless man, whom I'd hand picked for the job, since he looked positively medieval in his hooded jacket, floppy woolen hat and baggy trousers.

He was as good as his word, and when we arrived at the park Alice spotted him immediately, standing under a tree, playing his tin whistle as eerily as ever.

'The Pied Piper!' she said excitedly, and it was all we could do to stop her from rushing over to him.

While the piper played under his tree I took the trap to a shrubbery and released the captive mouse. It hesitated for a few seconds then dashed into the undergrowth.

When I straightened up I put my hand on my head, as prearranged, and the pied piper moved away from us slowly, his plaintive tune receding into the distance. My plan had worked perfectly. As we stood there in silence with our empty trap, the parents turned to each other and beamed. Alice was delighted and wrote a first novel about the experience when she was only ten. She is now one of the country's foremost nature writers and has won more awards than there are mice in your local branch of Computer World.

And so to the conclusion.

There is a folk belief that elephants are afraid of mice. Pliny the Elder recorded this enigma almost two thousand years ago. The TV programme Mythbusters conducted an experiment, which showed an elephant apparently attempting to avoid a mouse, so there may be some basis for this belief. And I am about to admit to you that I am the elephant in this room today.

Let me remind you that symptoms of a phobia such as musophobia can include extreme anxiety, shortness of breath, an irregular heartbeat, sweating, nausea, dry mouth and shaking. And I have little doubt that one member of the audience, sitting below me in the front row, is suffering some or all of these symptoms.

During my address I have looked down to see if I could detect any doubt or creeping uncertainty among you. I scanned your keen and attentive faces to see if anyone had begun to question the nature and substance of my lecture. But I am happy to say that all of you bar one appear to have received my message without quaking, or hurling insults at me, or rotten tomatoes (laughter).

But you have been badly misled, since I am not the person you think I am. The professional you expected to hear, and had every right to hear, was not in fact invited to this meeting. Instead, I have appeared in his place, at the invitation of one of your members, Professor William Morton LRCP, MRCS, MRCPsych (retired). As you well know, he's the clean-shaven gentleman with a red bow tie in the back row, near the exit. You will also know that he has been unable to practice for over twenty years, since he suffers from agateophobia, which is a fear of madness or of going mad. And that is the psychiatric equivalent, in my books, of writer's block.

And now the time has come for me to confess all and to tell you the naked truth.

I was Professor Morton's penultimate patient. I was referred to him as part of my rehabilitation in the community following a seven-year jail sentence for fraud and embezzlement. To put it simply, for well over half my life I was a con man preying on rich, vulnerable people. You may have heard of me, since I have made regular appearances on Crimewatch. My name is Andrew 'The Viscount' Moroni, though I am also known as The Great Imposter. You may remember my biggest sting – selling famous London landmarks to gullible American entrepreneurs.

In his autobiography the famous con artist Joseph 'Yellow Kid' Weil, who stole over eight million dollars, said: 'The desire to get something for nothing has been very costly to many people who have dealt with me and with other con men. The average person, in my estimation, is ninety-nine per cent animal and one per cent human. The ninety-nine per cent that is animal causes very little trouble. But the one per cent that is human causes all our woes.'

Ladies and gentlemen, I said earlier that none of you showed any signs of having a phobia during my speech. And that was almost true, but there was in fact one person who began to show signs of fear whenever I left the lectern and moved to the front of the dais. People sitting next to her may have noticed that she showed signs of deep distress; she shrank back in her chair, and at one stage held her hands over her eyes. I won't identify her, since that would be indelicate. Suffice it to say that today she is facing her final test in a long programme of treatment for a rare and difficult phobia.

And what is that phobia, you might ask. The clue, ladies and gentlemen, is in my noble visage. During the course of the last hour you may have observed that I possess a full and bushy beard. Indeed, I could pass for one of the Pilgrim Fathers. But in keeping with my career as a con man, my beard is in fact bogus. It was glued in place earlier this afternoon by Professor Morton himself, and let me tell you that many guffaws and giggles passed between us as we went about our business. The result, as you can see, is most convincing. But what has that to do with the woman who has spent the last hour cringing and shaking in the front row?

The answer is simple. The woman in question suffers from pogonophobia, or a fear of beards. And today she is being put to the test. The final test. Because if she can live through this ordeal she will have finally conquered her phobia. And wouldn't that be marvelous. Wouldn't that be simply wonderful. Oh dear, can someone grab her? Quick! Stop her falling! Professor Morton....

This meeting was abandoned, and paramedics attended after a call from the secretary. Tea and biscuits were served. Mrs Harris proposed the vote of thanks. The next meeting will be on March 9, 2013, guest speaker to be announced.
A vacancy exists following Professor Morton's resignation. Please contact me if you know of anyone suitable.

Davina Froust, Secretary.

How Shall We Sing to Her?

Gary Raymond

If I think of her now I think of her in increments, in minute physical detail, in close-up, as if she is too much to see whole. I think of the silences and the glances. I think of the pin-prick pores of her scalp as she stands up to me fastening the buttons of my shirt, the breath on my chest from between her tacky lips, and my own breath gently waving through her mussy blonde bob. I think of the thin air between us and around us in that room, the enhanced sounds of fingers manipulating cotton, rustling through the quiet, that buzz just above the hush, our breathing, even the snips as our eyelids blink, the point of her tongue peeking out as she threads the buttons. She curves her back away from me, concentrating, her pelvis pressing at me, her t-shirt too big for her, creased from the night's sleep, one of her slim delicate legs moves a foot slowly back across the carpet a few inches and rests on the balls of her toes. A button pops through the hole. She does this slowly, almost sensually – everything she did was sensual. Everything she did was considered, performed, displayed. I look over her head out of the lead-latticed window, to the wintry crag of the brittle black woodland at the hilt of the valley. I look down at her, and she pushes the last button through its loop, she smiles, pats my chest with flat palms and looks up to me, the smile widening. She says something. A rare thank you, I think it was. We are alone and she kisses me gently, innocently. That is how I think of her now.

I would like to keep this moment as my most honest memory of Esther Delissen, but there comes a time when we are remembered in our entirety – it is irresistible – the whole novel pressed deep into one full stop, and I cannot see this moment alone.

It is a heavy, bloated feeling that accompanies the news of her death. A Paris hospital at age fifty-two. I imagine the white walls, the desert of pristine nothingness all around her, the fading bleeps of machinery, a nurse, maybe her assistant, a press officer.

It was a long time ago, that morning in that room in that place, her fingers moving slowly up the line to my collar, her soft fawn skin showing the first signs of tiny timid creases at the corners of her eyes. Esther had called me the day before from the only payphone at the retreat. I imagined her bare feet on the cold varnished wood as she explained where she was. I imagined a wide band in her hair, a cigarette in her hand, her head turning to look up the corridor, then down it. She would be in cropped trousers – pedal pushers, they used to call them – and a loose blouse, and she would have all the staff at her beck and call. I imagined her as she looked when she was young, when she was on the cover of magazines, before I knew her, when everybody knew her.

She said she was going insane with boredom in the Welsh countryside. 'All I can see is this long grey valley,' she said in her cut–glass voice. 'It's like God's latrine or something.' The insurance company for the movie she was doing had hired a limousine to take her up there from Pinewood. She had to dry out. They were treating her like a child, she said. 'Everyone is always treating me like a child.' She said I was the only person she knew in the whole country who had nothing to do with the movie business. It wasn't true. I had done script work in London and L.A., and she knew that. I had written a short book about my Hollywood sojourn. It sold quite well. She had read it before we knew each other. And apart from that she still had family dotted around – the Marches mainly – and they were a lot closer to the retreat than I was. They were certainly not a show business clan. They were gentry, in fact; she was of good stock. The Delissens had been doing eccentric things in cold manor houses, closed off from most of the world, for hundreds of years. But she didn't call them; she called me. The truth is she liked being hemmed in by her own stardom, she liked being hunted and bored, and more than anything she liked being unfathomable to her kin.

Esther Delissen was the youngest of a large family, which was, as far as I could ever tell, made up of rambunctious older brothers, an open-mouthed father, and a dusty, charming alcoholic mother, all of them falling about each other in the wake of a legacy from some kind of agricultural ancestry. Long expired baronetcies (if those things do indeed expire). She said to me once how privileged she had felt at being able to spend her teenage years watching her parents grow old; to see them go senile and rotten just like people with no money did. It was her idea of a social experiment, a Freudian opera: the drama and the science. Her father was the beneficiary of some precedents who were often portrayed around the dinner table as working-class heroes. There was a much-lauded distant forbear who had come eyeball to eyeball with Richard II at Smithfield, or so the story went. The whole family was a peculiar mixture of the gentry and the peasant, although nobody ever really knew the truth to any of it. There was something even further back about being related to the Earl of Pembroke and the family having 'souvenirs' of the Battle of Monmouth. 'Being stuck on the edge of this valley is even worse in that context,' she said. 'It's like coming home.' I'd asked her, a little nervously, as we stood in the lobby of the retreat, what she thought of Wales, and this is how she replied.

There was not a nation on earth she could not find a connection to. But she doubted the familial claim. As was the fashion with all the mongrel English dynasties who hit their nadir in the mid-twentieth century, she had always suspected the Delissens were keen to align themselves with ancient glories in the hope that if they could stretch time backwards, they might stretch it forwards also.

Oscar, her father, whom I met only the once, was a man who had more words than thoughts. He reminded me immediately of all those career politicians I had encountered when working for the Sunday Times in the seventies; all those cheap smiles and vacuous phrases used to veneer a genuine lack of charisma. Her mother, who was known to all as Hattie, smiled with a lopsided mouth and bright, glazed eyes. She was beautiful in increments, the sum of the parts not adding up. And she had nothing to say, but I always had the feeling this was through nurture rather than nature.

Esther spoke of her parents with a practised indifference and often changed the subject swiftly. But she was the queen of her own conversation, and topics never lingered once deemed done. I interviewed her in a restaurant in eighty-two; the year we first met. She drew long on a cigarette and said, 'I cannot really credit my parents with any of my successes nor blame them for my flaws. They let me be and I became what I am: naturally, unchained, only my physical weaknesses to hold me back. I am made up entirely of Original Sin.'

I kept notes back then, of what people like Esther said to me. Like a diary of dialogue, much of it less incriminating in hindsight than I had hoped at the time. People like Esther were my trade. Only not quite people like Esther. As a student I had planned to become a great novelist, and then I became a journalist in order to pay my rent, and then my novels failed to sell and I lost my publisher. Opportunities to write biographies came along. My fear of the ephemera of journalism was abated. I came to be writing what I saw were novels of the living; even when many of my subjects were deceased. And as had been my style when writing fiction, I was drawn to the darker figures for my subjects. I had convinced myself that the brightest stars were beneath me, too bright to get a good look at, and that the shadows held the most interest. That is why I went for Arturo Pansattio as a biographic subject: the brash, philandering, Mussolini-sympathising, arch gentleman. The genius photographer. He seemed like the life I had been waiting for. I had the canon call of his death in eighty-one, the pricked-up ears of my publisher, but really I was interested in the ugliness of the prospect. He was a famously difficult man who got much of what he wanted because he had an unknowable talent for instilling depth and character in the faces of those on whom he trained his lens. I was not long into my research for the book before I was told I would have to speak to Esther Delissen. She knew him better than anyone.

Meeting with Esther meant stepping into that light. She did not live like people live. She lived like the religious man who spent his life perched atop a pole, trying to get closer to God. Her God was a brilliant mixture of oblivion and omnipresence. That she had missed the Golden Age of Hollywood (she made her first film aged seventeen in nineteen sixty) was an unspoken disappointment to her. In every other way she was classical. Esther experienced herself, rather than the conventional method by which people go about their lives, that is, experiencing the world. Her drinking and her drug abuse, I am sure, was entirely an attempt to self-medicate. It wasn't escapism, but it was an attempt at freedom, in a gnostic sense, and yet it made her more flesh than ever. She knew she could never be as frozen, as perfect, as when her image was trapped by Pansattio's clicker. She could never hold that pose; she was cursed that way, her motionless image glaring at her across the globe.

She had been to this retreat at the edge of the valley, overlooking the tongue-grey slate roofs of the town of Tanddaerol, many times before, and she was happy to walk the grounds, breathe in the air, pick buds from bowing branches and picnic near the brook in the clean frost. She was so very glad to see me. During the drive I had been working out topics of conversation. It had been two years since we had last spoken, and my nervousness had overrun my memory of how Esther was the person who chose the topics.

'I saw your last film,' I said as we set off for a long walk through the wood at the far end of the grounds.

'That wasn't *my* film,' she said. 'I am forty now. I play mothers. I'm trying to get more prostitute roles,' she said. 'You play them just like mothers only the costumes are better.'

We strolled for some hours, much of it lapsing into silence. It was fulfilling to see her again, and I was sure she felt the same way. Maybe, until she came to me in the lobby of the retreat, she had not realised how much our friendship had once meant to her. I was afraid to ask why she had called me in the first place. She had always said she didn't think all that highly of writers. She said it to get a rise out of me, I know. She said writers always seem to have too much time on their hands. She knew I wouldn't be busy, she said picking the petals from a small daffodil she had plucked from the ground. I *was* busy but I dropped everything and followed her vague directions as far as I could before I had to ask someone where I was going. I went north at Newport toward Tanddaerol and turned off to climb wooded hills, past a monument to Nelson, past a ruined Abbey, a brewery, and to the grand seclusion of her keep.

The retreat was an old stately home that had served as an orphanage and a girls' school before it became a hideaway most often for those who found themselves wealthy, intoxicated and chronically noticeable. Esther knew the place quite well by this time; she had a 'retreat' in every town, they used to say.

'What would you have done if I had not come?' I said.

'Who does not come?' she said with a straight gaze. 'You remember when I came to visit you in London?'

I said that I did. She stepped up to walk a few paces ahead of me.

'We held each other in the frost – much like it is today,' she said.

I said that I remembered it.

'I told you that writers are no fun; they are the easiest to ensnare. They are drab, and always on the lookout for jewels. One can wrap around a writer in just a few sentences, like Baudelaire's pipe smoke.'

'You still think that?' I said.

'You're here, aren't you?' she said.

Esther was never more dazzling than when playing herself.

She was an English rose who had become nationless; adored, she belonged to everyone, and felt homeless because of it. She said to me once that the world thought of her as a person she did not recognise. They thought of her, first and foremost, as the summation of the goodness in all the characters she played on screen. She had been a nun who died at the hands of fascists, a school teacher who stood up for orphans, an orphan herself searching for her long lost brother thief; she had played Guinevere, Esmeralda and Kitty Shcherbatskaia, all before the end of the sixties. The photographer Pansattio saw something terrible, triumphal and vulnerable in those eyes as they trembled at the edge of tears on that mighty silver screen, and he took her and froze her.

'I am not so good and not so vulnerable,' she said. Pansattio knew that. He gave darkness to her eyes, put sex in her vocabulary.

We, all of us, have that striking profile of hers in our mind's eye whenever we think of her; the Arturo Pansattio photograph on the veranda in Venice from the late sixties. It is a remarkable image of light greys and thick blacks, a snapshot of a joust between the middle-aged reclusive genius photographer and the nymph. And it was the beautiful child captured at the very moment, the crackled second of time, when she became a woman. The portrait is bursting with sexual energy, either spent or coming to fruition. The fact is it is impossible to tell, which is part of the allure. She is still credited with inspiring young girls to pick up the smoking habit even now, so many decades later. In the photograph, you see, she does not hold her cigarette like a cigarette, but like a violin bow, like a flute, she holds it as if music is about to come from it. And the smoke could even be the notes.

I even remember the first cigarette we shared. We walked through Regent's Park. It was unbearably cold and she tucked herself into my lapels, her scalp pressed into my chin. By this time she was twice divorced and yet to turn thirty-six, professed to be 'off drugs', which could have only been true were alcohol, caffeine and nicotine not drugs. She did not want to speak of Pansattio – she had found his passing too traumatic – when we first met in Madrid. It was to prove typical of her.

I had flown to Spain for the purpose of the interview, her enthusiastic invite still ringing in my ear from the phone call, only to be told she could talk of anything but 'Satti'. We spent three afternoons drinking wine and talking about our lives, I making her laugh with stories of growing up in the crawling greyness of a northern industrial town; she ruminating, skating over delicious Hollywood anecdotes and sarcastic gossip. She did not seem lonely, but I suppose she was. She never mentioned anyone other than ghosts from her past. She told me at one point that she suspected she was adopted, a token gesture to a mother who had borne so many boys. 'That is why', she sighed, pluming smoke into the sticky Spanish air, 'I've been treated like a pet all my life. I've been treated like a pet and was conditioned to behave like one. And retaliate like one.' She looked at me and gave a clipped snap of the jaws through a cruel grin.

One story I think could possibly explain Esther as a young girl, one that I was told by a student friend from her time at Balliol, was that it was her and her alone who pressed for the production of Swinburne's *Atalanta in Calydon* to mark an anniversary of the poet's birth. Perhaps in him she saw a kindred spirit, and perhaps she would have faired better had she been taken in by a man such as Theodore Watts-Dunton, Swinburne's life-saving patron. Perhaps she would have faired better had she been a poet rather than a muse, a playwright rather than a character, but she would have been the first to admit we are assigned our roles in life and have to make do. (She certainly did not have the stamina or the focus to sit for hours at a typewriter). When I heard news of her death – and I, like so many who crossed her path over the years, read about it in a newspaper – I thought of Swinburne's verse from that play: *Where shall we find her, how shall we sing to her, Fold our hands round her knees, and cling? O that man's heart were as fire and could spring to her, Fire, or the strength of the streams that spring!*

Several months after our Madrid rendezvous she contacted me to say she was to be in London for the foreseeable future. It seemed she had fallen in love with an art dealer and was intent on getting him to propose to her. So, with no sign of or another mention of the art dealer we spent the next six months drinking wine and quite often talking about Pansattio. Her proclamations on his character formed the basis of my most successful biography to date. If for nothing else I owe her that. During those six months I may have fallen in love with her, but it seemed not to matter then, and less so now.

At the retreat I felt a great thirst had been quenched merely by laying eyes on her. I don't know if that is love, or if it is something else entirely. A need for a certain force. We walked and walked, the frost eating away through my shoes to the bones of my feet. Esther was warming up, and as the retreat became hidden by woodland and hills, a village came into sight.

'How far are you allowed to walk from the retreat?' I said.

'As far as I like,' she said. 'It's the insurance company who think they own me. As if I need to make another film ever again in my life.'

But of course she did need that. It was not a financial necessity, but something deeper, haematic, elemental.

She carried on down the hillside toward the village.

'You know the Delissens originate from this area,' she shouted back to me.

Not quite, I thought. I followed her.

'We hail from the Earldom of Pembrokeshire, or so the story goes. My ancestors fought one of the Henrys up on those hills.' She vaguely swiped her arm to the horizon without looking.

'I just wondered if you needed to be back at a certain time before they come looking for you,' I called after her.

But she was close to the edge of the village now; she was at a canter, and heading for the building with the bellowing chimney.

I found her in the pub, at the bar looking sheepish. The landlord, a tall thin man with red cheeks and damp curly hair, was saying something to her, gesturing downwards with both palms. She ran to me at the door and took my wrist.

'I ordered a vodka tonic before realising I have absolutely no money on me,' she said. 'And this delightful man said that I could have it on the house as I looked frozen to the core and, you know, seeing as who I am.' She gestured to the landlord who was now shrugging, his shocked grin fixed. 'You have money, don't you?' she said, patting my pockets.

'A little,' I said, and dug out the wallet from inside my overcoat.

The pub had a rustling open fire in a large stone fireplace, and two high-backed armchairs positioned in front. I paid for the drinks and we took the seats.

'Obviously, you're not supposed to be drinking that,' I said as I took off my coat.

'I am constantly at loggerheads with the insurance company. It's part of the game. Nip and tuck. Tug o' war. It's how they get what they want from me: the middle ground.'

'I suspect what they want is for you to finish the film,' I said.

'I always finish the film,' she said, and she sunk back in the chair and lifted her now bare feet up to the flames. She let out a sigh.

I watched her as she sipped at her V&T and talked at length about an apartment she was renting in Knightsbridge while she was shooting the film. She told me about the flowers in the window box, the view across the street, the furniture, the neighbours. 'Everybody is excited to have me as a neighbour,' she said, 'but nobody knocks my door to say hello.'

She was talking about a special kind of loneliness. I asked her whatever happened to that art dealer she had fallen in love with. I had not had the courage to ask her during the time we spent together in London.

'I think he married a Greek princess or something,' she said, gazing into the flames. 'Women are all interchangeable to that sort. High end is high end. I was high end enough until the billionaire's daughter came along. I didn't keep tabs on him, you understand, but I believe he had a stroke and now her billions pay for a nurse to spoon gruel into his mouth.'

'You've never thought to marry again?' I said.

'Are you asking?' she said.

I smiled and sipped my beer.

'We could be happy together for a short while, sure,' she went on, looking back to the flames. 'You could travel the world with me and write your books, dotting from hotel room to hotel room. All you'd need was a typewriter and a suitcase full of shirts. But you'd go insane. Just like the others did. You'd plead with me to cut back the work, to take some time off. Because *you* would need to. I wouldn't need to. And then I'd have to go it alone and you'd become pointless, another memory, after the fact. You think I'm making this up? You'd hate me within two years. You'd write a book about it. Out of spite. Out of disappointment at the high life. And then you'd grow to hate yourself for even having done that. Either way you look at it, it's all corrosive. The only thing you'd know is that there's not much worth knowing behind what you knew already, before you even met me. So let's just save ourselves the trouble.'

She held out her empty glass to me.

'We should head back,' I said.

'One more,' she said, in a soft, youthful, edgeless tone.

Before we left Esther was further recognised. A professor came in. He lived in the village and taught at the university in Tanddaerol.

'I thought you were sublime as Sister Anja,' he said, grinning from ear to ear, his long arm reaching across the mantelpiece of the fireplace. 'And I remember taking my now wife to see *Lancelot of the Lake* at the Odeon. She will not believe me when I tell her you were sat in our local pub.'

'You're very kind,' Esther said, brightly. 'All a long time ago.'

'But classics,' said the professor, who, it seemed, was intent on going through every one of Esther's silver screen personas in a perfunctory roll call.

Esther, I know, hated *Lancelot of the Lake*. 'The director saw me as some kind of rag doll to be emotionally tossed about between these two honourable brutes of King Arthur and Lancelot,' she had said to me once. 'I asked the director why I was supposed to be in love with Lancelot, what was the motivation of the character. "Because he is handsome and brave and chivalrous", he said to me. "But such a bore!" I said to him. "But women went for that in those days," he said. "And men love women who go for that nowadays." I thought him an idiot. I was young and had more faith in men than he did, I suppose.'

I looked at her, her legs tucked up, her chin resting on her knees, as she listened to the professor sermonising on her career from the mantelpiece. Her face was kind, open, her eyes attentive and the reflection of the flames from the fireplace glistened in them, and I could see she was remembering that conversation with the director of *Lancelot of the Lake*.

As we walked back up the hill, the sun beginning to dip over the far edge of the valley, she turned back to the village and smiled sadly for a moment. And then she said, 'We have to keep this place our little secret. And the vodkas. They must be a secret above all else.'

It was on our return that I was made aware that the retreat was not a glorified secluded hotel for the rich and plastered. It was a certified medical institution. Esther had her own personal nurse who had to report directly to the insurance company. She was a pretty but broad-shouldered Irish woman who was red with apoplexy as we sidled into the warm glow of the lobby, the sun now set behind us. The nurse said she was about to call the police and send out a search party. Esther waved her arm dismissively: 'I find that very hard to believe.' Esther took her to one side and gave a hushed speech that calmed everything down, drained the rouge from the nurse's cheeks. Coming back to me standing awkward and guilty at the door, Esther said that as long as I swore on my mother's life and spit in the dirt that I have no intoxicants on my person then the nurse would allow me to stay for dinner, to be taken in Esther's room. Esther delivered the news with a wink out of sight of the nurse, who now was looking relieved, indeed grateful, to her charge for her return.

In London we had not been this close. There was a mischievous, childish side to this renewed union; two orphans bonded in their espionage against the system, against the cold crushing night of reality. In London she had seemed directionless. I was not even sure why she had come, and why she had found me. It was a link to Pansattio – our conversations were. She spoke of him as if in a trance, as if I had placed her under hypnosis and she were recalling every detail of his being. Every sip of wine took her deeper under his skin. We walked for hours, visited museums, galleries, ended up at house parties of the rich and famous – actors, philosophers, writers. All her life she had whisky-sodden older men leaning over her slight frame, her large eyes looking up to them, her mouth about to utter words that would tie them up as she made her escape. Now these men wanted to know who I was, the adjutant of the perennially delectable Esther Delissen. Richard Burton, ashen with the creeping death that would claim him, once said to me at one of these parties, that I looked like her bagman, yet she looked at me like I was her priest. He wanted to know if I was a cult leader or something. I told him I was just a friend. 'Rasputin,' he barked at me.

I believed her when she said that Pansattio had never made a move on her. I grew to realise that he had taken her in, put his cloak around her shoulders. Others assumed this a vampiric gesture, but I saw it differently. At the retreat we sat at a small round table and ate goulash and potatoes looking out over the blackness of the valley's edge. She ate very lightly, tiny morsels. I commented on the meagre feasts of the upper classes and she said, 'I read the book – did I ever tell you?'

'The book?'

'Your biography of Satti,' she said.

'I wondered. I never heard from you about it.'

'I meant to write you to thank you for it,' she said. She was looking down at her plate. Her one leg was bent under her, and she used only her fork, cutting down through the potatoes with its edge. 'Many would have given the old man a difficult burial. He had a bad reputation by the time of his death and I was worried some hack like yourself would come along and cash in on it and spread disease. But you did an honest job.'

'What can I say? I grew to like him,' I said.

'You did?'

'You sold him well.'

'He was good to me,' she said and her thoughts, I could see, drifted away from the table, from me, and from the retreat. Her delicate jaw line grew defined and she gazed long out of the window, her eyes misting, and she looked ever so much like that portrait Pansattio took on the veranda in Venice.

I did not leave that night. And in the morning we did not speak. We glided around each other like ghosts, attached to each other by some moment of contact, but ethereal, apart in our true forms. We held each other for some time, just the sound of our breathing between us. She curled around me like smoke.

She slowly pulled my shirt up and onto my shoulders and began looping the buttons into their holes. I watched her. She walked me to my car and kissed me again before I got in. I remember the dryness of her lips, the slightest creases to the corners of them, and to the corners of her eyes. And I remember seeing her on the steps of the retreat in my rear view mirror. The last time I saw her.

I think I will come to look back on her life as one long exhalation that lasted fifty-two years, sixty days and however many hours and minutes, and perhaps that night we spent together was a brief moment when she held her breath. That is how I will think of her.

Fabrications

Tyler Keevil

It's impossible to say, after fifty odd years, how Lowri and I found the shop, with its missing floor and collection of rugs and that rambling man who had so many stories to tell. All we know is that it was in our town (that picturesque hamlet formed around two cross streets, nailed to the earth at the point of convergence by the old market hall) and that it was on Longbridge Street, not Shortbridge Street. But whether the entrance was behind the curry house, or the knick-knack shop, or the Unicorn hotel, or further along towards HSBC and the Red Lion, neither Lowri nor I can say with anything resembling confidence.

At that time the knickknack shop wasn't even a knick-knack shop. It was a vintage clothing store. And the Unicorn was not the Unicorn, but a less successful pub called the Plough. In the intervening years both those places have cycled through various permutations; the first a hobby shop, an auto supply specialist, and a teahouse, the latter the Daffodil, the King's Arms, and the ill-fated Sow's Ear. So a certain amount of confusion on both our parts is understandable, even expected. Just as time heals all wounds, it also erodes all memories – until your own past seems as tattered and patchy as a swath of moth-eaten fabric.

For a long time I was convinced we had reached the shop via a narrow passage, marked by a wrought iron gate, which still lies between the ever-changing pub and the (then) retro clothing store. However, when I went back recently, hoping to relive the memory, I found myself at a dead end – marked only by a newly (and poorly) built brick wall. Lowri, for her part, is convinced we reached the shop by passing through another – possibly the retro clothing store, with its racks of thin, faded T-shirts and wrinkled trousers. The more I consider it the more I suspect she's right, and that the clothing store acted as a kind of passageway to the rug shop. If that was the case, then the woman who ran the store must have had some kind of understanding with the old man. It's even possible that she was the one who'd put up the sign that lured us off the high street of town: Sale: Wondrous Rugs of the World. As to that I can only speculate, since neither of us can recall where, exactly, that sign was located. I can visualize the lettering – an antique, old-fashioned font – but not its position.

In the end, I suppose it doesn't matter where his shop was, or how we came upon it, because we couldn't go back even if we knew the way. It now exists only in the past. And so, somehow or other, we came to a courtyard tucked behind the buildings of Longbridge Street, and thereafter the details of that day are much easier to recall.

*

The uneven concrete of that square was filled with cracks, and the cracks filled with tufts of grass. Affixed to the wall on our left was a crooked wooden staircase, precarious as a Jenga tower. As we ascended it seemed to sway and totter beneath us. At the top was a plain blue door, the weathered paint peeling back in layers. Pinned to it was a small, hand-written note: Enter, Please. Despite that, I felt obligated to knock, setting loose a cascade of paint chips that fluttered like tiny flower petals to the floor. They were still in the process of settling when the door swung inward.

And there he was. For all the uncertainties about the location of his shop, my memories of that old man are indelible: tall and loose-limbed, with a mass of Mark Twain hair and one brown tooth among dozens of yellow ones – like a single rotten kernel on a gleaming cob of corn.

'Come in, come in,' he said, beckoning us with a nicotine-stained finger. 'You've arrived just in time – I'll be closing shortly.'

He had a habit of gazing at your shoulder, or ear, or chin, or just past your head – never quite looking you in the eye, perceiving the world as he told his tales: from a sly, slanted angle.

'For the day?' I asked.

'No, no,' he said, studying my hairline. 'Forever.'

That kind of comment, uttered with such calm finality, would ordinarily have warranted a more inquisitive response from Lowri and me – had we both not noticed, as we crossed the threshold, that his shop lacked a floor. Instead, a metre-wide walkway, or catwalk, had been built into the walls of the building. From it (we were standing on it) you could see right down through to the ground level, where we presumed he lived. I say 'we' even though at the time, of course, I could not have said what, exactly, Lowri was thinking. But later on we both agreed that we'd been looking down upon the man's living quarters, and therefore his life – the specifics of which could be read in such details as the unmade cot against one wall, the rusty hot plate, the overturned bookshelf that served as a table, the sink with its clutter of rusty tin dishes, the Persian carpet of near-biblical proportions that dominated the room's centre, and the cat creeping about, oblivious to our presence, its haunches rippling beneath its dirty black pelt. I had the impression that we were gazing into the guts of a temporary encampment, as of somebody on safari, or a military expedition.

'You must watch your step,' the old man said, pointing; there was no rail or barrier between the catwalk and the space below. 'I could have put a floor in, you see…' He trailed off, looking at the space, at the place where a floor might have been.

'But you didn't want to?' Lowri prompted.

'Quite right, quite right,' he agreed. He had an accent I found impossible to place – but coming from Canada that's quite common for me. He wasn't Welsh. I couldn't even be sure he was British. I thought I detected a soft Australian drawl, maybe even a dash of New England. Later Lowri (who has a better ear than me) would confirm it wasn't just me; the man's accent was wonderfully ambiguous, both educated and guttural, refined and coarse, rustic and worldly, with dashes of Northern intonation mingled with Southern slang, and the faint inflection of foreignness just tangible, as of a tongue influenced by many languages, many dialects. 'I had this high-ceilinged room, you see, but dividing it into two floors would have required planning permission, and lighting, and windows. This way my treasures are lit from below, which I find delightful.' As he spoke, he moved his left arm in a slow sweeping gesture that took in the treasures to which he was referring: a collection of sumptuous, vibrant, astonishingly varied rugs and tapestries that adorned the walls, like doorways to exotic, mystical worlds.

'Are you interested in buying?' he asked, and I thought I saw him wink. He had one lazy eye. Or rather (more accurately) one dominant eye, which seemed to be forever scrutinizing the world through its constant, roving motion. 'A rug for your new home, perhaps? Making a nest?'

We laughed, since we had, indeed, just bought our first house, but also because we could tell, at a glance, that these rugs were far more expensive than anything we could afford, than anything we could ever dream of affording. We professed our poverty, together, like two beggars, but the old man waved the concept of poverty aside – as you might a fly.

'Nonsense,' he said. 'A poor pocket and a rich heart are synonymous. At least let me show you around. I would rather chat with a young, local couple than the predatory antiques connoisseurs who I deal with so often – who think small-town equates to small-time, who think they might know more about rugs than me, though I have spent a lifetime seeking and collecting only the most exquisite of carpets. As if I wouldn't know their exact worth! 'He shook his head, chuckling at the thought. 'This world is a boat of vice bobbing along on a sea of greed – though no doubt it will be scuttled soon. 'That idea seemed to cheer him. 'But come. See for yourselves.'

He had adopted the pose of a museum curator – one arm folded across his midriff, hand cupped to support the opposite elbow – and he spoke with such authority we felt compelled to follow as he turned on his heel and moved off down the creaking walkway.

*

He marched past several hangings, apparently intent on beginning with something impressive. He stopped before a large rectangular rug, covered in complex patterns, dyed red and brown and beige.

'Now this rug,' he began, 'is something special. Some of the colours have faded, as you can see – but the design is as intricate as the day it was woven, over five centuries ago.'

Lowri and I exchanged a discreet, secretive glance, both of us silently agreeing, yes, this old man is crazy – obviously – but let's humour him for a while.

'That's amazing,' I said, studying it with a theatrically critical gaze, hoping to make Lowri laugh. Yet soon my affected air dissolved. The rug was faded, as the man had admitted, but not so much that you couldn't discern the design. And what a design! At the centre was a shimmering sunburst, the pattern as fine as a snowflake viewed beneath a microscope. Smaller, oval-shaped decorations radiated from each spoke of the central motif. Every inch of the field had been incorporated into the abstract, symmetrical design, so complex it played tricks with your eyes.

'Shah Tamil,' the old man said, 'was a great lover of the art of weaving. When he discovered he was dying, he held a contest for the weavers in Ardabil – the centre of Iranian rug-making in those days. Whoever could weave the most intricate, the most beautiful rug the world had ever seen, would have his work selected as the carpet for the Shah's tomb, and guarantee himself a place in paradise. To complete such a task alone was impossible. Teams of weavers formed, ready to take up the challenge. But the high stakes provoked squabbles, bickering, in-fighting. In the end only half a dozen rugs were completed.'

Lowri and I stood and gawked as he explained this, as casually as if he were telling us about a walk he'd taken the other day. 'You're not going to say,' I said, 'that this is the rug that won?'

'It placed second, actually. But that is where the judge and I disagree. You see, Shah Tamil never lived to see the finished products – he died of what many suspect now to have been a stroke shortly before the contest finished. The selection was left to his Grand Vizier. You can find his choice on display at New York's Metropolitan Museum of Art. It is a masterwork, of course – but the Vizier lacked Tamil's discerning eye. I am certain if the Shah had lived to see it he would have chosen this rug. The medallion pattern is typical of Iranian carpets, but what sets this piece apart is the tightness of the weave – over a thousand knots per inch. And yes, I have counted them.'

*

The next rug he showed us, at first glance, didn't seem to be nearly as impressive or remarkable. To my eye, the weave looked coarse, the colours drab, the design relatively simple.

'And this rug,' he said, as if ready to launch into a well-prepared speech. Then he paused – catching himself. Instead he asked, 'Tell me about this rug. What can we deduce?'

'It's pretty plain,' I said.

'Ah – but look closer at the colours. Isn't this brown reminiscent of a farmer's field, these greens bright as a Welsh hillside, that grey like the waters of the River Wye on an overcast day?'

And the longer we stared the more the woven features seemed to adopt the characteristics of those comparisons, blurring into the geographical features he'd suggested, until I had the impression that we were looking at –

'A map,' Lowri ventured.

'That's right,' I agreed. 'A map of mid Wales.'

And our words seemed to settle it, crystalize it, make those statements true. I recognized, now, several local landmarks: the snake trail of the A470, the blue bends of Llyn Clywedog, the patchwork of Hafren Forest. All very rough, of course, or else we would have noticed it before.

'This rug,' the man said, neither affirming nor refuting our claims, 'will show you the way home. Each to his own.'

We laughed, assuming he was joking, seeing if we would fall for it. But the longer we stared at the mottled patchwork of colours, the more details seemed to miraculously emerge.

'That square of green...' Lowri murmured.

'The soccer pitch?' I pointed to a spot adjacent to it. 'And this deep slate-grey?'

'Our terrace.'

The old man nodded, accepting our discoveries, and continued:

'This is one of my oldest items, and native to these shores. Woven by an unknown artisan of an ancient Celtic clan, before the Norman

Conquest. Those were the days of myth and legend – when what we might now call magic was still an everyday reality. The warriors of the clan took this rug with them when they waged campaigns against enemy settlements. In those days paper and parchment were not used in Britain, so the map it contains was the best means they had of returning to their wives and families.'

We look at him, half-believing this outrageous lie.

'But conquering is a dangerous business. One day they looked at the map and saw nothing – only patterns on plain cloth. They knew then that their village had been attacked, their kin wiped out – retribution for one of their many conquests. For the rest of their lives the remaining warriors scoured the land, searching aimlessly for some ruin, some evidence of what had been their home, and found none. It may seem obvious, but you can only go home if you have a home to go to.'

He pinched his lower lip, giving us time to digest this axiom, before moving on...

*

'I came across this next tapestry, and the people who wove it, while exploring the Sahara. Men tall and lean like me, but dark-skinned, their faces scarified by sun, sand, and wind. They walked with me for many days, guiding me along unseen trails in the desert. At night we slept in tents, warmed by their camels – though in actual fact we slept little, talked much. It was during one of those dark, sand-hissing nights that they told me their purpose.'

'To weave this tapestry?' Lowri asked.

'They were nomads, and had been weaving it for generations, outlining the entire history of their people – beginning with their first ancestors who'd come to Africa from a land of parrots and persimmon. They had no written language, so they'd woven their lore into the rug itself, a rich history that went back centuries.'

Withdrawing a magnifying glass from his pocket, he held it up against the fabric. Beneath its lens, the tendril lines morphed into complex pictographs: a man with a spear, a woman giving birth, a desert oasis, bonfires, some kind of wedding ceremony, two children paddling down a river, all etched in detail as fine as the cut of a diamond, in colour as ripe and vibrant as fresh fruit.

'They could not explain how, exactly, they'd attained such level of intricacy – but please, look for yourselves.'

He handed the glass to Lowri, who held it close to her eye, her face intent, a caricature of a detective looking for clues. She saw (she later told me) the waters of a flooded river, a series of caves where the tribe buried their dead – each skeleton in the pictograph no bigger than an ant, but just as detailed.

I asked, 'But why would they give it to you? For them it must have been priceless.'

His face cracked into a grimace, like a brittle mask, and he said, 'The tribe had long since brought the tapestry up to the present. Upon reaching the point where they were weaving the events of the previous week, and yesterday, and today, they saw no need to stop – but continued weaving the rug into tomorrow, and the next day, knotting the threads of their future. They saw the babies they would have, and the famines they would face. They saw the ongoing cycle of birth, life, death until, at a certain point, there was nothing but darkness – black threads entwined like vipers, the patterns of oblivion. Convinced they'd foreseen the end of the world, believing that some calamity would befall their tribe, they gifted the tapestry to me – the first foreigner they'd met in centuries – to ensure the history of their people would never be forgotten, that their story would not end with them.'

Lowri handed the magnifying glass to me, and I knelt to examine the bottom corner of the tapestry. I saw a great feast, a bonfire the size of a burning match, and then…nothing. Panel upon panel of darkness, which ended in a tangle of loose threads – as if the weavers had been so startled by what they'd foreseen that they'd abandoned their weaving without tying off the knots.

'But surely it was just superstition?' I said. 'Once they realize they were in error, you can return it to them.'

'If only that were true. But shortly after I left Africa that area was carpet-bombed by the Libyan government, who thought it a rebel stronghold. I have been back since then, and there is no trace of them. Their apocalypse was real. Yet I sometimes wonder if what they'd foreseen was only their own future, or if it is still waiting to happen to the rest of us. Did they foresee their end or our end? Is it possible the fabric of our civilization will soon unravel, the threads of our lives be cut off, as if snipped by the Greek Fates?'

I smiled uncertainly. I could tell all this talk of doomsday unsettled Lowri – as it unsettled me – and in an attempt to lighten the mood I gestured at the rug further along.

'What about that rug?' I asked. 'Does it have a story?'

He smiled, seeing through my ploy. 'They all have stories, my boy,' he said.

*

The one I'd pointed to was the plainest of them all. It was a small, dusty oval, perhaps three feet wide by four feet long, divided into rings of colour: blue, red, green, yellow. That was all. No intricate designs, no patterns, no hidden map. Just some tattered frills around the circumference.

'You're probably thinking,' he said, 'that this rug looks out of place among all this finery. Perhaps. And in auction it would fetch no more than a few pounds – if that. Yet at the same time it is the most valuable item here, the closest to my heart. You see, if it weren't for this rug I would not be alive. 'He reached out and touched it, the only time we saw him make physical contact with any of his treasures. 'I was born in Berlin, you see, a few years before the war. We were not Jews but we were sinti – travellers – and there was little difference in the eyes of the Nazis.

'You know all this, I imagine, from your history texts. But what those texts miss are the little moments of villainy and heroism that mark such times of crisis. On the last day that I saw my parents, they took me and my six siblings to the toy shop at the end of the street, which was run by an ex-army engineer of whom we were all afraid. Since retiring he had put his skills to designing all sorts of mechanical toys. This rug lay in the middle of his shop. I do not remember the specifics of the bargain, or how my parents had known to come to him, but I remember him pulling it aside, revealing the trap door beneath. The seven of us descended into darkness. I looked up and saw my parents' faces; then the circle of light was obscured, as in an eclipse. I lived beneath that rug for five years, with my brothers and sisters, the man's wonderful toys our only source of joy. During the day, we would hear the creak of the floorboards and the clink of cash exchanging hands. We grew to recognize, and fear, the thumping of army boots, when some member of the SS came in to buy presents for his little one. At night, the trap door would open; the chamber pot would go out and food and candles and new toys – occasionally – would come in. And each time the frightening old engineer would whisper to us that help was coming soon, that our parents sent their love, that it was only a matter of days before we would be free.'

The man tilted his head, as if just noticing something. 'I think those years of entrapment led to what came after – to my life of wandering. I had been confined and now I wanted only freedom. When the trap-door opened, and hands helped us up, we were all rail-thin, pale as corpses. It took days for our eyes to adjust to sunlight, and just as long for our stomachs to adjust to full meals. The engineer wanted neither gratitude nor reward. He could not bear to look at us as we emerged. He said, "Go, children. Go from this place, this city, this country, and do not look back. Do not return." And I didn't, for many, many years. When I finally did, he was gone, of course. But the shop remained. And would you believe that this rug still stayed in its spot on the floor. I told the new owner of its history, and my collection of carpets. She gave it to me with tears in her eyes.'

Even as he said it, he looked at us, with tears in his eyes. We were both near tears, too.

'So in a way, this rug was my chrysalis. It covered me for most of my childhood – those five years of incubation. I emerged fully grown, ready to escape, ready to fly.'

*

'But come,' he motioned us to follow, rounding the corner to a rug on the wall opposite the entrance, 'let me tell you about this next rug – from a little known weaving community on the outskirts of Alcaraz, in Castile. There the art of rug making is prized above all others – and the competing guilds jealously guard the in-house techniques they have developed, be they soumak, embroidery, brocade, pile weaving, hand tufting, or a combination of these and others.'

As he spoke, he pointed to various parts of the rug, which was large and colourful and gorgeous. It depicted two young people, dangling from a series of strings like marionettes. Yet instead of a puppeteer, the threads hung suspended from a pair of looms. The couple were straining to kiss each other, but the tension in their strings prevented their lips from touching.

'This piece is assumed to have been woven by Catalina Calino, a child prodigy – the sixth generation in a famed line of master weavers. The Calinos had, through carefully arranged marriages, bred their children for particular physical traits beneficial to the art: long fingers, hand-eye coordination, a natural nimbleness and ambidexterity. Reputedly, Catalina was able to weave before she could walk. By the age of five she was making her own thread, by six she had invented a new dye – a particularly vibrant red made from the shells of cochineal insects. Unfortunately, the demands of her craft – and her overbearing parents – meant she was plagued by neurosis and mental illness. She drank her own dyes. She killed butterflies. She had an obsessive attraction to felines in the great cat family. She saw – and frequently spoke to – the ghosts of her ancestors. None of these idiosyncrasies affected her craft, and her parents were willing to tolerate them, until, on the day of her sixteenth birthday, she fell madly, wildly, deliriously in love with a boy.'

'Why would they object to that?' we both asked, which is what we were expected to ask. All his stories had such breaks, in which a line seemed to be scripted for us, waiting to be spoken.

'The boy was a weaver himself, the offspring of a guild that specialized in the use of synthetic dyes made from chemicals. The

Calinos despised aniline dyes. Though inexpensive, they faded and deteriorated quickly – and her mother thought it symptomatic of an overall decline in the craft, which more and more sought to cater to vulgar, American folk-art tastes. None of this mattered to the girl. Neither did the fact that her lover's skill as a weaver was mediocre, which made him an unsuitable match for a virtuoso like herself. Against her parents' wishes, the two of them continued to meet in secret, exchanging tiny woven tokens of their affections. When her parents forbid her to see him again, she eloped – essentially defecting to the other guild. Violence between the two families ensued; several people died. Tensions reached a peak during the annual Alcaraz rug weaving competition. The final was between Catalina and her mother – Calino vs. Calino. The whole town gathered to watch the event, which reputedly lasted for days, both parties weaving themselves to the point of exhaustion, subsisting only on water and salt tablets, as the rules decreed.'

'And who won?' I asked.

The old man sighed. 'Sadly, we don't know. Before the competition finished, Castile was hit by a devastating earthquake. Both families perished – including Catalina and her mother. This rug was found among the ruins, though we have no way of knowing for sure who the artisan was. The obvious choice, given the content, would seem to be Catalina. Yet survivors maintain that her mother was working on a similar portrait – perhaps as an act of appeasement, a means of healing the rift with her daughter. To use a phrase as worn as some of these rugs, we'll never know.'

*

It went on like that – each rug a story, each a gateway to a flood of memories and fantasies, and it seemed to me he was purging himself of them, as a monk before meditation, a Catholic seeking absolution – passing on the accompanying tales before his journey elsewhere. The old man was such a consummate salesman and raconteur that it didn't matter whether his anecdotes were fact or fiction, myth or history. If the proof is in the pudding, then the truth, perhaps, is in the telling, and in that place, at that time, we believed his stories – even those ones I can no longer remember. My only regret now is that I did not write it all down immediately after, for my memory is sound, but not perfect. Yet had I gone in as a reporter, seeking to take advantage of him – like the antique dealers he was fond of disparaging – I doubt he would have been so open and forthcoming.

As our tour wound down the light outside the windows was fading. The last work he showed us was unfinished, something he'd recently commissioned – thin and delicate and woven from white mesh.

'A friend is making this shroud for me out of silk from old cocoons,' he said. 'I am not there yet, and perhaps have a few more years of collecting in me. But in some ways that is of little significance. The shop will close today; as far as my customers are concerned I'll already be gone.'

'But why?' Lowri asked. 'You clearly love it – so why close your shop?'

The old man shook his head, as wearily as an old horse in the traces. 'The people have stopped coming, my dear. And those that do have stopped listening. 'He turned to survey his collection. 'They see only material objects, not the stories behind them – and I am sick of spinning my yarns for an unappreciative audience.'

'Isn't there anybody to carry on your work?' I asked. 'Somebody to train up?'

'I've had apprentices over the years, it's true. But none willing to invest the time to commit to it. Your generation is so flighty, so quick to flutter on. But then, who am I to talk, having never had a real home, or a long-term relationship? 'He grinned, patting us both on the shoulder, as if claiming us as comrades. 'Perhaps there are those who take up the mantle in their own ways, on their own terms.'

As if to seal that declaration, he clapped his hands together, startling the cat, which had settled into sleepy reverie below. 'But tell me – you strike me as a discerning young couple, with good taste. 'Have any of these rugs taken your fancy?'

Dazzled and dumbstruck as we were, we immediately professed our ignorance, and our poverty. We knew we couldn't afford any of his treasures. He let us stammer and babble our way into silence.

'Let's play a game, then,' he said, rubbing his palms together, as if warming them. 'Just for kicks – as you youngsters might say. If you could afford my overpriced fare, in another life, which would you prefer?'

We didn't have to answer; we betrayed ourselves by looking back across the room, across the missing floor, to the rug hanging nearest the door, the one that showed the way home.

'Ah-hah,' he said. 'So it goes. I'll admit to being fond of that one myself. There is something so comforting about being able to imagine your way home, especially for us travellers. But in this case, also, perhaps particularly appropriate – given that you are beginning your new life together. 'He led us back to it, walking with certain swagger. 'And tell me – again in jest – how much do you think I'd ask for this heirloom of a clan from ancient Wales?'

Lowri and I looked at each other, then at the floor, hesitant to even proffer a guess. It was like being asked to bid on a piece of the man himself, a part of his body. Instead we again reiterated that it was no doubt priceless, that we had no hope of being able to afford it.

The man chuckled. 'Yet you must realize you are in a position of great advantage, this being my final day of sale. In many ways you would be doing me a favour, in saving this piece from being relegated into storage, or ending up as part of some soulless museum display. In fact – and no arguments here – I will sell it to you for the money you have in your wallets, and that's it.'

Before we could contradict him, he held up both hands.

'No arguments, remember?'

He was so adamant we had no choice, but we were almost embarrassed to open our wallets, and reveal the paltry, crumpled bills within. I had a tenner; Lowri a five and two-eighty in change.

'This is more than sufficient,' he assured us, alleviating us of our money. 'And I hope you may always find a home to go to – even if it's one you don't expect.'

Those words, as enigmatic as the rest, were the last he said to us –

at least that I remember. I have a feeling we lingered for a little longer, exchanging pleasantries, reluctant to bid him a final good-bye – though Lowri isn't sure about that. We both remember him walking us to the doorway, and leaning there as we descended those rickety stairs. I carried our new rug, rolled up and slung across my shoulder, like a body I'd rescued from a burning building. It was surprisingly heavy. I looked back once, saw him smiling, and looked back again, and saw that he was gone, the door shut, though I hadn't heard it close.

Back at our house we unrolled the rug, but in the dimness of our terraced cottage the colour seemed less vibrant, the patterns less defined. For a few months (or maybe longer) we had it on display, but we squabbled often over what represented what, where our house was, and where our town – debating those details that had been so clear beneath his coaxing eye. Like a flower plucked from an exotic garden, it seemed to wilt and fade over time. We never dared to get it appraised, for fear, I imagine, of discovering it was not fifteen hundred years old but barely fifteen, terrified that the magic of that day might be dispelled by some expert declaring the rug worthless. But neither did we relish the questions the mottled tapestry always evoked from curious guests. Nobody ever saw anything in it, and eventually it found its way to our attic, where it remained for many years.

It's only recently, perhaps spurred on by a bout of nostalgia, that we've got it out again. Fortunately the moths of memory have not been at it. And strangely enough, maybe because my eyes are going in my old age, I feel I can again perceive something within the field of the rug. And we are no longer embarrassed to keep it on display. When our grandchildren come over, they often ask us to relate the story of the mysterious carpet salesman, and our visit on his last day of business. We tell them about the myth behind the rug, and encourage the little ones to pick out those features that show them a way home, which they always manage to do. And I think it's only lately, through passing these tales on to them, that I've begun to understand the gift he gave us back then, a gift which had less to do with the rug, or any of the rugs, and more to do with the art of weaving a story.

The Plagiarist

Richard Redman

Upon completion of his film-script – an adaptation of the short-story *The Gospel According to Mark* by Jorge Luis Borges – the then obscure, but now justly famous writer, Phillip Morris,[1] contemplated the strange and complex issue of its copyright. We can consider the word strange as particularly apt in this case as, from Morris' highly subjective point of view, ownership of the aforementioned story was not a straightforward issue.

The collection of Borges stories *Brodie's Report* had been recommended to the young writer by a brief acquaintance,[2] as something that would be of *interest to him*. This proved to be an uncannily accurate supposition, as we shall see. In deference to his mother's religion, Morris began with *The Gospel According to Mark* – which he rightly guessed to be some form of instructive parable.

The opening paragraphs of the story delineate the perverse, ironical nature of its central character, Baltasar Espinosa.[3] As Morris read on, he couldn't fail to notice the number of disturbing parallels to be drawn between Espinosa and himself, at the time of reading he was thirty-three[4] – just like Espinosa – and he also had a mother, a devout Pentecostal, who similarly obliged him to make a daily show of religion in spite of his atheism. It required little more than these few coincidences, and a profound sympathy with Espinosa's penchant for nuance and self-correcting thought-processes, for Morris to believe he had chanced upon his exact literary double.

It often bewildered the young writer that even in the shadow-worlds of his fictionalised autobiographies, the characters he designated his alter egos were inevitably puffed-up or idealised self-images, or wizened, partial glimpses of an interior self. Yet here he was in *The Gospel According to Mark*, the work of another, replicated in almost every detail, excepting the superficial.

Morris cautioned himself that he had thought similarly of Mersault in Camus' *The Outsider*, and Joseph K in Kafka's *The Trial*, and even Nick Carraway in Scott Fitzgerald's *The Great Gatsby*, only for such comparisons to embarrass him later when he came to reread those novels. Yet with each rereading of *The Gospel According to Mark*, his initial identification with Espinosa only increased. He copied out the story in long hand – hundreds of times – in order to understand it more completely. His decision to finally adapt the story into a screenplay stimulated further this bizarre fascination. The story began to affect a change in him, until he came to regard himself as the story's one and true author. *The Gospel According to Mark* belonged to him, and not to Borges.

For the cattle-ranch where Espinosa is trapped by the floods, Morris envisioned the farm that clung to the side of Twmbarlum Hill, which he visited weekly in his youth. It was during childhood that the terrible fancy suggested itself to him that Twmbarlum was actually the very same Golgoltha where Christ was crucified. And, rather than accept Daniel's half-Indian and half-Scottish servants, the Gutres[5] as 'tall, strong, and bony with reddish hair', he recast them, in his mind, as short, stocky, dark-haired and Welsh. The Gutre Bible (printed in English) that Espinosa discovered in the farm's main-house, Morris felt sure resembled in every respect (five inches thick, two feet by one foot across, cloaked in a hard, black cover with the words 'Holy Bible' embossed in gold leaf on its front) the same Bible that sat on the table in his grandparent's living-room.

This cross-fertilisation of imagery was made possible by the central idea of *The Gospel According to Mark* – that people, being fickle and paradoxical, inevitably kill those who offer themselves as their redeemers – being one that had lodged in Morris' imagination long before he had read a single word of Borges. The theme had become quite emblematic for the young writer, to the extent that he became convinced that somehow Borges had plagiarised him. Time was Morris' enemy, confounding his hopes of claiming authorship. For it was stated clearly at the bottom of Borges' foreword to *Brodie's Report*:

J.L.B
Buenos Aires, April 19th 1970[6]

Three years before Morris was born!

He entertained briefly the possibility of challenging Borges' copyright, before concluding that the laws of intellectual property would not bend to metaphysics.

Morris' claim was indeed difficult to prosecute, even in the case of Borges, who had once written: '*The fact is that every writer creates his own precursors. His work modifies our conception of the past, as it will modify the future.*'[7] The implications of this idea tantalised Morris. The argument was clearly there to be made that in crafting his film-script of *The Gospel According to Mark*, furnished with the new setting of the Welsh Valleys, he had effectively created Borges as his precursor upon whom he now exerted a *retrospective* creative influence. The task of proving such a transformation had taken place, unfortunately, was a job for a literary theorist and not a lawyer.

Morris was apprehensive that his script might languish, unmade, in his bottom drawer, unless a direct appeal was made to Maria Kodama.[8] It was she who currently exercised the copyright of Borges' complete works. There would be little consolation for Morris to be had in the continued existence of the film as a platonic ideal in his mind's eye. Quite the contrary, he needed the film to exist so that the past could be modified and the original story supplanted. It was the only way to show the story belonged to him and no one else. He felt sure that when audiences saw the rolling Welsh hills substituted for the sweeping long grass of the Pampas, they would understand it actually made sense to relocate the action of the story there. Concerning the depiction of the rain-floods, the inciting incident that keeps Espinosa isolated on the farm with the Gutres, where else other than Wales is it known to rain endlessly?

Aside from this relocation, Morris' script shared with the original story only the motives of its protagonists, the fate of its hero, its central theme of superstition and redemption – and nothing more. Both versions of the story followed identical narratives, related a chain of events in precisely the same way, and began and ended at corresponding points.

He wrote a long letter to Ms. Kodama but didn't send it. There was little doubt in his mind that the widow of Borges would be open-minded enough to consider intelligently his authorial claim to *The Gospel According to Mark*, yet surely by some sentimental pang of loyalty to her late husband she would still maintain the story belonged solely to Borges.

It should be made clear at this point that Morris wasn't seeking to avoid paying a royalty to Ms. Kodama for his putative screen adaptation. He merely wanted to credit his film thus:

> The Gospel According to Mark
> A film by Phillip Morris
> Based on the Short-story by Phillip Morris[9]
> – as suggested by Jorge Luis Borges

The co-author credit would reflect the fact that the story resulted from a relationship between both writers. Morris considered it a neat way of acknowledging their respective roles in the story's genesis; making sure he was proclaimed the story's author, whilst also conceding that Borges had had the privilege of telling it first. It was an elegant solution but Morris eventually convinced himself that Ms. Kodama would oppose it. He suspected pride in her husband's work would lead her to reject Morris' claim that his achievement as a reader of the story was as important as her husband's writing of it. And, no doubt, she would maintain her sentimental view even though Borges had written: '*Poetry is the encounter of the reader with the book, the discovery of the book.*'[10]

The imposition of Ms. Kodama as mediator mitigated the intimacy Morris had supposed existed between him and his illustrious Argentinean collaborator. He wished to negotiate with no one other than Borges, yet that was made impossible by the immovable fact of Borges' death nearly twenty years before. The young writer struggled for weeks and months to find a solution to the problem. He couldn't sleep. He refused to read the works of others. He wouldn't start another project. Then, on the verge of surrendering to despair, he happened upon the expedient of contriving a meeting with Borges in a story he would write. This story would have the form of a dream, possessing its own reality.

He picked up his pen and started to describe the journey, by foot, from his three-bedroom suburban home into the city-centre of Newport; writing of the Malpas Road and the Lyceum Tavern and the canal that passes underneath a motorway bridge. He could not resist the observation that Chartist rebels had walked the same road in eighteen thirty-nine, marching towards the guns of a troop of dragoons. His visual and historical imagination thus stirred, Morris took the decision to add to these local descriptions, the evocations of Buenos Aires from Borges' work.

He copied out these words from Borges' text: *the street corner on Cabrera where a mailbox stood; two cement lions on a porch on Calle Jujuy a few blocks from the Plaza del Once; a tile-floored corner grocery-store- and-bar...*

He wrote them down, again and again, until the repetitions took on an incantatory power and the walls of his study began to shake. Books fell from shelves. In moments the Welsh home around him was torn down to reveal sudden and sweeping vistas of Buenos Aires. Morris required no more than those few words above to work this magic. No mere photograph could stimulate as complete a vision of the Argentine capital as those scant details selected by Borges. Their very sparseness opened up imaginative spaces large enough for the young writer to build his city of dreams. With decreasing astonishment, Morris found he was able to populate his Buenos Aires with buildings and parks that Borges hadn't described. It had become more real to him than Newport.

He wandered the streets, absorbing the sounds of Spanish and Italian; until he was sure he'd acquired some understanding of these foreign tongues. He searched for an arch of an entrance hall with grillwork on the gate (as described in *Borges and I*) and found just such an arch and just such a gate around the corner of a large public building – The National Library of Argentina. He found Borges' name on a list of professors' mailboxes and climbed up three flights of stairs.

The door to an office was open; inside a balding old man with dry, yellowing skin sat at a desk. Morris recognised him immediately – it was Borges. In spite of his prior confidence, the young writer grew nervous at the silence of his great precursor. He wondered momentarily if he had indeed travelled back through time to engineer the encounter, or whether the old man was a ghost. On reflection, this question of time became increasingly important to Morris.

On Borges' desk was a wood-carved chess-set, with opposing sides missing one of their rook's pawns.

'Do you play?' asked Borges.

Morris could not recall later if Borges had asked this in Spanish or English.

He looked down at the chessboard, and then at the misty, sightless eyes of the old man. He remembered how the writer Bruce Chatwin had once described the entire genius of South America as having funnelled down into the personage of Borges, and thought it prudent to avoid the battle.

'Not really, though I do write about the game quite well.'

Borges nodded sagely. 'A proper story has much in common with a good game of chess. There should be nothing accidental about it. As Poe once said – in reference to his most famous story *The Raven* – the work should proceed, "step by step, to its completion with the precision and rigid consequence of a mathematical problem". Does your story unfold in such a way?'

'It does,' Morris replied.

'You must know that my father once explained Zeno's famous

paradox, choosing to make his example through a game of chess?'

'Yes, and I can think of no better preparation for your games with time and infinity.'

Dispensing with this chitchat, the old master brought them round to the business at hand. Morris chose to be bold and, with a tone that suggested he anticipated no denial, said he'd come to claim ownership of *The Gospel According to Mark*. Borges expressed no surprise at this, but simply asked if, like Pierre Menard (the author of the Quixote), the young writer was proposing a word for word rewrite of the story, making no alterations to the text. To achieve this, Borges explained it would be necessary for Morris to know Argentina as well as he, to understand its culture and landscape as a native, to be steeped in its myths and literature.

'Have you read *Facundo*?' asked Borges.

The young writer confessed that he hadn't.

'My boy... Facundo is the most memorable character of Argentine literature.'

Morris said that he had no doubt of it, but that it wasn't necessary for him to study Argentinean literature, or spend any time in the country, to be the writer of *The Gospel According to Mark*.

'With respect, the story is closer to me than it is to you Señor,' Morris countered. 'To the Welsh, religion is as dark and superstitious as it is for the Gutres. They must be neither Indian nor Calvinist, but Celtic non-conformist protestants. Place them in the landscape of my country and you have a more fitting theatre for Espinosa's tragedy.'

The old man shrugged his shoulders and asked to see the script. Morris handed over his copy, and was pleased to watch Borges trace his gnarled fingers over the surface of each page. Despite the fact that the script hadn't been written in Braille, Borges appeared able to read it. With a couple of gurgles, which sounded something like laughter, he finished reading.

'My original is unfaithful to your adaptation.'

'I'm glad you think so.'

'I am much impressed by the penultimate line of your script, there you have written – "A bird screamed; *it's a goldfinch*, Espinosa thought." Whereas I write – "A bird screamed; *it's a goldfinch*, Espinosa thought." I believe your version is infinitely richer than mine.'

Morris caught the scent of a passionflower and breathed deeply.

'Tell me,' Borges went on, 'is the goldfinch native to Wales?'

'It is. Nothing is lost and something is gained by transferring the story to a Welsh setting.'

The old man smiled thinly, 'I'm happy to have met you in this Patagonia[11] of our imaginations. I believe the story is yours.'

The young man rose quickly to his feet and thanked the old master. He paid fulsome and lengthy tribute to the brilliance of *Death and the Compass* and *Funes the Memorious*, and said he was certain he'd always be learning from them.

'No, no... It is I who should thank you,' said Borges with a wave of his hand. 'For you came to me in this dream and brought me your story. I shall look forward to waking and committing it to paper.'

The End

Authors Note: In the autumn of 2005, a cataloguist working for The Jorge Luis Borges Center, at the University of Aarhus, Denmark, unearthed an early draft of *The Gospel According to Mark*. The manuscript (dated 1966) had a note attached, in Borges' own handwriting. It told of the curious genesis of the story, which Borges claimed was delivered to him in a dream, complete, but in the form of a film-script, by another writer.

1: The reader will no doubt recall Morris' screenplay *The Seduction of Bel-Ami* (after the novel *Bel-Ami* by Guy de Maupassant) and his religious satire *Sadhana*.

2: The novelist Gregory Norminton, author of *Ship of Fools*.

3: The Spanish reader will sooner or later associate the character's surname, Espinosa (thorny) with Christ's 'crown of thorns'.

4: The age of Christ at his crucifixion, a foreshadowing of the story's denouement.

5: It is revealed that 'Gutre' is a corruption of their Scottish ancestral name Guthrie.

6: *Brodie's Report*, J.L. Borges.

7: *Kafka and his Precursors*, J.L. Borges

8: Ms. Kodama was a student of Borges, later his amanuensis then, in the final year of his life, his wife.

9: Mr. Morris has become somewhat notorious for his collection of credits.

10: See Borges' lecture *Poetry*.

11: An area of Argentina settled by the Welsh in the 19th century.

Swansea Malady

Georgia Carys Williams

Its breath is the strongest, stifled by something in the pit of its stomach, green with grumble and blue with malady. It catches you, and like the fish around Mumbles pier, you can't quite let go. You open your nose to the sickly-sweet smell of seaweed and you hear the farcical shriek of gulls in the air, pining for you to look up. Then you're thrown, out of the sea and straight into rain.

I've heard people speak of water having a memory and I wonder if it's better than my grandfather's is, as I look at the sea trembling in and out of Swansea Bay like a tired hand. As I step across the quilted impression of the sand, I wonder what it's seen. Does it drift in and out in the same, slow manner, with every base of its stories strewn upon the seabed, only the shrapnel of shells to be dragged back in?

Head over shoulder as I see the prints of my toes among the pinned shells, my feet have led me to a large mound of sand; they've crept into a circular castle built at the end of the bay. Stopping to observe its structure, I'm glad I haven't done much damage other than a slight indentation in the side and although I feel the urge to sink my foot entirely into it, remembering the striped tail of apartments overlooking the dunes, I tell myself to resist. I remind myself of how it must feel for someone to build something so intricate and then witness it being reduced to rubble.

Mesmerised by the exhibit, I crouch down to its lopsided shape, which is layered to resemble a decadent birthday cake. It has spindles for turrets as though it belongs to a realm of fairies and phantoms, and the only article missing is the roaring dragon of the Welsh flag upon the top.

I stand up, feeling the ache in my thighs stretching out and as I drag my feet along the damp sand of the bay, I think of all that remains of the real Swansea Castle; its grey, carcassed elbow joint at the centre of town.

This is I, it would project with a gravelly voice if it could speak, like the proud, stubborn voice of my grandfather who has smoked cigars since the war. He sometimes speaks about the smoke during The Blitz and I look to the left and see the long sewage pipes stretching out into the sea like two, long arms.

As boys, we used to dive right off those, he'd say.

This morning, before attending an arts afternoon called 'Transitions', I walked through the centre of town and heard the guitar's hollow pluck of a song I recognised to be Jeff Buckley's cover of 'Hallelujah' disappearing shyly behind the murmur of Swansea Market, then ringing through town. I couldn't make out what the musician looked like but through the hoard of people, I saw a splatter of silver upon the black felt of his open guitar case. I filled in the lyrics I could remember as I walked past. Then it was the instrumental in ascending steps before it broke out, then hid again, ebbing into the market.

My grandfather said the market used to be the best in Wales, a grandiose glass-iron structure around all sorts of stalls: cafés, fishmongers, clothes, vegetable and clock stalls.

We used to love laverbread and Penclawdd cockles from the market, he'd say, lovely with a bit of bacon fat. Sometimes, we'd have black beef or salt marsh lamb at the weekend. Over six hundred stalls, it had!

He'd start one story and, without ending it, begin another about the picnics on the top of Kilvey Hill or The Lion's Head, and I'd feel the shrapnel of memories hitting me as his eyes looked into mine. Sometimes, he'd stop talking altogether.

There have been especially good days, where he's almost told a whole story, but I only know this because he will have certainly told it before. He asks me questions as though I'm someone else, his old friend, his brother or even my passed away grandmother. It's when things alter around him that he becomes confused, suffers from forgetfulness. At that moment, it feels just like the sand slipping through my toes.

It was at the arts afternoon that people spoke about water having a memory. There was the verbal kind of art, poetry and storytelling, the kind that can speak loudly from some place deep and there was music, yet it didn't seem to transcend as emotively as the strum of the busker's guitar I'd passed earlier on. There had been paintings, but they were too abstract for my taste, too undecided about their own motives and I was desperate to leave. More shrapnel hits me:

without the cracks, we have nothing to fill, without the empty canvas, we have nothing to paint.

So I quickly paid my respects, then stepped out of the theatre and onto the cobble-stoned Marina where the Helwick ship was perched like a smoked-out dragon, dead on its back.

Here on the beach, I see the sand-cemented walls of the castle before me and wonder how easily I could move it. I place two arms either side of the castle's curve and close my eyes, ready to turn it over like a just-baked cake but the base doesn't budge, only the edge begins to turn to dust and fall as grain in my hands. I step back, wondering where the rest of Swansea went in my grandfather's memory. *The beach is always here*, he'd said, *it only changes shape*. I wonder where its laughter lines are, feeling the sandbanks bowing around me.

After The Blitz, Swansea's face wasn't smiling anymore. It was shattered. The sandcastle stands there so proud that I ask myself what the urge is to break something so beautiful that someone else has created. I think I'm alone, but I look up and notice a couple, their arms in a figure of eight as they walk down the slope and onto the beach:

> foreheads together
> but lips not,
> words together
> but tongues not.

My rucksack is full of glass tumblers, equipment intended for this afternoon's performance, but I didn't use them, I told the other artists I'd forgotten my material, and then hastily walked towards the door. Afraid they could hear the clinking of the hollow, glass harmonica upon my back, I didn't turn around but kept pacing away until I'd escaped the building and reached the gull-filled air, bubble-wrapped glasses behind me. I was intending to fill each with a different amount of water and hear Welsh tunes upon the glass by striking them with a wooden pencil, but it would have sounded so mediocre.

I let go of my rucksack and place it upon the sand next to me, removing the glass stack. Tumbler after tumbler, I press holes for each base to sink into, just a few metres from the tide. I save the eighth to be the water collector, scooping the sea into it before pouring it into the others, steps of memory from left, to right. Sitting cross-legged in front of them, I use a wooden pencil to try and mimic the beautiful music I 'd heard on my way through town. Not much happens other than the dull ding of different tones that could be played by the hand of a child.

I glance to the left, past the imposing, charcoal wall of the harbour and towards the Marina. If I close my eyes, I'm there, in whatever moment I choose. Last time, I walked right to the end of the harbour wall, where there were newspapers foot-stepped so hard to the ground that there were some from the 1970s. My grandfather and I bought salted chips and ate them under the archways until the evening drew in, the Marina's black water growing solid beneath the reflection of its dusky, yellow lights.

Now kneeling behind my octave of glasses, sunlight glimmers through the beaded glass, clammy sand grasping onto it. I lie on my stomach and look at the sea through the smudged lenses. It rolls in and out, creeping over me like the murky sheets of a penny slot machine at the arcade and leaving remnants of white horses jumping over my flattened palms.

Then I see the blur of a girl nearing the fairytale sandcastle, her coat a bold blue, magnified in the side of one of the tumblers. Sitting up, I see that she pokes her fingers through its windows and doors, and then places them flat on each step. This castle has two levels. With less thought than I, she sits in the centre, squashing the sand so it makes the circle a little larger around her, only laughing quietly enough for herself and I to hear. She leaves as it begins to rain.

Leaving the glasses to their own devices, I draw another circle around the castle's moat, giving it more depth than before. The castle looks a little stunted but sturdy remnants of it stand tall with the foundations still laid. I trace the space of a graveyard, for all the people who used to walk there, their booming voices and the incantation of necromancers echoing from the turrets. I provide each grave with a shell for a headstone and dig elongated dips into the sand to leave room for their bodies. I look to the tide, which is moving in.

I can still hear my grandfather speaking about the same, magnificent things. *There was talk of a tunnel under the seabed, running from Swansea Castle, all the way to Oystermouth Castle!* Once again, I place my arms either side of the castle, wanting to break it before the waves reach it, but even with gapless fingers, I'm incapable. I peer into one of the sandcastle's windows, and then picture myself standing inside it.

I imagine curling up within the remains of Swansea Castle, its voice luring me towards the top of a cobblestoned Wind Street, a compact watering hole for the sober eager to topple. The corner is marked by a building with a Tudor skin, which is also a bar, and I begin to feel out of place. On this oddly warm, spring evening, I'm drawn in by the aroma of chips and hot dogged air, I see women ahead of me with empowered looks but sparse clothing, and men roaring above club music that already vomits out onto the street.

As always, I find myself at the storm-less No Sign Bar, a more subdued and authentic pub, which I've heard has a yearning for journos. I'm not one, but I prefer this portrayal of Swansea, where the live music of folk band sings up the fire exit steps from The Vault. After drinking a glass of their house wine, I remember why I'm here in this haze, so I walk back out into the air where it's still light.

I often visit Mumbles, so I've seen the green-bellied hill of Oystermouth Castle and been one of a couple holding each other's hands, afraid to wipe the white of ice cream from the corners of their mouths. *There used to be a tram from the bottom of Wind Street, which ran all the way to the end of Mumbles Pier*, says the voice of my grandfather. From here, my mind is on the tram and with each retracing, my grandfather's voice is chiming in. *I courted your grandmother in Mumbles*, he says, and as we reach the dismantled, old stone bridge, I imagine him pointing to the right. *You could hire deck chairs and take donkey rides along the beach.* His stubby fingers change direction. *Oh! The Patti Pavilion! That's where I first saw your grandmother, waltzing around the mirrored pillars. Her reflection was never as good again once she started dancing with me!* It's a restaurant now.

After a few blinks, I vacate the haze of my imagination and I'm back here, at the sandcastle. The breeze has grown colder and the water's icy bite is catching up with me, rain having already soaked my face. My feet are numb and the wind is trying to push me back as I look at the waving, long grass of the dunes. I've been here before, throwing shells at the foam-crested waves. I've been here before.

I see that the little girl who played with the castle has returned and noticed the additional gravestones. She's brought a friend slightly smaller than her and they're moving the headstones around, and then using them to build another bridge over the moat. In awe, I watch their little fingers poke more windows into the structure and even more scrupulously, positioning a tiny twig on the top to represent a flagpole. They laugh, then leave, running towards the distant silhouette of a dog and its owner.

I crouch once again, to strike the wooden pencil against each glass before me. The final glimmer of sun is coruscating through the blistered pattern and as the rain drops into each small current, it permeates with a dull tap in different notes to create an odd scale. My glass harmonica has begun to play itself, bases beginning to agitate in the wet sand of the overflowing tide before the froth is soon the same height in every tumbler, the heads of white horses bobbing above the surface then galloping over the sides. Feeling water splash up to my palms, I stand up straight again.

My feet are now covered in water and with each new lap of the sea's tongue, it's rising up to my ankles, so I step backwards, away from the tide, only the eight, faint circles visible in a line in front of me.

'You want to get yourself dried off,' interrupts a voice and I at first think it's in my head. 'I've been waiting here for you all morning!' The gravel of this voice is familiar, crackly like that of a habitual cigar smoker. As I look at him, his stern smile disappears under the thick, white moss of his eyebrows, the leftover laverbread tarring his teeth.

'Bampa, what are you doing?' I link his arm and try to guide him away from the water.

'I walk here every day,' he says.

This was true about five years ago. I see how content his face is, something of an old independence creeping into the wrinkles. 'You want to get yourself dried off,' he repeats, peering down at my feet for longer than is necessary, from a face perched upon the wrappings of a large scarf.

'I walk here all the time,' he is saying again. 'I walk here all the time.' His face has turned sanguineous from excessive sea breath. He begins to look around and his feet start to get wet too, the leather of his shoes growing darker. 'Lovely,' he says and I wonder how much he means it. I can just about see the outline of Mumbles Lighthouse in the distance, the light here is fading quickly now.

One by one, I pick up each glass of water and tip it back into the tide. Sludges of sand that were stuck stubbornly inside are dropping out with a dense flop. I stack the glasses in my rucksack with no time to wrap them safely, the water already reaching my knees.

'I walk here all the—' my grandfather continues, but I interrupt him.

'Come on, Bamp,' I say. I link arms with him and we begin to walk along the bay, our trousers weighty from rain and seawater.

'Abertawe,' he sighs, idling sideways. He hunches ever so slightly but has a back so broad that it manages to centre the gravity of us both. The rain beats heavier but our pace remains the same as the tide continues to nag at our feet. I think of the evenings I've watched it roar with laughter, felt its saliva spitting onto my own, its lines creasing its corners into my memory, the wet tremble of the sea's palm broadening and nursing my malady to sleep.

Beyond the Perforation

Rhian Edwards

I didn't really believe in marriage counselling. But then I was married to an American and he could do all the believing for me. He was convinced my antipathy was embedded in some kind of Welsh stiff upper-lipness; that we attributed some kind of stigma to therapy and regarded the whole thing as an admission of failure.

My aversion stemmed from the fact I was cheap. I regarded it as an exorbitant way of stalling the inevitable demise of our marriage. 'The Welsh have no qualms discussing their failures,' I pointed out. 'We're just not accustomed to paying for the privilege.' After all, that's what family and friends are for, not to mention the occasional stranger in a bar. But for £85 an hour every week, our counsellor Erin was the human equivalent of rent. For that kind of money, I expected our notes to be scribed in calligraphy. For that sort of money, I expected our mediator to be a C-list celebrity.

Surprisingly my husband was something of a closet glutton when it came to counselling, which you would never think to look at him. You certainly wouldn't think it to listen to him given his dogged conciseness in conversation. Information was something you waterboarded out him. It was seldom donated, least of all at the behest of a question.

To my amazement, he was also well versed in relationship

counselling, having dabbled with the dark art with his previous fiancée and his long-term girlfriend before that. Perhaps couples' therapy was a rite of passage in the US, akin to taking things to the next level, fifth base. Instead of throwing car keys into a hat, you resolve to seek professional help.

I suggested his perennial return to marriage counselling was indicative of a chronic ineptitude at relationships. Whatever lessons these marital shrinks were trying to impart, the penny just wasn't dropping. Nothing was changing apart from the girl in the chair next to him. These were precisely the types of comment that weren't constructive to our relationship. This was also why we were here.

Erin, our counsellor, was a lovely dumpling of a thing. She always ran to greet us at the door of her Newport house. Her enthusiasm usually outraced her legs and behind the frosted window we would hear her tripping and tumbling over hallway obstacles. She would always appear full of zealous hellos, a mess of mousey hair and a litany of excuses for her clumsiness. I adored her; she was utterly human and marvellously unprofessional.

She was also American, at my husband's insistence. It meant she satisfied the exacting qualifications of a US therapist. (Apparently anyone in the UK could be a counsellor.) It also meant she would hopefully understand where my husband was coming from. He would never have trusted the advice of a Welshman, not in a million years.

The bookshelves in her front study were full of jibes on her profession, *Psychology for Dummies*, a pair of Freudian slippers, Lucy's psychiatry stall from the Peanuts comic strip, cards of purple sunsets with italicised nuggets of wisdom. I wondered if she had a version of *Guess Who?* where you could play multiple personalities simultaneously.

Erin also had a sandpit in the hollow of her coffee table, which was also therapy-related. I was rather keen for 'our process' to graduate to the sand castle level. I knew I would win hands down. My competitive nature was also a hindrance to the future of our relationship.

Our first session solely consisted of my husband 'sharing'. This was a good thing given his sparseness of conversation ordinarily. In essence, he stated he could only do his job effectively if we moved to London. Erin concluded that he might experiment with living in London during the week and returning to Wales on weekends. You could have cut my husband's silence with a diamond as he wrote the cheque.

The second session was uncannily similar to the first. Though on this occasion my husband stipulated that we had to move back to New York, as that was the only place where he had ever really been happy. Erin nodded sympathetically. She closed the session with the possibility of him returning to New York with us visiting him as and when we could. The cheque ripped beyond its perforation.

During the third session, my husband conceded to the possibility of Cardiff, but even then it wasn't relevant to his job. He was pandering to my desire to remain in Wales.

It was during the fourth session that Erin pointed out that I hadn't uttered a word during our past three meetings. My response was that I wasn't fucking moving anywhere. And thus the ribbon was cut and the channels of two-way dialogue were officially declared open. Erin identified that this may be a source of conflict. She was good. Real good.

After this, I started rather looking forward to our counselling sessions. I treated the whole thing a bit like 'date night' with Erin as our rather overpriced chaperone. These were the rare occasions I heard my husband talk in successive sentences. Our domestic conversation had become cumbersome and perfunctory and usually only pertained to the baby. I probably should have mentioned that earlier. Yes, we also had a baby.

I suspected my husband approached the sessions like a lapsed Catholic returning to Confession. Did the sheer act of attendance absolve him from being a feckless member of the flock for the remainder of the time? Were the other six days of the week the marital equivalent of penance?

During our seventh session, Erin suggested we get the crayons out. This felt like a precursor to the sandcastle stage. She wanted us to draw our 'vision' of family and home. I started clapping my hands like a demented sea lion. However, I knew my husband would not mirror my enthusiasm. This was precisely the type of Mickey Mouse, cod-psychology, he would never espouse.

'I didn't come here to draw any goddamn pictures!' he muttered, plucking phantom fluff out of the IKEA cushion.

Despite Erin's gentle coaxing, my husband refused to partake of the arts and crafts therapy. Instead he decided this was the optimal time to critique some of Erin's chosen methods, in particular her willingness to offer advice. Apparently that was not *noblesse oblige*, the done thing. After all he did have a wealth of therapists to compare her to.

He also chastised her for making judgment calls. The previous week, she had described him as the angriest person she had met in eight years. My wholehearted agreement, which bordered on a high five, was also deemed unsupportive by my husband.

I was bemused. Judgment calls and counsel were the least I expected for £85 an hour. They were the least I expected from anyone. I think I would have torched the bookshelves and the Freudian slippers, had I merely got the nodding dog routine and the occasional mantra of 'how does that make you feel?'

Erin resumed her ferocious scribbling and barely said another word for the remainder of the session. Poor Erin. I felt sorry for her. He shouldn't tell her off like that, not in her own house. She was only being nice and doing her job, just not the way he liked.

I suppose he was right about the crayon pictures though. They would have proven very little apart from our retarded doodling abilities. I think we probably would have produced identical cartoons, a one-dimensional house with cross-hatched window panes, smoke coming out of the chimney, the three of us prancing outside the front door grinning rictusly with a blithe sun smirking down at us.

The question was where to anchor this family and home. I wanted to remain in Wales; he wanted to return to the US. That was the fundamental irreconcilability, we thought. That was why we were sitting here, why we failed to get on.

The truth was Wales was killing him, especially living in Bridgend. Somebody once said there was something in the water that had caused that epidemic of suicides some years ago. And in less than two years, the confident, relaxed man I met in Manhattan, had paled into a ghost of himself, an angry monosyllabic one.

He couldn't make sense of anything here, he said. After two years, everything was still unfamiliar, nothing worked, nothing tasted as it should. He felt like a fraud, inventing and improvising his existence in the 'Boonies' of this Cardiff suburb. He still had no real friends or family here apart from the baby and me and even we were dissolving before him.

Which begged the question, why was I refusing to move? Because somewhere along the line, I had stopped sympathising with him. I had stopped feeling guilty for the sacrifice he had made to be with me, moving all the way from New York to Bridgend. Instead, I was annoyed at him. I was sick to death of his never-ending indictment of my hometown, its backwardness, its drunkenness, its commonness, even the maternity ward at the local NHS hospital reminded him of a makeshift wing in *M*A*S*H*.

I knew Bridgend was imperfect. I knew it better than anyone. But your hometown is like the black sheep of your family and only blood relatives have the natural right to slag it off. If anyone else tries to trash the place, you turn into a poor man's Braveheart, willing to defend the place to the death with a broken pint glass. The more he complained, the angrier I became and the more I wanted him to leave, the more I was desperate for him to leave, both for his sake and mine.

But here he was, stuck. Stuck in the quicksand of this sham marriage, stuck in a town he abhorred, tethered by a wife's unwillingness to budge and bound by a daughter he wished to see everyday.

Added to that he was now living here on borrowed time. His two-year marital visa was due to expire in the autumn. Now he had to summon a small fortune to apply for indefinite leave, just to continue residing in a place he loathed. And if he failed to get that, he would have to return to the States, relegated to visitor status, only getting to see his daughter for a handful of weeks a year. And I didn't wish that upon either of them.

One of my money saving ideas was to discontinue the marriage counselling. After all it wasn't getting us anywhere. It was more of a vanity project really. Without the therapy, we would save nearly £400 a month.

But my husband was no fool, despite my usual insistence to the contrary. He knew it was buying our marriage time. After all, Erin was the angelic optimist of our wedlock, the lone cheerleader for team US. She was literally the only one invested in our future.

There was no doubt in mind that he had chosen a fellow American as a therapist on the assumption that she would feel more sympathetic towards him, that she would relate to his disdain for this country, that he would not feel alone.

But my motivations for attending marriage counselling weren't entirely honest either. I still resented paying someone an obscene amount of money to witness our domestic tug-of-war. But then maybe it was in Erin's interests to observe and corroborate just how vile we could be to one another. This wasn't polite company where we had to temper our tongues. She had a fiduciary duty to sit there and take it, playing umpire to our endless bickering.

The truth is, I wanted her on my side. I wanted the American therapist who met my husband's exacting standards, to say in no uncertain terms that we should end the marriage. I wanted her to bite the hand that fed her.

I was secretly gleeful when my husband corrected or chastised her; or refused to answer her questions or spurned her crayon exercises. Surely that underlined just how impossible he was to live with. Surely that undercut her ability to like or empathise with him. Surely she could now understand why I so desperately wanted to leave this marriage.

I needed her validation. I needed him to hear it from her, a fellow American, a professional therapist. He had to hear it from someone who was impartial and calm. It had no credibility coming from me any more. I was the irrational, crazy one. I was the unreliable witness in my own marriage.

And then something shifted.

It was our eleventh session and Erin was more giddy than usual. Apparently, she was going away on a camping trip for two weeks with her family, immediately after our appointment

The realisation hit me and I started to panic. She was going to miss our weekly session. She had never missed a session before and more importantly neither had we. We were going to have to wait an entire fortnight until we could defend ourselves, self-justify our positions. We would have to wait two whole weeks for a positive appraisal on how well we were coping.

I became fidgety, I had become dependent, I had become addicted. I thought I could handle it, once a week for fifty minutes, just a bit of fun, no harm done. I wanted to ask if there was anyway of contacting her while she was away, in case we went into meltdown, Skype, texting, instant messenger. Would she even have reception at the campsite?

It was official. Counselling was the new crystal meth. No wonder the whole of the US were at it. No wonder my husband was mainlining on both sides of the Atlantic. This was how he could afford to be reticent. Behind the scenes, he was gushing to a paid stranger, concentrating a week's worth of conversation into an hour.

Even my attempts to discuss our relationship at home had been curtailed with the response: 'I don't think we should be discussing this outside our sessions with Erin.' Our marriage had become a taboo subject inside our own house.

Erin was no longer the plush chaperone. She was now an extension of the marriage, an alter ego. She was our middleman, candy-coating the insults that were being thrown like crockery. His criticisms of me weren't actually about me, they were about himself. They derived from fear. They were a cry for help. She even apologised on his behalf, reassured me I was a good mother, thank you Erin, thank you Husband. She even told us we were actually agreeing with one another, even though it appeared we were incessantly at loggerheads. She told me he still loved me.

She was brilliant! And I had fallen for it. She was the quintessential con artist, playing us in favour of each other. Therapy had blurred my perspective. It had made my trademark cynicism woolly, pastel-shaded, italicised. Erin had plumped me up like one of her IKEA cushions, delivering unadulterated flattery under the guise of 'constructive feedback'. It proved just how little kindness was required to keep our flimsy marriage fastened together. We just weren't capable of propagating it ourselves.

If I was going to endure cold turkey for a fortnight, I thought, I may as well sever the supply altogether. After all, my sadness had now curdled into pure exhaustion. I couldn't muster the will to be angry any more. Apathy had doused that too. Nor could I summon the energy to leave him. The mental effort required to even conceive of the logistics, the disassembling of our inextricable lives, was enough to make me want to curl up in a corner.

All I could do was sob, uncontrollably and pathetically. I kept spluttering that I no longer loved him. I kept repeating it and repeating it like a broken record. I couldn't understand why this piece of information was being so plainly ignored by both of them.

My husband's rebuttal was that this was somehow a flaw of my character, an emotional handicap, a patent lack of gratitude.

Erin's response usually erred towards setting us homework, asking us to try and remember what we originally loved about one another. 'I thought she was someone I could co-operate with,' my husband said.

'I think the two of you should think about separating,' Erin said. 'Just for a while. Just to see how things go.'

We paused. I even stopped weeping.

'And I can perhaps help you with that transition if you want me to. What do you think? Shall we book something in for two weeks from now?'

From behind the tattered tissue, I looked at my husband, sniffed and nodded. Erin was already peeling her way loudly through the pages of her thick diary. My husband shook his head, more out of disbelief than contention, as he tugged at the curled chequebook caught in his back pocket.

I'll See You On Sunday, James

Rhys Milsom

Mephedrone: also known as 4-methylmethcathinone (4-MMC) or 4-methylephedrone.
Formula: C11H15NO

Synonyms: Miaow, 4-MMC, MMCat, MD3, Roxy, Bubbles, Rush, Plant Feeder, Drone.

Most common modalities of intake: Oral ingestion by swallowing capsules or 'bombing' (wrapping mephedrone powder in cigarette papers and swallowing); insufflation.

According to users there is a highly addictive quality to the substance i.e., a strong compulsion to redose (this may be related to the duration of effects). This addictive quality means that binges in which large amounts of the substance are consumed in single sessions is common. Users also report the development of tolerance to the substance after prolonged use.

Sustained use of mephedrone can result in flash headaches, intermittent pain in feet, numbing sensation on left side of head/scalp, tinnitus, ulcerations, vasculitis, kidney pain, cardiac problems and respiratory problems.

Most desired psychoactive effects: euphoria, empathy, stimulation, increased insight/mental clarity, intensification of sensory experience stimulation (particularly auditory e.g. music appreciation), decreased hostility/insecurity.

Most common physical/medical untoward effects: loss of appetite, insomnia, numbness and lack of tactile sensitivity, influenza like symptoms, painful joints, fatigue, anxiety/paranoia, hallucinations, depression, tremors and convulsions, loss of concentration and memory loss/amnesia.

The duration of mephedrone effects are on average: come-up 10-20 minutes; peak 45-60 minutes; comedown 60-120 minutes.

*

In May 2010, my best friend committed suicide after three slow years of addiction had become too much for him to bear. He was twenty. He overdosed and was found by his sister. He was lying on his bed, wrapped under the covers. She thought he was sleeping until she noticed the white foam on the sides of his mouth, a purplish tinge underneath his eyes, and dried vomit on his pillow. There was a piece of paper next to him. That piece of paper was his suicide note.

However much you think you know someone, you never really do and never will. That suicide note ensured that sentence will always be embedded inside of me, because that was his final sentence in that note. It was an A4 size piece of paper, and he'd only filled one side in. It was the hardest and longest thing I've ever read. Knowing the torment, anguish and sorrow he'd gone through, while he'd put on a very different façade, really opened my eyes up and gave me the push I needed to kick my own addiction. Knowing that someone who was more like a brother rather than a friend, someone who I'd known since childhood, someone who I loved, had been in so much hidden pain without me knowing or without him even taking the first step and telling me, someone, anyone, not only hurt me, it destroyed my world. As cliché as the saying is, when he went, a part of me went too. It's never been more true.

The first time we did drugs was when we were seventeen. From then on in, we were hooked. Addicted. It went from smoking weed to popping valium to sniffing coke to swallowing acid to sniffing glue to snorting ketamine and then, eventually, the one that pushed us into a state of decline, mephedrone. At first, it's the best feeling in the world. You know everything, and want to talk to everyone, and aren't afraid of anything. The world is yours. That is until you develop a state of 'walling' – where a few grams doesn't have any effect anymore. Leading to more and more of it being taken to have the desired effect. In turn, an addiction of it ensued. And there was no way out for him. Because of him, I got out at the right time. I didn't want to die, I didn't want my friends and family to carry my coffin, I didn't want my dad to have no-one to watch the rugby with, I didn't want my mother's laughter to stop, I didn't want my sister to grow up without a brother. I got off the drugs within a year of his death and haven't touched them since. I don't want any sort of congratulations for that because it's not needed. I got myself into the mess and I got out. He didn't. That's it.

He was a beautiful person. You hear friends say that about lost ones all the time, but he really was. When you were around him, everything was so much brighter. I remember him telling me once, after a poem got rejected by a magazine, to keep doing what I do and to not let anything negative get in my way and that something will come. His words turned out to be right. Actually, most of the things he said turned out to be right, he never let a word go to waste. He didn't say much but what he did say he meant. His words were to be treasured, to be collected and hoarded and to be brought out in times where you really needed some sun to break through the clouds. I've lost count how many times his words helped me after he went, and even now I think of what he'd do when I'm feeling low. One look at our sixth form prom photo together makes me realise that I'll only have one chance and the fact that he can't be around to see what I'm doing gives me much more incentive to succeed. He may be gone but he'll always be around.

James, I can't forgive you for leaving me but I want you to know that I understand. I don't know if I'll see you again, I'm still unsure of believing, but every word I write has part of you in it, every bottle that goes down is shared with you, and every cigarette – yeah, I've cut down, don't start – brings back memories of us sat in a beer-garden somewhere. Smoking and drinking, waiting for the future. You don't need me to say that your future never came because it sort of did. With me. Wherever I go, you're there. I still go round yours and your mam and dad are doing alright. So is Bethan. She's growing up now, man! It'll be boyfriends and all that next. I'll take care of her, though, don't worry.

I hate you for leaving me.
But I'll always love you, man.
You'll never be forgotten and will always have a place in my heart.

I've meant to do this for a while but now I have the chance. I'm not going to write a misery memoir, because his life wasn't miserable. I'm going to tell you about some of my most cherished memories of James, without any of the bleak memories. I want to celebrate who he was, and you're invited to the party.

*

I first met James in infant's school, Craig-Yr-Eos Infants, which was in Pen-y-Graig, wrapped in the heart of the Rhondda Valleys – where I grew up. The school has been demolished now and instead of a huge, intricate, Victorian-style building which was once satiated with young laughter, flowering friendships and yellowed maths books, there's now a blank tarmaced waste-ground with the walls decorated in unintelligible graffiti and the corners piled with corner-shop waste.

It was at dinnertime, after the actual dinner, in the school-yard when we first met. I remember it being a really warm day so I was sat on the wall in the shade while everybody else was playing games; games that children play at that age. I was quite shy and introverted so I didn't really have friends, I didn't talk to people and they didn't talk to me. I was pretty content being by myself. I'd look forward to going home so I could be with my parents and to finish the jigsaw I'd started that morning or to finish another *Mr Men* book.

Just as I started to drift in and out of my thoughts about why Mr Grumpy was as miserable as he was, a football slowly rolled towards me and glanced against my feet. I ignored it, whoever's ball it was they could come and get it themselves. I didn't like football. I wasn't joining in with any of their games. I picked a small, loose stone from the wall and started to roll its cold, sharp edges against my palm, the taste of warm milk dissolving from my senses as shouts, screams, whispers, laughter, cries, filled and echoed around the school-yard.

I started to pick more stones from the crumbling wall and lined them up, making patterns, faces, anything. I was so engrossed in this that I didn't realise there was someone standing in front of me until he spoke.

'Wanna game?'

'Don't like football.'

'Let's play your game then.'

He sat down next to me. A dark blonde bowlcut, piercing green eyes and a constant grin. He started to pick up the stones and copied what I was doing. Before long we had loads of patterns on the wall. A mini-army of circles, triangles, rectangles, squares. Next, we arranged the stones to spell our initials, then our names. That was how we first knew what each other were called. This pattern-making was performed in silence, until James said:

'C'mon, this is boring now, let me show you something.'

I didn't think the stones were boring but I followed James, anyway. This knee-high, bowl-haired enigma. We were out of the shade, into the sun, across the yard, to the gate that led to the lane behind the school.

'Go on,' he said.

'What if the dinnerlady sees us, though?'

'She won't. I've done it loads of times, go on.'

I pushed the gate but it wouldn't budge. I tried again, harder, and it dragged across the ground, moaning sleepily, crunching against the ground and scratching its dandruff-like rust amongst the gravel. It swung fully open and rested against the wall. The lane was strictly out-of-bounds, we'd probably be told on if we left the yard and went into the lane, but that was exactly what we did. We closed the gate after us and stood there, watching through the rusted metal bars as the rest of the children played. James started to run up and down the lane, like he'd won something, ecstatic. I stood there and watched. After he finished running, he came back to the gate and stood there with me. The bell went and we slid back into the yard.

Things were never the same again.

*

As we grew up, one of the things we did a lot was walk his Westie dog up and along the mountain behind James' house, which was just behind Craig-yr-Eos. His house rested on the mountain like a lower lip, the upper lip being the farmer's cottage which sat on top of the mountain with the sheep, barbed-wire fencing and the weird men with binoculars.

We'd pretend we were running away from something or someone, what we were running from was never clear but we spent hours, days, even weeks, kicking up dried dirt and scattering paths amongst the wimberry bushes. Molly, his dog, would be running around us and in front of us, occasionally stopping to sniff something, but she'd never be too far away. It was as if there was an invisible leash attached to her and James. Wherever he went, she followed.

This particular day was in the summer holidays. We were ten. On that mountain there's a huge quarry, deep and dark, as if it's the belly of the mountain itself. We were running around the top of the quarry, ducking and diving into the grass that textured its craggy claws. The snipers were shooting at us, weren't very good shots, though. We crawled and crouched through the bushes as the sound of the park (which was about a five minute walk from the mountain and viewable from our position on the edge of the quarry) – people shouting, laughing, dogs barking, the water in the pool splashing – echoed and carried through the air. It was strange, even though we could hear other people, they couldn't hear us and it felt as if we were in a place where no-one else could get to. The mountain was ours. They could have everything else, and they did. They slowly took over everything, even our mountain, when a fire raged and shrieked for days, a few years later.

Molly was on the edge of the quarry, looking down into it, when suddenly she barked. Something down there must have startled her, because as she barked her whole body juddered forward and her claws slipped on the silky stone of the cliff-face. I was nearest to her and I looked at her when she barked; hearing her bark was like Man United losing then, it just didn't happen, and as I saw her claws trying desperately to cling on to the stone, I rushed up from the prickly bushes and grabbed her back-end before she fell into the quarry. In one movement, I turned her body around so that her rear-legs were now facing the quarry, rather than her front ones. I pushed her and she scrabbled to the safety of the grass and to James, who was watching in a state of silent shock, his mouth hanging open like the gaping, curling aluminium on a half-opened tin. He picked her up and turned his back, probably so that I wouldn't see him kissing her.

As I pushed myself up from my knees, my feet slipped on the stone. I banged a knee and scraped a shin as I went down and I remember the pain being so sudden and hard that I winced and instinctively reached down. As I did this, I slipped further and the pain didn't register anymore. I was hanging on to the cliff-face, one hand on the stone, one hand clutching the dusty, greyed root of some forgotten tree. I was thirty foot from my death. I shouted to James and I heard him running.

'Where are you? Rhys, where are you?' his voice was laced with terror and worry.

'Down here,' I said, fighting back tears. 'Quick, help me. Grab my hand.' A tear danced down my face.

He reached down and grabbed my forearm on the arm that was hanging onto the cliff. He tried to pull me up but he wasn't strong enough. We were both about seven stone soaking wet, all skin and bone and hair.

His effort was enough, though, for me to get a better grip on the cliff-face. I was now able to swing my legs onto an out-shooting rock below me and I stood on it, hoping that it wouldn't slide away. It didn't. I composed myself, and pulled myself up onto the cliff face and onto the creased, old mountain.

The blood was streaming down my shin and soaking my trainers. There was already a lump on my knee. It hurt standing up, but James helped me as I struggled down the mountain. Molly kept looking back at us, as if she knew what was going on, as if it was her fault. I think I kind of felt it was her fault.

We got into James' house and his mother made us fish-fingers, chips and beans. I'll always remember the smell of the vinegar, freshly-washed clothes and the faint smell of his father's cigarette drifting in from the back-garden. She repaired my knee and my shin, and after we ate our food James and I played on the Playstation until my mother came to pick me up. He never mentioned my tears.

*

Being part of something, anything, when you're young is really important. It gives you a sense of protection and allows you to interact with other children who're not in your school or live in your street. James and I were part of our local rugby team, Penygraig. I played scrum-half, he played wing. I was faster than him, but he wouldn't admit it. He played on the wing because, at that age (we were fifteen), he was bigger than the rest of us and having a big player on the wing used to kick fear into the opposition's guts even before kick-off. He also couldn't pass that well so he just used to run with the ball. He wouldn't even look around to see if a pass was on. A proper winger.

We'd reached the semi-finals of a ten-a-side tournament, which was pretty exciting because we hadn't won a game all season. We were playing Pontypridd in this game, and they were one of, if not the, best teams in the tournament. We were shitting ourselves.

It was raining, puddles were flowing into other puddles. Mud was caked onto our boots, socks, faces, hands. For some reason, there was sand mixed with the mud and whenever you rubbed your hands together, it felt like pebbledash.

We knew we had to keep it tight, but our pack wasn't the biggest. Kick-off came. They scored straight off it. And then again and again and again. Before we knew it, it wasn't even half-time and we were 28-0 behind. Our coach was going crazy, shouting, spitting and jumping up and down on the sidelines. Everyone else was huddled into their coats or watching from the safety of the club-house.

They were targeting our pack, they were much bigger and stronger than us in that aspect so we had to change our game-plan. As scrum-half, you see the game more than any other player. You hear everything and the team listens to you. I remember telling the forwards to just set the ball up after kick-off and for us to go through the phases instead of rushing. To get some rhythm going. They listened. It worked. Before long, we'd scored two tries and went into half-time 28-14 down. Our confidence was high.

The second-half was a stalemate until the last ten minutes. We scored one length-of-the-pitch try from a Ponty mistake and then with five minutes to go we were camped on their twenty-two. They gave away a penalty. I slotted it over. Three minutes left. They kicked to us and the forwards set it up again. They were like exhausted wildebeest, their legs looked like pieces of cotton swaying in the wind. They wouldn't have lasted another ten minutes. The crowd were going mental, shouting and watching with avid concentration. Even other teams who'd been knocked out of the tournament were watching the game now. The underdogs were giving it to the big-boys. Big time. You could see it on the Ponty players' faces – we had them scared.

From a ruck, I passed the ball to Damien, our fly-half, who hoofed the ball in the air. James chased after it and I watched as the Ponty full-back waited for the ball to land in his arms. It never did. James leapt in the air just as it was about to be gathered by the Ponty full-back and he caught it superbly. He handed-off the full-back, who crumpled to the floor, holding his face, and James kept running. The Ponty winger was chasing him and was catching, but I knew James would score. The fourteen on his back, the one covered with mud, and the four a fading white, kept getting further and further away, just as much as the rain kept falling. The winger did catch him but all he could do was cling onto his shirt as James flung himself over the line, into the thick mud, and thumped the ball down.

Everyone went mental. Drinks went flying, coaches ran onto the pitch, Ponty sat on the field, desolate. I ran to James, he picked me up.

'We won!' he shouted. 'We won!'

I clung to him tightly and as my nose pushed into his hair, I could smell the deep odour of soil and the reek of vaporub. We lost the final but we didn't really care.

*

It is dark now,
The sun has been lulled into sleep -
I look past the sky and see nothing;
The day has gone.

My senses sullen,
A frozen rose in my chest
And a map of a hundred faces
Cloud my emotions and sight.

The sky will fold with light;
The tides will turn,
Sun is the greatest lie –
I want to stay, but I must run.

*

I'll see you on Sunday, James. I've told everyone you don't like flowers
but no one listens.

Distance

Dic Edwards

It's Edward Hopper's painting *Gas*. There are three pumps and the attendant is wearing a long-sleeved white shirt and a waist coat. You can't make out what he's doing, the attendant. But more importantly there's the road with its unkempt verges going to wherever you might imagine it could all dwarfed by the bank of conifers on its far side, dominating and indifferent to time and story. And the diffident Mobil gas sign on its pole, an emblem for the passing insignificance of man.

What you can't see is my café and now I'm looking out on two rows of pumps and no attendant but an occasional driver serving himself. I'm looking out from my seat in the café on the A487 north of Llanon.

And then there's Hopper's attendant dressed in that shirt and waist coat and I'm with him as he goes back inside his station like a small chapel with spire and inside is the woman we can't see who I imagine came with him about a year ago – about the time I first turned up here – a simple woman with modest expectations who came out West because it sounded good. And now she has become my waitress who's been here for well over twenty years. She comes in each day from the cottage she rents in the hills above Nebo. You feel the job is all she's got to keep things going. But that sense of just hanging on is what it's all about – it's what I'm all about because the alternative, the world where there's some kind of certainty, where things are all screwed down firmly in place for now and into the known future, is a place of doctor's waiting rooms and slow, monotonous decline. Even the successful in their world of success and comfortable certainty can't dodge that. And I am with the waitress, the silent unseen fact in Hopper's painting who knows about transience and the unfathomable road.

And that's how I like things. I like looking at things like that – from a distance. Getting inside them. In my mind. Things like paintings. Other things. And sometimes I like to think I'm in a painting with people looking.

Every day I come here and every day I look out at the food vans and artics and the caravaners traipsing the coast road to the North and almost no one ever stops for tea. Occasionally I'm aware of the waitress behind the counter at the other end of the café from where I habitually sit, making the small sounds of unexacting industry. She told me her name was Carol not long after my first visit. Yesterday I was working on a piece I'd worked on many times before – many drafts, never knowing when it's done. Just travelling the road.

Carol's about 50 I'd say but that seems irrelevant in her case – her time is peculiar to her, determined by the pace and urgencies of the dirt-track life. She's petite with an attractive turn in one of her green eyes. In fact, she looks like one of those women Hopper portrays alone in hotel rooms.

Yesterday when she brought me my tea I was her only client and she seemed about to say something when the door opened and the golfers came in. It was Friday. Every Friday late morning they would come in after their couple of rounds on the nine-hole up the road. The group includes an aboriginal man in his forties, large with an embracing smile and the personality of a stand-up comedian doing his routine. He would always engage with Carol and she would respond with giggles and cheeky digs. But not yesterday. I sensed her going to them and after some talk they suddenly went silent and when I turned I could see surprise and dismay while Carol stood beside the table awkward and unsure of herself.

I tried to imagine what she had said to them. I'd heard the words 'thirty years' and 'the rising cost of gas' and then heard a chair scrape and turned again and the large aboriginal had stood up and was holding Carol tightly in a sympathising embrace.

I've spent so much time over the years in cafes that my life is not described or even coloured by anything I've written but by the waitresses I've watched and the people who have come and gone. This place had become the one I liked best and I would flirt with the idea that I would have lived life well if my mind's final image was of someone like Carol in her heyday flashing a toothy smile and opening up the morning for someone like me. So it was not in the natural order of things that Carol would receive the kind of attention the aboriginal was giving her and I knew something was wrong. Whatever she had said was not to do with, say, a death or some other local tragedy but was something that would compromise our world. At that moment I stopped writing, or trying to write and turned around fully. I was able to make eye contact with Carol and that caused her to come to me.

She said: this is the last day.

I said: until when?

No. They're shutting it down for good.

She said it as if she was annoyed with me. She wasn't, of course. Her anger and dismay was just so overwhelming it left her bewildered and unfocused.

Later, at three o'clock I parked my car near the car wash. I saw the lights go out in the cafe – a Hopper scene the simplicity painting the sadness. I looked a little to the left to see the steeple of the church that now seemed forlorn where before it had been a delightful decoration in the village and to my left the caravan park whose new cafe offering breakfasts by the sea had, I'd found out, caused the catastrophic decline in the number of visitors to Carol's place. The place I had so selfishly appreciated.

While I waited I ran back over cafes I'd written in and recalled the Honey place which had been white and silent until it was sold to a yuppy who painted it and installed a hi-fi. It was there I read Marquez's beautiful and outrageous *Love in the Time of Cholera* and Aberaeron, the town of the Honey shop became Macondo and the chestnut trees almond; that book wherein the saintly 14 year old Americo Vacuna kills herself when she is jilted by the 80 year old Florentino Ariza. That was twenty years ago and there was a young woman who I remembered was called Claire and there would be times when the place was almost empty with just me in my corner and Claire stationed behind her till. And occasionally our eyes would meet. She would colour up a little and I would play with a smile and quickly look back to my work. And we would become characters in the Marquez, me a young Florentino and Claire the bewitching Fermina Daza, the woman Florentino would love all his life; the woman he would wait fifty years for; the woman he left his fourteen year old for. In that way we had a kind of affair. And in the evenings I would sit across the harbour from the cafe and look through my binoculars at her moving around at her work in a medium of film-like mystery. I became voyeur of the illicit affair I had created. That distance between my eye and her image in which I could linger as one immune from codes of goodness. Until one evening when she suddenly appeared away from the cafe while I was walking with my wife. I turned quickly down a side lane, taking my wife with me, to avoid the two meeting. I said I saw someone I owed money to coming towards us.

Then I saw Carol come out. As she walked to her small old car I looked for the misery in her step but saw none – she was too proud to allow that. I drove around and stopped by her car. I got out and went to her. From that spot I could see the sea which released me from any doubts I had about whether this was a good idea. She looked indifferent.

I said: that news was.....devastating. What will you do now? Will they give you a different job in the shop? There was a small supermarket attached to the cafe.

She said, no. It's over. Sunday. After we've cleared the place out, that's the end. They're shutting the place to save on our wages. Me and the other two who work there.

O right. Don't often see them.

One's the cook. The other's the cleaner and dishwasher.

I said: I don't know what I'll do now. I've loved this place.

You always look as if you're writing.

Yes, I said, I like writing in public places. Like restaurants. You don't get many places like this one. So quiet.

That's their excuse for shutting it.

It's crazy. You think they'd be flocking here. The main road between north and south.

We used to get the caravaners. From the park.

I said: it would be good if we could see ourselves as if we were in a painting. People looking at us. Because, as long as they are, the painting goes on. That's how it works. The story of it.

She said: I don't get that. Then she said: there's one difference between us. Between you and me. You've got something to fall back on. Your writing. Some of us are so out of luck that when ends come they really are the end.

She seemed cold. But then I remembered one time in the cafe when a story I was reading made me cry. Nothing too obvious. She happened to see me. The water in my eyes. But there was no response from her. As if she lived too far away from me to be moved by it.

When I lost my wife I made a decision that I would never succumb to the heartbreak of it. I felt that what's gone is gone or, rather, I determined that that's the motto or mantra I would live by. But you can't escape the effects like the way time and air pits and discolours the richest and most cared for painting or other public art. Last night as I lay alone in bed, to distract myself from the deep melancholy brought on by the news and the attention of my suppressed grief, I imagined Carol as she may have been when she was young. I wondered if she'd ever married. I wanted to paint a picture of her in good times. Her and maybe a couple of sisters. Sitting before a hearth and in the centre of this little community a bassinette in which her new baby lay. And they are discussing when to have the christening and would she ask the landlord of the Black Lion for a room to celebrate? And the centre of gravity of the picture would rest firmly with her, her hair auburn and carrying the breezes of youth and the light fire-flies of her words that we can't hear. But in the morning, when I woke, I realised I'd been thinking about my wife.

But I did wonder whether, if I followed Carol and waited for her that one day I would see her walking some wind-swept lane fearing the mysteries that have no outcome.

This morning I got up feeling as if I had lost my job. The street I could see through my window was wet. Gloomy. The cafe was four miles up the coast and now carried a sign saying: this cafe is closed for the foreseeable future. The foreseeable future – that awful phrase that teases with the hope that there may be something beyond the foreseeable. I would go to the cafe and stop in the parking area across the road from the garage, just in front of the caravan park. And I would watch her wrap things up through my binoculars. I knew I was in a bad way because as I watched her I recalled a small event from my childhood. We were not well-off and my mother would try things out on us – cheap meals – and I recall sitting at the table in the living room of our council house but alone with her and she's put before me a dish in which she's soaked a slice of cheap processed bread in a very unattractive gravy. And I can remember clearly that she was in her late twenties with black hair that fell in waves onto her shoulders. I always remember thinking that there was distance in that hair – though I suppose that was a notion I would have come up with later. When I started writing. She is looking at me with fire in her eyes. Expectation. I remember that she is very beautiful and that in some way she is tragic as she thinks she has failed in life because she was such a romantic. And I can see her across that expanse of time. As though she is in a film. It's an event I realise that I often recall when so many are forgotten. An isolated moment that exists as if in the lens of a pair of binoculars. And it makes me feel lonely. Like I feel now having lost Carol. And as I watch Carol moving mysteriously through the glass of my binoculars and the glass of the windscreen past the intermittent sweep of the wiper blades and through the glass of the restaurant window I know that that distance between my eye and the image where the power of the voyeur resides and where stories are written, preserves in us that fast separateness.

Fear

Linda Ruhemann

She was doing that thing again, the little hints, the nosing into his bedroom to see if he was playing *Assassins' Creed* or learning French vocab. He had the curtains drawn against the thin April sunshine.

She said, Did you want to meet later to do some French together? She whisked the curtains open. The Blorenge Mountain appeared like a sleeping mastodon, breathing wreaths of mist. Why are you sitting in the dark?

He sighed.

She didn't look directly at his laptop where he had clicked shut the page about landing a jet. Hmm? she said. You said you'd like me to do some with you because it was less boring.

Maybe, he said.

Well, when? she said. Because I've only got a couple more days' holiday. She smiled. It was a thin line. Up to you, of course.

She would do that. Speak lightly to show she wasn't worried for him, so as not to undermine his confidence. It was maddening. He laughed. It's ok, Mum, honestly. I'll be fine. Let's do it later, he said, about four? Think I'll go out on the bike now.

A flicker of the brows.

Get some fresh air, he said. Magic words. Sounded healthy and sensible.

Nat hauled up the steep lanes to St Mary's Vale, surprised by the pleasure of the physical labour, the breath sour in his chest after a mile but his legs powering on. The thought of the downhill rushes to come gave them force. Between the trees, swathes of wide green valley, the Sugar Loaf tempting on the other side. Past the plants, green against the stone wall, that his mother had told him were Dog's Mercury, very poisonous. The entrance to the Vale a muddy gateway, and the cool gloom of the wood closing in as he cycled down the track soft with ancient leafmould.

She'd come with him a few times, once, up towards Clydach, where she'd struggled to stay in the saddle, then eventually slid off and panted up slowly, pushing the bike, him circling back down like a hunting dog, calling her on till they reached a stony downhill gully he wanted to try. They stopped at the top, looking round at the hills, the old lime workings, the July blue of the sky one day last year. He'd asked her to wait while he cycled off slowly on the green bank, looked at the obstacles, found the good lines. And then back to her where she gazed anxiously at the rocks underfoot and the barbed wire fence to the side. She hardly had time to say 'Be careful' before he had plunged down the track.

This you can't beat: rocketing down the mountain at maybe thirty miles an hour, relishing the air beneath you as if you really can fly, just briefly, and might get the hang of doing it all the time if you just keep looking ahead down the track, finding the line, and don't stop, don't worry that you might be going too fast, just relax and get the rhythm, your body always in the right place for taking the berms, the drop-offs, the roots and corners.

He was half-way back up again before she'd got very far, brakes shrieking as she inched down. Oh my God, she was muttering, and again when he curved round towards her at the bottom of his second flight. Oh my God. You don't know fear, do you? She said he'd been like this as a small child, always first to the top of the climbing frame, crossing the rope bridges at the climbing centre, abseiling. It was a good day.

Alone now he savoured speed, power, control, amidst the mud and beech roots of the slopes by the Nant Iago. Up then, towards the Sugar Loaf, in quest of new ways. He rambled round the mountain, trying this and that track till he realised he was lost. Well, if he went downhill he would eventually get back to the town. But fences and ravines might mean retracing miles. Heigh-ho. He circled round again, eyes alert for familiar configurations of rocks and trees. How similar these things can be when you need them to be distinct. At length he realised he was heading towards a wood that he knew, where paths crossed at a cattle-trough. He slowed down to make sure and passed an old man standing in the shadow of the oaks. He was wearing a wide-brimmed hat with a shallow crown like the old pilgrims, and he was strangely still and brown in the tree-shade, as if he was made of earth.

He pedalled on faster, down a pleasant green track where the valley spread out to his left, on the home run. But ahead of him again was surely the same old man, standing by an open gate that should be closed, black as a crow this time against the bank of spring grass. Cycling on too fast for clarity he had an impression of an impassive face, something missing – no teeth, perhaps, or sightless eyes, and was so afraid he might see the man again that he hardly dared raise his head till he reached his own streets.

And it was gone six.

She was not pleased. She tried not to show it but the mouth was set again and the voice pitched down a tone to convey calm.

It's under control, Mum, he said, I know what I need to do.

She rattled the pans. Look, she said, I don't mind how you do as long as you feel you've done your best. You were disappointed before.

It was true. He'd done pretty well in the GCSEs but he knew he could have done better with a bit more work. Some kind of dry grey wall always rose in front of his eyes, and a dark ache in his marrow. School made you focus on silly details of stuff when your mind was restless for all the knowledge of the world.

Oh, thanks for the reminder, Mum. Look, it's my exams, ok? Stop –

Take those off the table, she said.

He grabbed his muddy gloves and went to the back door. I'm going to put my bike away.

You'll have to be quick. It's almost ready.

He didn't slam the door. He washed the bike down and left the hosepipe snaking in the yard. He kicked off his cycling shoes and sat heavily at the table. He waited for her to look out at the jumble of kit.

I'll do it later, he said sourly.

You'll forget.

One more word and he could stamp off upstairs. No French vocab.

But there again, a tense atmosphere over dinner at the least. And maybe a little revision wouldn't hurt. He went and took the shoes and the bike out to the shed, and came back through the still-bright garden and told her about how he had been scared by the eerie old man.

The exams came and went like a series of discouraged beasts. He waited for them, he pounced; somehow, he got by. They slunk off into the undergrowth, biding their time till August. In July he embraced the freedom of the summer, camped out with friends on the side of Sugarloaf, went biking, or messed about by the Usk. Often the carefree holidays of his childhood seemed to wave at him, almost within reach.

One night in the first week of August he met with friends by the river. They did the usual: someone brought a tinny sound system, they had a few cans of booze; some weed was going round. He had a beer, sat chatting. Then something strange began to happen. He found himself forming the intention to get drunk. This he had never done before, hated the idea of such loss of self. Now, though, he set about it. Someone offered to go and buy vodka if they all chipped in. He held out money. He lay back on the river bank and considered the lights of the main road beyond.

In a while he was swigging Ben's idea of a brilliant drink – a sweet potion of vodka, cider and Ribena. The lights across the river began to dance up and down, and, later, a couple of girls from Year 12 were dancing too, right out on the Usk, oddly on the water not in it, and the tinny beat from the CD player was merging with a sound like bagpipes. He looked around for the source of the wailing music, and Rhian and Meg and Rhys and Ben reared up around him and floated past his eyes, waving slowly, they and the trees and the water circling till he felt quite sick. Then the old man from the mountain was standing before him with a hand held out, and he knew he had to take it, but he was very afraid, and said, No, and fell back on the bank with a groan. He heard weird laughter, then, and struggled to sit up, and Rhys said, You ok? and helped him stumble a few feet away to puke.

That improved things. Rhian and Meg resolved back into ordinary girls laughing in the summer night, their black-rimmed eyes glittering in the light of a big torch, flirting with him and mocking him at the same time, the older boy who couldn't take his drink. There were other things, he thought, you could not take. Sometimes you could not take yourself. He walked with purpose towards the water. The sign, he remembered, said SWIMMING IN AND BOATING ON THE USK IS PROHIBITED, but in the summer you often saw kids paddling by the Bridge Inn despite warnings about dangerous currents. For some reason Rhys was grabbing hold of him.

Don't be a knob.

They collapsed together into a knot of brambles.

Fuck's sake, said Rhys, unhooking bits of his clothing.

Sorry, mate. A new idea occurred to Nat. I'm going home.

Not on your own. Come on, I'll see you back safe.

Which he did, because Rhys was a mate, they told each other at least twice on the way home, as Nat remembered the next day, and also that he and another friend had done the same for Rhys quite recently. What was surprising was the way his mother took the situation. The next morning he knew, from the wrong duvet on his bed and the bucket next to it, that he must have been sick some more when he got home. That she must have helped him into bed, taken the mucky stuff away, left him sleeping on his side with a glass of water and some kitchen towel handy. But he could recall no alarm, no crossness, just a vague sense of her hand on his shoulder, holding him as he bent over the toilet bowl and got rid of some purplish puke.

Even when he surfaced in the early afternoon she just looked at him a tad ironically and asked how he was feeling. And he was going to say nothing about it all, but it felt like a betrayal, when she was being so gallant, and so he went so far as to say Well, a bit, when she asked if he was nervous about his results.

I'm sure you'll be fine, she said, and she smiled at him without biting her lip, and he realised he could easily cry.

I could have worked harder, he said. He wasn't sure what he was most upset about. That he'd set his heart on Warwick and then been too cocky or lazy to get the grades, or that he'd let her know it mattered.

And he didn't know any more whether he was afraid that she would be upset for him, or he for her, or whether the real problem was what he now understood was his first hangover.

She patted him tentatively on the arm. Chocolate and lemonade, she prescribed brightly. What we used to have the morning after the night before, when I was – ooh, younger.

He tried to smile, understood they were to cheer each other up. I think I'll just have a cup of tea, he said. Maybe go for a ride to clear my head.

Something made him take the track up Sugarloaf that went through the grove of oaks, as if it was a rendezvous he could not avoid. His head pounded as he drove the pedals but he would not stop or slow, anxious to grind something out of himself through the pain and sweat. He stopped at last by the cattle trough, sick and panting, and reached for his water bottle. It was muggy and grey under the trees, and flies were feasting on the trampled dung and mud. A mad place to stop; he would come out of it and find the cleaner air, look down towards the town and out to where in clear weather you could see the Bristol Channel and even the Somerset hills beyond.

He knew before he turned that the old man would be there. He stood, a tall figure cradling a large-brimmed hat in one arm and leaning on a stick. He gazed absently at Nat and said something.

Nat shivered. Sorry?

Mushroomth, the man said, indicating the hat. He was missing some teeth. Nat, surprised at himself, went close enough to look. A few moon-pale objects nestled there, and a fresh strong scent rose from them. The man gestured with his stick. Always get them here, he said. More in a week or two. He smiled slowly, showing gaps like a seven-year-old. Take them back for Olwen. He glanced down towards the farmhouse in the valley.

Nat nodded.

Every year, the man added.

Nat replaced his water bottle and made to mount his bike but the man spoke again, and waved his stick at the sky where the rain clouds were huddling in a sullen mass.

Rain coming, he said.

Looks like it, said Nat. I should get going.

You'll be all right, said the man. You'll ride fast.

Nice to meet you, Nat said, as if they were at a tea party.

The man smiled his slow smile again and set off down the path to the farm, quite briskly.

On the way down the mountain the storm broke and the rain pelted through Nat's cycling top. Sodden hair escaped from his helmet and snaked over his forehead, and his knuckles were chilled and pale on the handlebars. On the way down the mountain he was soaked and cold, and the rain trickled down his neck and back. But he felt he could keep on going, down this slope and up the next, descending and climbing track after track, the old man with his pilgrim hat appearing now and then with gentle talk of years of mushroom-gathering. And when he came into the kitchen splattered in mud he felt he was glowing despite the cold.

Hello, love, his mother said, smiling at the state of him. Feeling better?

I'm fine, he said. No worries.

Seriously?

Seriously, he said, shaking his wet head like a spaniel. I'm OK. It'll be OK, whatever, he said.

And he put his arms round her waist, and hugged her like he hadn't done for years. He covered her tee-shirt in mud, and she didn't complain, and they stood like that for a minute before she said, I think you really will be OK, whatever. But –

Ye-es?

For God's sake get in the shower.

OK, he said.

He rested his chin lightly on her hair, and looked out of the kitchen window at the drenched yard. Beyond lay the mountains, washed and hazy in the pelting rain.

The Reading

Richard Gwyn

Owen drove in silence, and with care. He had slept badly the night before, which is to say he had not slept at all, and now the act of staying awake for the duration of a two and a half hour drive had become an endurance test, since the mechanics of his insomnia dictated that while unable to sleep at night, he was perfectly capable of sleeping for stretches during the day, especially following a meal, and even, shamefully, while driving. He was also prone to dozing off during performances by his fellow readers at the events he was required to attend; for apart from being an insomniac, Owen Price was a poet, and today he was on his way to a reading. He had published a new collection, his third, and today's visit to the mid-Wales town of Newtown was a fixture on his launch tour. He had already read at other locations throughout Wales, including the launch at the Dylan Thomas Centre in Swansea, which had attracted around fifty people – a good number, he thought, for a poetry reading. Owen was certainly not a household name, but he had a modest local reputation and had been referred to – by a critic who was considered (or considered himself to be) a leading arbiter of judgement in such matters – as one of the more talented emerging writers of his generation, at least in Wales. Elsewhere, he was practically unknown. He was, in the articles of literary achievement, a very minor poet.

As he drove along the twisting roads, he felt the need to sleep wash over him. He knew he should probably pull over and take a rest, but could not afford this: he needed to be on time for his reading. Clutching at the wheel as though at the helm of a storm-stricken vessel, he forced his eyes wide open and began to sing, loudly, inanely, and tunelessly, his jaw clenched, lips barely moving. The hills of the Epynt rose in a green tide to his left as he negotiated an interminable bend in the battered estate car, the road descending into a valley charmingly populated by Friesian cows and through which a narrow river tumbled, its water refracting silver light. It was a bright June morning. He knew he should appreciate this bucolic scene; but he was too tired, much too tired.

Approaching his destination Owen tried to locate his favourite radio station for the one o'clock news, but the reception was awful, drowned out in loud crackling and buzzing by Radio Telford. Typical, he mused, slipping by default into a mode of thought that manifested as an unending clamour of complaint: you can't get radio reception for a Welsh station in Wales. You can't even get Radio Wales in Cardiff without Radio Bristol wading in like some colonial intruder. Or mobile coverage, for that matter, not that Owen owned a mobile. Technology was a source of limitless bewilderment to him, and his rejection of a cell phone, along with his ineptitude when faced with the practical matter of computer technology, was simultaneously a source of pride and embarrassment to him.

He had set out from his hometown of Cardiff at ten and was on schedule to begin his reading at the Newtown public library at two. He had brought sandwiches and a thermos of coffee and would find somewhere to enjoy his packed lunch – perhaps a bench in a nearby park – before turning up to his event a quarter of an hour before the advertised time. Owen was a methodical and punctual person, in spite of being a poet.

Having driven around Newtown three times without any success in identifying his venue (but unwittingly passing it twice before noticing the sign that designated it a Public Library) Owen pulled into the car park of the unexceptional red-brick building. He wasn't optimistic about a Saturday afternoon poetry reading in this curiously voided town. Who had organised the event? Not his publisher, but a London-based PR firm which had won the franchise to promote literary events for a consortium of publishers, of whom his was one. Their name, he seemed to recall, was Con Art Promo, which might have sent out warning signals, but this had evidently not deterred whoever organised such matters at his publishers, or at the Welsh Books Council, which ultimately held the purse strings. Owen wondered how much Con Art were getting paid. Considerably more than his eighty pounds plus fuel allowance, that much was certain.

Outside, the sun had retreated behind grey clouds, which threatened rain. Owen took his sandwiches from a paper bag on the passenger seat and decided to eat in his car rather than search for a bench and risk getting wet and flustered just before his reading.

Inside the library, a monasterial silence greeted him. He inspected the notice board in the hallway, expecting to see some kind of poster advertising his event, like the one he had been sent in his Tour Pack by Con Art Promo. There was nothing of the kind. Behind the counter a woman was writing in a ledger. Owen moved over to her.

Hullo, he said. I've come up from Cardiff for the reading. I am Owen Price. Even as he said his name, he felt like a fraud.

The woman peered up at him, slightly startled. She made an expectant noise in her throat, as if presaging speech, and inspected the diary that lay open on the desk in front of her.

There doesn't appear to be anything down, she said. Not any events at all for today, in fact.

Owen touched his cheek, because, inexplicably, it felt as if the wings of a bat had brushed his face. His first instinct was to flee, to return straightaway to Cardiff, but he held firm. All the same, he knew that his own credibility was struggling for survival.

He decided to adopt a chipper approach. Don't tell me, he interjected – as though she had not said what she had just said – that you know nothing about any reading.

I'm afraid I don't, said the librarian, and she smiled a nervous smile. Are they born that way? Owen wondered, or is it something in their DNA that predisposes them to that particular line of work, a sort of bookish determinism, a call of destiny; or do they grow, like Lamarck's apocryphal giraffes, into the prescribed physical form? She was aged somewhere between thirty and sixty; trim, agreeable, owlish (obviously), but somehow crushed into premature nonentity by working in an institution paradoxically bereft of any qualities relating to the soul, condemned to a daily routine of doling out and stamping polyethylene-covered editions of works by Danielle Steel and Jeffrey Archer to a readership whose lives demanded a weekly dose of something more bracing than they were ever likely to encounter in this or any other town on the Welsh Marches.

Owen felt swamped by an overwhelming and almost tactile sense of pointlessness: about his being there, his stupid choice of occupation (he dared not consider it a profession), his inane pursuit of the written word as a means of personal salvation. Not for the first time, he contemplated – in a highly abstract manner, of course – the notion of suicide, before deciding that Newtown was not nearly exotic enough a place to end things.

He handed the librarian the schedule he had been posted from Con Art Promo, and she inspected it dutifully.

I'm sorry, she said, there must have been some kind of a mix-up. We haven't been told anything about this. We do hold readings from time to time, in the Function Room, but I know nothing about this one, Mr Price. I am sorry. Sorry, she repeated, a little more quietly, as though a single enunciation were not sufficient.

Owen recalled the one phone conversation he had endured with the man from Con Art Promo, to check on details of his tour, having waited two months for an itinerary to arrive in the post (and which had eventually materialised in the wake of his phone call). The phone had been answered by a man possessing the implausibly Welsh name of Llewellyn Rhys ap Madoc, which didn't quite go with the plummy voice that reminded Owen of a seditious and gravelly magistrate he had once had the misfortune to cross in his one and only encounter with the law.

He suspected the Con Art man was a professional crook, who had seen an opening and had adopted a fallacious identity in order to get his hands on the loot. It was not an entirely improbable interpretation.

Ah well, he said, more to himself than to the librarian. I should have known.

Would you like a drink perhaps, a cup of tea? The woman asked.

No thanks, said Owen, I am weary of cups of tea.

I'm sorry?

I have an allergy, that is all.

To *tea*?

To something in it, I think.

The woman looked at him strangely, and straightened herself.

You are welcome to sit in the Function Room, to see if anyone arrives, she suggested, softening a little. Perhaps they sent a mail-out to interested individuals without informing me.

I doubt it, Owen said, but thanks anyway, I will.

He began to walk towards the room she had indicated when she spoke again.

I have a friend, she began, hesitatingly, who writes. I could give him a call, if you like. See if he is free. He met R.S. Thomas once, and several other writers of note. It would at least be company for you, after coming all this way.

That won't be necessary, said Owen. Though it is very kind of you to offer. I might sit for a while and rest. Give it half an hour in case someone turns up.

The librarian ushered him into a large room with children's paintings fixed to the walls with sticking plasters, as though they were, each one, covering an abrasion or a wound. A long window looked out onto a wet patio. The sun had given up for the day: a dense mantle of grey now stretched across the skyline from east to west, and the rain came down.

Once the librarian had left, Owen sat down in one of the chairs surrounding a large table. He took a book of his poems from his shoulder bag (he had come equipped with a dozen copies, as part of the deal with Con Art Promo was that he bring his own books to sell). He tapped rhythmically on the table-top with his fingers for a minute, then opened the slim volume at random and stared at the far wall, the one which was empty of children's paintings.

When the golem entered the room, awkwardly, as though battling an invisible tide, Owen was slumped at the table, his head resting sideways on folded hands. He stirred, it must have been the sense of another body nearby, or perhaps the shuffling of the golem's flat feet on the floorboards; he stirred and raised his head and looked uncertainly towards the figure in front of him. Its shape was amorphous, as though still in the process of being formed. The head, set upon slanting shoulders, was oval and – at least, at first – almost featureless, containing only the dim outline of eyes, a nose, and a mouth, as though a gossamer covering were stretched over the face, obscuring those features. The golem had skinny arms and legs, its grey flesh almost translucent. It was naked, but sexless. It trembled almost imperceptibly as it stood before the table. It did not speak, and Owen knew at once that it was a golem. He had read of such things, knew of their role in Jewish folklore as unformed beings made from mud or clay, brought to life by some incantation, the speaking of a secret word or name. He also knew that it had come for him, and that he was somehow responsible for its existence. Both of these realisations filled him with a dim, nebulous fear, or perhaps joy. Without moving from his chair he stared at the dumb and unmoving creature in front of him until it emerged fully into the landscape of the room, its features sharpening a degree, coming into focus. Simultaneously the golem began absorbing and then reflecting aspects of Owen's own thought, the limitless capacities of his imagination and his memory. Owen remembered – or else memory sought him out and presented him with – an image of the interior of the Aghia Sophia in Istanbul, of watching a cat wash herself in one of the wide spaces of that cathedral; he saw a rocky island at a small distance from a beach where he was standing at night, forlorn and alone, pondering whether or not to swim out to it; he saw a scarecrow in a field on an early summer's day and he wanted to lie down in the warm ploughed soil; he remembered the first time he had witnessed death, the crash of colliding machines, the splintering of glass, the stench of burning metal and rubber. And then he saw himself reflected in the golem, and he tried to remember how he must either manage this encounter or else escape it. Without thinking, he tore the opening poem from his book, folded the sheet of paper over several times until it was only a few centimetres square, and he approached the golem. He walked around the creature carefully, in a clockwise direction, before standing directly in front of it, face to face. The golem was the same height as Owen, but lacked his ease of mobility. Indeed, the golem seemed to find it hard to move at all beyond those awkward, jerky movements with which it had entered the room. Owen raised the folded piece of paper containing his poem to the level of the golem's mouth and, moving his hand slowly so as not to alarm the creature, he gently inserted the multiply-folded sheet of paper between its slightly parted, dry and chapped lips. He placed his gift carefully on the golem's small, leathery tongue. At first nothing happened, and then Owen noticed the tip of the tongue retreat inside the mouth, and the jaws begin to work, as the golem chewed slowly, methodically, on his poem. Elated, Owen returned to the table to retrieve his book, and carefully tore out a second page. The same thing happened: the golem received the folded piece of paper onto its tongue, paused for a moment as though weighing up its import or content, and then commenced its slow chewing. In this way Owen fed the golem his book, page by page, and he was fascinated by the way in which, with each offered poem, the golem would pause, as though wishing first to appreciate the flavour of the text, before beginning the process of mastication, and then swallowing, a process marked by a barely perceptible fluttering on the skin of its neck.

When the golem had eaten all of Owen's poems, it stood still for a while, and then turned slowly to its left, before beginning its strange shuffling walk towards the door. But it didn't open the door; instead it seemed simply to merge into the woodwork, to disappear back into the organic world from whence it had come.

Owen returned to his seat at the table, still holding in his left hand the cover of his book, its forlorn shell now devoid of any content. He took from his bag a bottle of water and drank thirstily. He wondered whether he should leave, and thought for a moment about the librarian at her desk, thought of her sitting there, oblivious to the appearance of the golem in this place she had called the Function Room. He wondered how she might have responded had she seen the strange, unformed creature. He wondered too about his own reaction to the encounter, how unremarkable he had found the thing, its willing subservience and malleability, how unquestioningly it had consumed the word-filled pages he had proffered it. And he wondered whether he had correctly understood the golem's passive stupidity, its inert stumbling defencelessness before the world. He had fed the golem his words, but a kind of transference had taken place as well. He himself felt oddly purified, scraped out, reconfigured.

Owen took his time driving home. He took the back roads. In one village he stopped off at a pub, spending an hour over a pint of beer and a pasty of indeterminate content. At another point, on an empty stretch near some woods, he passed a solitary church. He reversed along the road and parked outside. The church seemed ominous in the dusk. To his surprise the big handle on the outer door turned freely, and he entered. How strange that they should trust people enough, in these godless times, to leave church doors open. The air inside the church was cold and smelled of mould. He stood for a while at the entrance because there was a poem posted in the porch: he read it twice in the half-light, but could not make sense of it, even though there was nothing much to understand; a poem that drove relentlessly into the depths of the void; a joyless, and to Owen's mind, entirely pointless poem by one of his country's most famous sons, now dead, a priest who had apparently preached here on some occasion. And he wondered at the capacity of anyone to be a poet in this age, when any foul-mouthed cretin with celebrity status has his words repeated stratospherically by millions, while poets of the abyss go unheard in the darkened portal of a country church.

When he arrived home in the capital, it was past midnight and the street where his house lay was quiet. As he got out of the car he heard the febrile wailing of a Saturday night drunk somewhere nearby, followed by a smashing of glass. He closed the front door quietly, draped his coat over the banister and crept upstairs. His wife appeared to be asleep. He undressed and climbed into bed beside her, and she made a kind of chirruping sound, and turned, letting out a long sigh. He wasn't so certain now that she was asleep, but he didn't feel like speaking. The burden of irritation and burgeoning despair that he had felt on arriving at the library, the sadness and rage with which he had reacted to the poem at the church on his way home dissipated and he lay back on the pillow with his hands behind his head. When he remembered the golem he felt again the strange elation he had experienced that afternoon, the mix of joy and fear, the clarity and the possibility of a new beginning, and he did not know for certain whether he had fed the golem his poems, or whether the golem had fed him; whether the golem had read him, or he had read the golem. He lay facing the bedroom window. There were no curtains, as his wife had tired of the old ones but had not yet replaced them. A black mark in the vague shape of a spider caught his attention on the pane, and he stared at it for a very long time.

The Visit

Kate Hamer

The stone cottage slides into view through the taxi window like a painting, a memory being wheeled across frame.

There it is, the house in a sort of Gainsborough tableau; the crookedy path leading to the door and the trees outlining it with the heavy feathers of their branches. The edges fade into many shades of blackness because there's dark woods all around, leaning and dripping on the roof. Every time I come back the trees have grown a little.

'Didn't even know this was here,' says the taxi driver. He's smoked the entire journey, one arm resting on the windowsill. But somehow I hadn't summoned the energy to ask him to stop.

'Whenever I visit I always think it might have disappeared. Just like that – into the night,' I say. But the taxi driver doesn't know what I mean so I pay him and wheel my suitcase up the pocked path to where my parents have come out, alerted by the slam of the taxi door, to greet me.

'Hello, hello.' The breeze whips up their white hair exposing pink furrows of skin. Mum raises her hand to wave. Even from a distance I can see how she can't hold it up straight, how it folds into itself like a wing.

'Happy Christmas,' she calls out, waving her wing around. 'Happy Christmas Stella.'

Because today is the day before Christmas Eve and I have come from London to have the holidays with them in Wales in the house where I spent my childhood. It's awhile since I last saw them and they seem a little more bent over, their feet shuffle back and forth on the front step slightly more uncertainly. The door behind them has peels of green paint and wafts back and forth in the wind.

'Inside,' I scold, 'you'll catch your death out here.'

Inside: a cottage with the ground floor knocked into one, kitchen on one side, sitting room on the other. Stone flags. Wood burner, not yet lit. Sofa with patchwork cover thrown over it to hide the threadbare fabric.

I have a moment of vertigo. The walk down the path was one I'd taken a thousand times after being dropped off by the gate – the last stop of the school bus. Long ago: every evening coming home from school. In the winter it would be dark already, twilight. The woods tip tapping all around me. One lit window in the house shining out. The long evening would stretch out – Mum, Dad, me. I would know inside a stew will bubbling, flub, flub, and that was the sound of divorce. There'd be treachery and betrayal around the bottom of the stairs, rolling with its thin fingers stretching out, ready to poke you.

But now my Dad is merely marvelling over my suitcase on wheels, he's never seen anything like it. He holds the handle and pushes, the body of it like a hard black giant turtle, up and down on the flags, making a rumbling noise.

'Dad. It's the twentyfirst century, how is it possible you haven't seen a suitcase with wheels before?'

He looks slightly hurt. 'Don't get out enough I expect. I just don't understand why anyone didn't think of doing it before. All that lugging I used to do with my great suitcases all the way up Paddington station. Down into the tube.'

My Dad used to be an engineer. Simple, practical solutions delight him. 'No.' I unwind my scarf, decide to keep my coat on for a bit. 'It's true, why did nobody think of it before?' I realise I'm smiling for the first time since I arrived.

But he's still engrossed in the suitcase. 'I just like it is all.' He says and I realise he hasn't set eyes on me once since he's noticed it. Oh, buck your ideas up Stella, I tell myself. You're only here for three days for fuck's sake.

Dad sets a match to the firewood and newspaper already laid in the wood burner and we have tea, sitting at the kitchen table. I look down and notice the chair I'm sitting on has a burn mark down one leg.

'So no Charles?' my mother asks. She has soft brown moles on her face, flat against her skin that I don't remember.

'No. No Charles this time.'

It's nearly dark before the Tesco online shop is delivered.

'We couldn't find it,' the men in overalls apologise. Their van is parked right down by the gate and they have to carry the plastic boxes of food all the way up the path. They stand in the doorway and wipe their foreheads despite the dark evening chill that's falling all around us. When they've gone Dad takes a packet of cheese from a blue striped carrier bag and sniffs at it, as if it might not be real.

'So you bought it all in London? Before you even came here?'

'Yes, Dad. It's one of the joys of the Internet.'

I look around the tiny stone cottage. The walls must be two foot thick and I wonder if broadband could even penetrate here.

'Well I think that's absolutely marvellous,' Dad bursts out suddenly. 'Marvellous.'

I unpack the shopping, bustling round the kitchen. Cranberry sauce, a good Stilton, mounds of vegetables in plastic bags, butter, bacon, wine – lots of wine. The turkey is huge – I think I must have made a mistake when I clicked on the size – and I wonder if it will fit in their oven.

I'm to sleep in my old room and I take my case up the wooden spiral staircase in the corner. Inside the room's become jammed up with junk. The energy saving bulb hanging from the ceiling casts a strange, dim light over boxes where Dad's half finished paintings stick up like ice burgs. A green tea set is in another. The golden stars I once stuck to the wooden headboard of the bed shimmer weakly. Mum and Dad are hovering behind me. Two lumpy shadows in the narrow hallway.

'You've kept it as a sort of shrine I see,' I mutter it to myself but they can hear.

'We started to give it a clear up but it got a bit too much. We thought maybe you could give it a go while you're here. It'll be something for you to do,' my mother says. She was always big on doling out jobs.

'Thanks,' I say.

Stop it. Shut up, I tell myself. Just stop it. Everything from your mouth sounds like a wasp's angry buzzing. Just because you moved to London. Just because you think you got away.

I sleep, marooned amongst the boxes and wake up, cold, and lie in bed for half an hour worrying about them managing in this house. I think of my lovely warm flat in London. My yellow silk curtains at the gracious living room window. When I left there was a spray of broken glass on the kitchen floor. But I just left it as it was, closing the door on it.

It's Christmas Eve. I decide to cook the turkey today.

In the proper light of day I can see how dirty the floor is. I fill a bucket with hot water and find an ageing crusty scrubbing brush under the sink.

'Is this all you've got?' I brandish the scrubbing brush at Mum and she eyes it like she's never seen it before. She has a slightly rheumy look to her face and a grey curl flops down over her forehead.

'Mmm, mmm.'

'There's no need for you to do that,' Dad interrupts. He's spooning teabags out of three mugs by the sink. He's smiling and I look over and realise what he's smiling at. It's Mum, standing there with her blouse slipping off one shoulder exposing a pale, blue veined shoulder and a pink ribbon strap. He's looking at her adoringly.

'It's fine.' My voice is brisk. Grown up. Efficient. 'Let's put the cooker on first to heat up for the turkey.'

The door of the cooker won't close.

'Use the chair,' Mum says. 'Push the chair against it to keep it closed.' With a kind of dawning horror I make the connection with the burn on the chair leg. I look to Dad for help but his head's to one side with a quizzical smile on his face and looking like he might be sharing a joke with his wife.

I say nothing, wedge the oven closed with the chair and start scrubbing at the quarry tiles with steaming lemon scented water.

When the black and red tiles have been sluiced and the water in the bucket turned black I stand up. 'You should think about getting a cleaner in,' I say to Mum. 'A few hours a week in here wouldn't do any harm.'

Her eyelids lower slightly. She hasn't lost it, that look. She doesn't like this, I think, all their little ways being exposed.

I look down and see my adolescent feet on the wet floor. Naked, vulnerable. Itching to head out of the door.

While the floor is drying they both walk around like cats with stiff legs and they only seem to settle once the floor is dry and patterned with their footprints.

In the evening I make supper. A Christmas Eve feast. Smoked salmon. Expensive out of season new potatoes. A soft whipped cream cheese from France. I open a bottle of wine while I cook and Dad lights the fire. I watch him as, once he's got it going, he takes a book from a pile to the side and feeds it into the wood burner.

'Dad, what are you doing?'

He stands up stiffly. 'Free fuel. We only burn stuff we don't want. We don't have to think about getting rid of them that way.'

'Honest to God, you're like the Nazis.'

Mum appears from upstairs. 'Stella thinks we're Nazis,' he says to her.

'What? What?' She sits at the table and pours herself a thimbleful of the wine.

'Because of the books. Our free fuel.'

'Oh that.' She giggles.

A thought occurs to me. 'You would tell me if you can't afford fuel wouldn't you? I can help you know. Buy a load in of logs.'

'No, no. There's a load out there delivered last Saturday.' It's true. I remember passing them now heaped by the side of the path. So it's not that. They just like burning books.

They exclaim over the exotic food and pick at it. The turkey is finally ready and I take it out to cool. Mum switches the telly on in the corner of the living room while Dad and I have pudding – a frangipane tart and thick Jersey cream.

'Everything alright Stella?' he asks.

I nod. 'Heard from Byron?' I ask, to deflect him. Byron – my brother. The one that got away properly. First into the woods as a boy, then working for local foresters and then Australia. But that was alright, according to my mother, when I complained about how he was allowed to do what he wanted and I not, because he was a boy. I had to stay at home. I had to be good.

Dad shakes his head. Then: 'You drink too much you know,' he says sharply, his woolly persona dissipating in one swift move. I think about denying it, but what's the point? Instead I raise my glass to my lips with an exaggerated elbow movement. 'I know,' I say.

They go to bed ridiculously early, it can't even be nine o'clock yet. A wind has picked up around the house and the wood burner slowly cools. I refuse to take part in their insane book burning and the log pile seems far away in the dark. Instead I wrap myself in the patchwork throw and open another bottle of wine. Sod it; I have to do something to get me through. But each sip seems to mine more memories. When, I think, did my parents get to be best bosom friends? They're like an aged Romeo and Juliet. Must have been when my back was turned. What I remember were murderous recriminations bouncing of the walls. Vicious voices heard from in bed. Divorce, flub, flub, and steam filling the house. Well just divorce and be done with it, I used to think.

I imagine Charles at home alone in our flat. He always hated Christmas with a spiteful passion. Why do we have to have presents, why parsnips, why baubles and a tree, why on this day? Why not on any day? It's not like we believe. We're just being suckers to commercial forces.

He'll have a curry tomorrow, I think. He'll love that – curry and a beer on Christmas day. The smell of tarka dahl permeating the rooms. His two fingers up to Christmas. To me.

I think of the arc of glass breaking in a shimmering fountain across the kitchen floor. His face was a volcano, bubbling with hatred. 'The thing is Stella there's nothing. Nothing here…I should walk away from this right now. In fact I will, leave you in your little palace.'

But instead it was me that walked away. What will happen now, I wonder? We'll have to put the flat on the market. My brain races ahead and I amaze myself at how already I'm looking ahead, planning. I wonder if he's doing the same. But we'll have to try and make new lives for ourselves, somehow, in our forties. New identities.

The second bottle of wine is empty and I crawl up the stairs and into bed amongst the boxes.

When I wake it's the middle of the night. There's an icy draught flowing underneath my bedroom door. I sit up; my mouth is dry and my heart pounding from all the wine. I seem more hemmed in by the boxes than ever before.

I wrap my dressing gown around me and come down the stairs. The front door is wide open to the night. Moonlight floods in through the front door. Blue and cold, illuminating the night air with a magic lantern feel. Outside my parents are standing on the path holding hands and looking up at the moon.

'What are you doing?' I whine. 'It's the middle of the night.'

I take a few steps towards them and look down at my feet. They're cold. Bare and child-like on the stone tiles. 'Come inside. You're making the house freezing.'

My Mum and Dad look back. The moon seems to make their faces bulge, giving them youthful contours again. 'Come and look. Come and look at the moon Stella,' they call.

I hesitate. 'But it's cold out there.'

'Oh come on. It's lovely. Come and look with us,' Dad says and I hear Mum laugh at all the beautiful recklessness of it.

'But…' My words fizzle and die.

I follow them out into the night to join them in the moonlight.

Long Haul Road

Robert Minhinnick

1.

Bowels of the fire.
Bonegrey driftwood.
Dead of night.

2.

She found she was singing to herself.
Two, two, the lilywhite boys,
Clothed all in green -o -o.
Then her brother came up, pointing at something, and she stopped.

Someone had put the plank back across the water. They examined the footprints in the mud, crossed, and decided to leave the bridge as it was. Neither had energy to conceal it.

It was humid here and birds were loud in the reeds. There was a flash of white and Ffrez thought 'egret'. They were nesting now but she couldn't be sure. The two walkers came around the last bend before the current left the saltmarshes and began its slide into the sea. A poor ending, Ffrez had always thought, even in past times when the river was high with meltwater. A shamefaced farewell.

She supposed the rains were heavier now, but this was a dry summer. Last month they had waded naked through the undergrowth, the flow up to her neck, she with her stiff hair tucked into a baseball cap, her brother shorn, hacked by himself.

She'd felt the chemical mud between her toes, the metal piping buried decades. But Ffrez had always loved this part of the coast. There'd been talk of abandonment but she couldn't visualise that. There were too many people, with too much to lose. Despite what had already been lost.

Yes…Bogart. She'd been thinking about him. And she'd smiled to herself. Bogie in *The African Queen*. Didn't he pull the boat upriver? Up? Yes, against the current. Leeches and all sorts on his scrawny frame when he climbed back over the side. And that river no wider than their river. Bogie's river was an idea hatched in the film studio, that swamp of fevers and dreams. Their river was a green patch she'd seen on the old Google Earth, strange tropical explosion between The Works and the beach, the Knuckle Yard and the sea. Their river was loud with creatures she couldn't recognise yet, not to mention the crickets in the dunes, the beach frenzy of sandhoppers. There seemed a mist of them in the failing light. A living veil.

And Bogart won the Oscar. Didn't he? Of course. But only because Jack Cardiff made him look good. It was Cardiff who filmed the makebelieve river, ensuring the audiences felt the slime of an impossible Congo.

Ffrez could still taste the sulphur in the water, see the petrol rainbow over her breasts when she had emerged on the bank. Now she scanned around for her brother, who was gazing east and brandishing that stick at the gritty beach.

Jellies, said Cai.

Yeah, well…she muttered, not bothering to look.

Like breasts, he said. Might be hundreds. There's more all the time. And is that their brains you can see? Or their hearts? Do they have brains? I thought you'd know. They're just….like huge breasts…

Only moobs, said the girl. Spare me.

The sun was setting and the sea was red. The rock pools might have been filled with iron although she knew it was coralweed. Walking east the pair were at the edge of the dunes. At times they found themselves on what appeared a smashed roadway under drifted sand. Maybe twenty miles behind was the Meridian tower. Occasionally there might have been a light at its top. Some evenings it was there. Others not. Apart from that, the bay was unlit. They were growing used to that emptiness.

Anyway, said Cai, I heard you last night. Talking in your sleep. *Peg, Peg* you were saying. Is that who I think it is?

They came to an enormous treetrunk. Ffrez reached out and touched a white limb.

This wasn't here last time we passed, she said, and noted it would take another storm to remove it. Its wood was bleached to ivory and stripped of bark.

Typical, said Cai. There's enough driftwood around in the debris. We'll build it here. This tree gives shelter. Sort of.

Both looked down the beach. There were no fires visible.

You do it, said Ffrez. I'm rough.

Again? Let's see you. He cupped her brow. Come on, sit.

S'okay…

Yes, you're wet, he said. And warm as a brandy glass. That's a quote. Who?

Don't care.

You'll be burning up again…

And you want a fire?

Of course. Smoke's the first deterrent.

And fire's the best giveaway we're here, she said.

Can't be helped.

It's just…unfair, she said, sitting down amongst the saltwort. All that talk about sterile mozzies and I get…

Loads of people have malaria. It's historic. The old man's grandfather came home from the war. One of those wars back then and he had malaria. All those blokes from pisspoor unpronounceable places but with a foreign disease. Used to get delirious regularly. Talked about all kinds of stuff, the legend was. According to the old man…If you can believe that.

Like me, I suppose.

You have your moments…

Do I go on about sex?

Pardon?

You heard.

Not especially. But wouldn't we all? Every ten seconds isn't it? But it's hard to tell what obsesses you. In those fevers. Those dreams… That's how you describe things, isn't it? Last time it was turnstones…

Christ.

Yeah. Let me quote, *da da da*…No, listen, I wrote it down. On this scrap. Thought it might be important. You being this autistic genius and all…Sorry, artistic genius. Okay, here it comes… *seven, eleven, nineteen, one hundred and thirteen, two hundred and three, one thousand seven hundred and ninety one turnstones up off the Gwter Gryn. Over the living limestone. Fossils that fly and…*

Stop!

And ferns that feel. Something like that. Nothing about who you want to fuck…

As long as it's not my brother, said Ffrez. Christ. Delirium, eh? Betrays your innermost…Boy, I'd love to hear what goes through your mind. Or what doesn't. Yes, bit rough now…

We'll all have to get used to that, said Cai. I'll catch it, no danger. So fire's good…

But…

Yes, you're shivering. Pull the coat round. And have a swig of this.

Ffrez accepted the flask. Thank God, she whispered, for the old man's stash.

Cai broke up some of the spills and splinters and made tinder. Then he pulled together a mound of driftwood and weed.

No wind for once, he said. Bet I can do this with one match…

Bet you can't. What happens when there's no matches? And Krazy Kremlin, isn't it? No thanks. This could unblock a drain. Why didn't he buy decent stuff?

It's all he could find at the end. We've had the rest. The good malbec, that Rioja? Gone.

You didn't stint.
Not that type of people, are we?
Boy, said Ffrez, we better learn.

3.

They were making camp on the edge of the Haul Road. The latest storm had sliced through the dune so that above the treetrunk loomed a twenty foot high sand wall. This was a regular feature of the new weather. Storms made changes to the dunes but the sand was usually returned by the wind. Occasionally the beach had been reduced to a plain of blue clay. Yet the sand never vanished. In the past it had inundated the area and hidden its features. But both were children of the dunes and understood sand's deviousness. Its dangers.

And before the delirium takes over, she said, I'll say it. Not fair. Is it? No, it's not fair. All that research on Peg.

Oh yeah, Peg. That Peg Entwistle?

Yes. She was the first, I was going to say. Burton and all the rest? Hopkins, Sheen? Then the telly people later on. Okay, most of them forgotten now. Like, who could care? Chancers. But Peg was the first... Peg clinched it for me...

And that letter she wrote? You say it apologised?

For being a coward. At 23? For being a woman, more like. In that prehistoric world.

And they found her..?

Under the Hollywoodland sign. The letter 'H' to be exact. Where a workman had propped a ladder. It was going to be the overwhelming image for my research. Her letter beginning everything. And here's me with...

You'll write it. Carry it in your head. Just stay alive. Keep thinking. And don't go mad.

Except...
What?
Nothing.
No, except what?
Who's going to publish? Now?

4.

Ffrez scooped hollows for her shoulder, her hip. In the first firelight the sand was violet. Both now looked across the bay. Once it had been a cave of lights. This evening nothing was lit.

No, I'll just lie here tonight rambling on about turnstones. Regurgitating my hopeless lusts... That's a male stat, by the way. It's different for women.

But how d'you know it's different for men?

Jesus. You know Peg worked with Bogart? Well, she did. I wonder how impossible a bastard he really was. Scrawny little...But yeah, she called herself a coward. Incredible.

Burning well, isn't it?

Okay, one lucky match.

But think of a world before fire, said Cai. I'm trying and I can't. Just can't. What came first, fire or stories?

Stories, certain to be.

Not so sure. Art is play. You only play when there's some form of comfort...You told me that.

Ffresni scowled. No, fire came first, she said. And this fire's the clearest signal we can give. Come and get me, I'm...

We're in an inlet here, said Cai. With a very narrow entrance. It's perfect. That's why the tree's stuck fast.

The girl rolled into the firelight. Even when I wake up, she said, it'll be a bad dream. That's right, you have malaria for life, people say. The mozzies have been ahead of us all this time...

Maybe you should have been a scientist then. Instead of bothering about all this film star rubbish...

It's about women, you oaf.

But you can't do it all. Writing, maths, it's..

Somebody has to. Not you, obviously...

I'm trying to stay practical. One match, remember. And making fire's a beautiful skill...There's nothing like fire.

Never seen you rub two sticks together.

Not yet. Anyway, what about that jelly on the way over.

The big one? Yes, and the others. But only moons...

Biggest I've ever seen, said Cai. No wonder people don't go in the water now.

Moons are almost harmless.

But what if you're swimming at night? And you meet up? That one was huge...

Who goes in at night? We got to adapt behaviour... Okay, they're bigger now. And there's more of them. But we've got other problems...

Ain't that the truth, said Cai into the bowl of the bay.

5.

He'd begun to patrol further from the fire, wearing a pair of steelies, the leather worn off the metal. There was a huge amount of driftwood lodged amongst the pebbles of the moraine and marine litter. Cai returned and placed a piece of pallet over the blaze, then dropped a bagful of sticks and nubbins into the flames. His fingernails were broken, fingers scorched by constant firelighting. Cai's right wrist was scarred where a spell had entered and he had botched the job of removing it himself. Both he and Ffrez were tattooed on the inside of this wrist to show they belonged to the local sect.

6.

Ffresni was waking up. Her brother cupped his palm on her brow once again.

How are you?

Ffiw...

Easy now.

Did I...ramble? Like before?

No. Yes. Different. Look, there's no need to apologise for what's in your mind. But boy, you're a dirty sod...

No, really...

Just stuff.

About what?

Not sure. Weirdness. Made no sense to me.

Did you write it down?

Christ no. Better things to do than try and catch your ravings. But you're okay?

Just coming to. Strange dream. About that man.

Man?

Bloke on the beach. Who called you Ethiopian. He called us both that.

What?

Ethiopian.

What does that mean, really?

He meant we were dark-skinned.

Well we are. Out in the sun all day.

But you're really dark, said Ffrez.

That's woodsmoke. That's fire. All these fires I light. Blowing into the ashes...Coaxing the embers. My face down in the ash. Hey, that's a bit like sex too. Isn't it? Sweet talking the fire. Aw, come on honey. Keep on going...So don't tell me there's no skill in that. Hey, I'm the great seducer! Keeping you alive. Just like keeping the fire alive... And all this wood I have to find while you're dreaming about Peg bloody Entwistle...

We're tripping over it...

Burning clean, though, isn't it? I love the green flames. That's the iodine in the dead man's ropes...

Imagine what Peg knew, though. And she never understood how it might be different. Thought men would be that way forever.

Can't blame men for everything...

Oh no? Oh yes.

It's different now, said Cai.

Yes, look what men have done with all that power...Given me malaria for the rest of my life. It's in my blood. Forever.

No. It's curable.

The new strains? Don't bet on it. Mozzies are just adapting to new conditions, but better than us...And they'll always be ahead. They're clever like that...

Thought they were going to engineer the genes, said Cai. Pipedream. Always was.

7.

Bowels of the fire.
Bonegrey driftwood.
Dead of night.

8.

She lay back in the bivouac, touched the white tree, its rind of salt under her nail. *One is one and all alone…*Ffrez knew the wall above her was recent. She understood too much about sand dunes to be happy about their camp. But couldn't have slept too long, she reasoned. There was Arcturus, passing into the north. When the fire was built it was immediately overhead, the only star visible. Now, it was a bonfire itself, gemstone in the woodash. That brazier she loved.

Ffrez shut her eyes then stared again at the sky. Her mouth tasted vile, the old chemical giveaway after all these years. No, they'd never rid themselves of it. Never. It's what had made everything. Built the world before their life. Built The Works, now a ruined city. So many were hiding out there. Five miles long, that warren. Not a place to enter, although she and her brother had penetrated a little way. Came to what she imagined was a quenching tower. There was evidence of settlement so they turned tail. Yes, The Works was unavoidable. Because…

It was as if she'd been drinking riverwater. As if some fool had held one of their bottles to the trickle where the river finally joined the sea. Then encouraged her to sip…

9.

She was staring at the stars. But started up. Christ, that cretin Cai had let her sleep for over twenty-four hours. No wonder there was so much ash. And he'd run out of water and used the obvious source.

She staggered to her feet and looked around. Silence. Ffrez estimated the sea was fifty yards away, and strained to think where it had been when she lay down. And cursed herself for inattention.

Be the death of us, she thought. Death of us. The book of tides was their bible.

Further down the beach someone might have been moving over the pebbles. But no shape. No shape and no shadow.

Her knife was already in her hand. You never knew, these days. You never knew. Too many feral children out of their heads, children of the salt and the sand, building heir own lore around the campfires.

Years ago they were all over the beach, driving buggies. The old man had told them. It had become normal. But that was when there was petrol. That other world. That easier world. And before the abandonments. In those days there'd been a beachmaster, trying to control the kids who poured out of the estates. A semblance of order.

10.

Mouth dry as saltwort. Her throat saltwort thorns. Yes, The Works. There were reports of men in orange uniforms patrolling the perimeters. She and Cai had thought the interior abandoned. But this had been naïve. The Works was a labyrinth that might conceal armies.

She strained to hear what the night revealed. The sea's pulse. A wave breaking. Ffrez had never been afraid of silence, its richness that nourished her study at the farm. Ten of them lived together, although maybe one of the boys was missing. And that study was made possible by the old man's chaotic library, its moldering shelves propped up in the barn, tractor oil and wrapped apples ripe in the air, sacks of jerusalems too far gone.

She loved that barn and slipped down at any hour to breathe its aroma, to rest her shoulders against the tractor wheel. Some of the tins of Super Universal were still unopened but the tractor hadn't moved in thirty years. There was a wren's nest woven into the front grille, hidden by dried grass.

The tractor wheel was solid. It comforted. So did the mud still attached, the grass seeds she chewed as she read or worked on her computer, plugged into one of the mini generators.

She was learning to look. No, to see. Those spiderwebs draping the tractor cab? The henbane on the track to the farm? They all walked past the flower every day. But never noticed it. The sulphuric petals had appeared out of the yard. Henbane was the colour of a corpse and an unhealthy corpse at that. She examined it but didn't dare crouch too close. Its fume was powerful. Neither had she told the boys how it could be an ingredient in beer-making. That might be a dream from which no-one awoke. She'd also imagined heating henbane seeds on a hot stone. Again, maybe not. But all those thoughts of cutting herself were gone. She was important now. Because they needed her mind.

11.

Yes, someone was there. Someone clumsy on the stones. Sounded like Cai. The greyest of light was leaking out of the south as she followed her brother's approach.

All right? he asked. I can see you're up.

You make enough noise.

Sorry, rushing.

Why?

How are you?

Rushing why?

He switched on his flashlight. Look at this, he urged, holding out a piece of plastic.

What is it?

Another drone, this one shaped like an insect.

It's a dragonfly, Ffrez corrected. The camera must be in one of the eyes. Or both. You know, I used to think they come from the Meridian. Got sent from the roof. Twenty-eighth floor, someone said. You used to be able to see all that tracking equipment that was installed, high up.

This is new, said Cai.

The old man said there was a restaurant there. On the top. Then the docks around it were abandoned, but he never believed in that story.

More than suspicious, he said.

Told me it was replaced by the radio station, said Cai. Then…

We should be thinking about how but also about why. It's important.

Oh, I have been.

That makes three we've found, said Ffrez. Nice design, too. Yeah, a black dragonfly. But hand-launched, no question. Like something you'd expect to see coming out of the saltmarshes. I think the green ones there are real. But these days, it's hard to know…

About the Authors

Stevie Davies, who comes from Morriston, Swansea, is a novelist, literary critic, biographer and historian. She is a Fellow of the Royal Society of Literature, a Fellow of the Academi Gymreig and Professor of Creative Writing at the University of Wales, Swansea. Her latest novel is *Awakening*.

Dic Edwards is an internationally acclaimed playwright with more than 20 productions to his name, including *Franco's Bastard, Utah Blue and Wittgenstein's Daughter*. His last production was of *Casanova Undone*, in Copenhagen in 2009. In September 2011, *Manifest Destiny*, for which he wrote the libretto, was produced by Opera Close Up at the King's Head in London on the tenth anniversary of 9/11. He is also the author of the poetry collection, *Walt Whitman*, while in recent years his short stories have regularly appeared in literary magazines. His latest play is entitled *Let's Kill All The Lawyers*. He is Director and founder of Creative Writing at Lampeter, Trinity St David, University of Wales.

Rhian Edwards is a multi-award winning poet and musician. Her first collection of poems *Clueless Dogs* (Seren) won Wales Book of the Year 2013, the Roland Mathias Prize for Poetry 2013 and Wales Book of the Year People's Choice 2013. It was also shortlisted for the Forward Prize for Best First Collection 2012. She is also the current winner of the John Tripp Award for Spoken poetry.

Rhian Elizabeth was born in the Rhondda Valley in 1988. Her debut novel, *Six Pounds Eight Ounces*, is published by Seren Books (April 2014). She will write some more.

Jon Gower is a writer and broadcaster who has seventeen books to his name: these include the novel *Y Storïwr*, which won the Wales Book of the Year in 2012, the coastal journey *Wales: At Water's Edge*, which was shortlisted for the 2013 prize and *The Story of Wales*, which accompanies the landmark BBC television series. He has also written travel books such as *An Island Called Smith* – as well as collections of short stories in both Welsh and English. He is a former BBC Wales arts and media correspondent, was an inaugural Hay Festival International Fellow, and is a Fellow of the Welsh Academy. Forthcoming books include a Welsh language novel about Central American migrants and an account of the Welsh overseas adventure in Patagonia.

Richard Gwyn was born and grew up in south Wales. In 1993 he began a study of illness, language and the body, an interest which he pursued professionally until 2003, resulting in the publication of two books, *Communicating Health and Illness* (Sage, 2002) and *Discourse, the Body, and Identity* (Palgrave Macmillan, 2003). He teaches at Cardiff University, where he is Director of the MA in Creative Writing. Richard Gwyn's poetry includes *One Night in Icarus Street, Stone dog, flower red/Gos de pedra flor vermella* (both 1995), *Walking on Bones* (2000) and *Being in Water* (2001). He is also the editor of an anthology of new poetry from Wales titled *The Pterodactyl's Wing: Welsh World Poetry*, launched at the Hay Festival in 2003. He is a regular columnist for *Poetry Wales*, reviews books for *The Independent* and has discussed his work on TV and radio. His first novel, *The Colour of a Dog Running Away* (2005), set in the Gothic quarter of Barcelona, is published by Parthian in the UK, Doubleday in the USA, and has been translated into many languages. His second novel, *Deep Hanging Out* (2007) is published by Snowbooks. His most recent books are *Sad Giraffe Café* (2010), a collection of prose poems, and *The Vagabond's Breakfast* (2011) a memoir.

Kate Hamer grew up in Pembrokeshire and after studying Art worked in TV for over ten years, mainly on documentaries. She studied for an MA in creative writing at Aberystwyth University. Her debut novel *THE GIRL IN THE RED COAT* is to be published by Faber & Faber in March 2015 and has sold in 5 other territories. Kate also won the Rhys Davies short story prize in 2011 and the story 'One Summer' was broadcast on Radio 4. She has two children and lives in Cardiff with her husband.

Carly Holmes was born on the Channel Island of Jersey and lives on the west coast of Wales. She's worked as a waitress, events organiser, bar maid, cleaner, admin assistant (where she crashed the entire office computer system), tenancy support worker and manager of a family centre. She has a BA, an MA and a PhD. Carly manages and hosts The Cellar Bards, is on the editorial board for *The Lampeter Review* and is the secretary for the PENfro Book Festival Committee.Her debut novel, *The Scrapbook* is available now.

Cynan Jones was born in 1975 near Aberaeron, Wales where he now lives and works. His work includes the novels *The Long Dry* (Parthian, 2006), *Everything I Found on the Beach* (Parthian, 2011), and *Bird, Blood, Snow* (Seren, 2012). Further work has appeared in *Granta Magazine*, *New Welsh Review* and various anthologies. His latest novel, *The Dig*, is published by Granta. He is currently at work on another book.

Lloyd Jones (born 1951) is a contemporary novelist from Wales. Born at Bryn Clochydd, Gwytherin, near Llanrwst, he lives at Llanfairfechan and has formerly worked on a farm and as a newspaper editor, a lecturer and a mencap nurse. He has so far published two novels, both through Welsh publishing house Seren. *Mr Vogel* (2004), winner of the McKitterick Prize, was based partly upon Jones' walking completely around Wales, a 1000-mile journey (he is the first Welsh person to do so). His second book, *Mr Cassini* (2006), was partially inspired by his walking across Wales in seven different directions; it won the Wales Book of the Year award 2007. His third book, *My First Colouring Book*, a collection of short stories and essays, was published in October 2008. He published a novel in Welsh, *Y Dŵr*, with Y Lolfa in June 2009.

Tyler Keevil grew up in Vancouver, Canada, and moved to Wales in 2003. His short fiction has appeared in a wide range of magazine and anthologies in Canada, Britain, and America. He has twice been nominated for the Wales Book of the Year, and recently received the

Book of the Year People's Prize for his novel, *The Drive*. In May, Parthian released his first collection of short fiction, Burrard Inlet, which includes the story, 'Sealskin,' a nominee for the 2014 Journey Prize in Canada. Among other things, Tyler has worked as a tree planter, labourer, and ice barge deckhand; he now lectures in Creative Writing at the University of Gloucestershire.

Dean Lewis spent the early '80s designing and airbrushing T-shirts and organising American hardcore gigs in Newport (including bands like Husker Du and Butthole Surfers) before returning to full time education and completing a BA animation degree at University of Wales College Newport.

For the last 12 years he has worked in Pupil Referral Units in south-east Wales working with pupils excluded from mainstream education due to behavioural problems and special education needs. Apart from behavioural management his focus has been delivering qualifications in ICT and Art and Design. While working in education he was also design editor for *The Raconteur*, a quarterly literary magazine. This role included creating all illustrations for the magazine, image sourcing and typesetting. He also designed the book cover and created illustrations for The Raconteur America book published by Parthian.

In 2013, with Somerset based printer, Jean Stevens, he set up #DrawingAugust on Twitter. This was a challenge for artists (professional & amateur) to produce a drawing every day throughout the month. This was such a success at producing an online artistic community that it was repeated in 2014 with even more participants.

Robert Minhinnick has twice been awarded the Forward Prize for Best Individual Poem and twice won the Wales Book of the Year for his collections of essays. His novel *Sea Holly* was shortlisted for the Ondaatje Prize. An environmental campaigner, he works for the charity, Sustainable Wales and is co-founder of Friends of the Earth Cymru.

Rhys Milsom lives in Roath, Cardiff, with his girlfriend and two cats. He grew up in the Rhondda Valley and has a BA in Creative and

Professional Writing from the University of Glamorgan (now known as the University of South Wales) and an MA in Creative Writing from the University of Wales: Trinity Saint David. He is the editor of www.wicid.tv – a website for young people aged 11-25 in Rhondda Cynon Taff, which showcases creative writing, poetry, photography, films, reviews and events. The website is also specifically designed for young people to make their first steps into the creative industries. His fiction and poetry has been widely published in magazines, anthologies and websites.

João Morais was 2013 winner of the Terry Hetherington Award for writers under thirty. His poem 'Oedipus Rex' was shortlisted for the Percy French Prize for Comic Poetry.

Thomas Morris is from Caerphilly. His debut story collection, *We Don't Know What We're Doing*, will be published by Faber and Faber in July 2015. He edited *Dubliners 100: 15 New Stories Inspired By The Original* (Tramp Press) and is editor of *The Stinging Fly*. He lives in Dublin.

Gary Raymond is the Editor of *Wales Arts Review*, and has had published a diverse range of fiction, arts and literary criticism, travelogue and journalism. As well as a regular voice in *Wales Arts Review*, Gary has written for publications such as *The Guardian*, *Rolling Stone Magazine* and the *Western Mail*, and is a regular contributor to local and national BBC radio on the subject of arts and culture. In 2013 Gary was the only western writer to follow National Theatre Wales' exploits in Japan as they collaborated for the first time with the New National Theatre Tokyo. In 2013, Gary published *J.R.R. Tolkien: A Visual Biography of Fantasy's Most Revered Writer* with Ivy Press. Gary is also the Welsh theatre critic for *The Arts Desk*, based in London. Gary's novel, *For Those Who Come After*, will be published by Parthian Books in 2015. Gary is also a lecturer in English and Creative Writing at the University of South Wales, as well as a mentor in critical writing on the Wales Arts Review Young Writers' Mentoring Scheme.

Richard Redman was born in Newport and trained as an actor at LAMDA. His work as a playwright has been staged at the Finborough Theatre and Riverside Studios In London. He has lectured at the University of Dubuque, Ohio University and the University of South Wales. His short stories have been published in the *New Welsh Review* and *Sparks*, an anthology from the MA in Creative Writing programme at Bath Spa University, of which he is a graduate.

Linda Ruhemann was brought up in the north and midlands (of England) and studied at Manchester University before moving to London. She now teaches English and Creative Writing at the University of South Wales. Her short stories have been broadcast on the BBC, and she was double runner-up in the Rhys Davies Short Story Prize in 2011-12. Having lived and worked in Wales for eighteen years, and having a grandfather who claimed descent from Owain Glyndŵr, on a somewhat uncertain basis, she dares to count herself as a Welsh writer.

Francesca Rhydderch's début novel, *The Rice Paper Diaries* won the Wales Book of the Year Award for Fiction, 2014. Her short stories have appeared in magazines and anthologies, and have been broadcast on Radio 4 and Radio Wales. She is currently working on a collection of short fiction.

Rachel Trezise was born in the Rhondda Valley, south Wales in 1978. She studied Journalism and English at Glamorgan University and Geography and History at Limerick University, simultaneously writing her first novel. That work, *In and Out of the Goldfish Bowl*, was published in 2001, attracting much critical acclaim and winning a place on the Orange Futures List. The book is studied in most Welsh Universities and is on the British Literature reading list at the University of Montreal. In 2003 *Harpers & Queens* magazine described her as 'the new face of (British) literature'. Her second book, a short story collection called *Fresh Apples* was published in 2005 and won the inaugural Dylan Thomas Prize in 2006. Trezise was writer of residence at the University of Texas in spring 2007. *Dial M for Merthyr*, her third book, was published in 2007 and won the inaugural Max Boyce Prize in 2010. Her first radio play *Lemon Meringue Pie* was broadcast on BBC Radio 4 in September 2008. Her most recent novel *Sixteen Shades of Crazy* was published in April 2010. Her work has been translated into several languages and has been published in Australia and New Zealand, Denmark, Ethiopia and Italy. She is married and still lives in Wales. Her second short story collection, *Cosmic Latte*, was published in May 2013, while her National Theatre Wales play *Tonypandemonium* was released in October of the same year.

Georgia Carys Williams was born in Swansea. She won third prize at the Terry Hetherington Award 2012, highly commended for The South Wales Short Story Competition 2012, was short-listed for the Swansea Life Young Writing Category of the Dylan Thomas Prize, 2008 and for the Wells Festival of Literature 2009. While working on a PhD in Creative Writing at Swansea University, she writes for *Wales Arts Review* and was commissioned by the Rhys Davies Trust to contribute to WAR's fictional map of Wales series. Most recently, she was shortlisted for *New Welsh Review*'s Flash in the Pen competition, published in Parthian's *Rarebit Anthology*. Her debut short story collection, *Second-Hand Rain*, was published by Parthian Books in October 2014.

Other titles available from The H'mm Foundation

R.S. Thomas – poet, priest, nationalist – came to dominate the Welsh literary scene in the second half of the twentieth and was nominated for the Nobel Prize for Literature.

Published on the centenary of his birth, these essays show the many ways in which both the man and the poetry inspired affection and admiration in others.

With contributions from:
Gillian Clarke
Fflur Dafydd
Grahame Davies
Gwyneth Lewis
Peter Finch
Jon Gower
Menna Elfyn
Osi Rhys Osmond
Jeff Towns
M. Wynn Thomas
Alex Salmond
Archbishop of Wales Barry Morgan

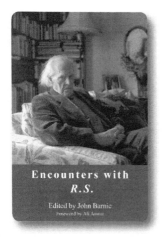

Encounters with R.S. | £9.99
978-0-9927560-0-0
Edited by John Barnie

Other titles available from The H'mm Foundation

To commemorate the centenary of another major Welsh poet and writer – and another Thomas – 2014 sees the publication of *Encounters with Dylan*, which features essays by academics and aficionados, poets and performers who have variously delighted in and engaged with the work of the self-styled 'Rimbaud of Cwmdonkin Drive'.

With contributions from:
Gary Raymond
D.J. Britton
Guy Masterson
George Tremlett
Steve Groves
Sarah King
Dai George
Sarah Gridley
Horatio Clare
Rachel Trezise
Jeff Towns
Michael Bogdanov
Kaite O'Reilly
Dafydd Elis-Thomas

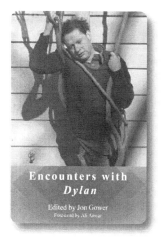

Encounters with Dylan | £9.99
978-0-9927560-2-4
Edited by Jon Gower

Other titles available from The H'mm Foundation

Nigel Jenkins – poet, encyclopaedist, campaigner, performer, gifted teacher and superb prose stylist – was a man of Gower, of Swansea and – in the deepest sense possible – of Wales.

Published in the year of his untimely and all too premature passing, *Encounters with Nigel* gathers tributes, critical essays and poems by fellow poets, prose practitioners and former students. Together they explore many sides of a fascinating man, who had an uncommon generosity of spirit not to mention the best reading voice this side of the Urals.

With contributions from:
Fflur Dafydd
John Barnie
M. Wynn Thomas
Mike Parker
Stevie Davies
Daniel G. Williams
Iwan Bala
D.J. Britton
Robert Minhinnick
Jane Fraser
Humberto Gatica

Encounters with Nigel | £9.99
978-0-9927560-4-8
Edited by Jon Gower

PARTHIAN

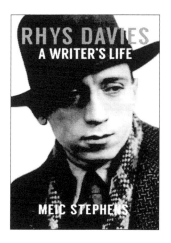

"[Meic] has done more than justice...to the black humour of Davies' writing and that of his life. This is a delightful book, which is itself a social history in its own right, and funny."
The Spectator

"In writing this informative, intriguing biography, Meic Stephens has done the reading public a great service."
Wales Arts Review

The first full biography of the important Welsh writer and a milestone in Welsh biographical writing.

Protecting his privacy and fearing intrusion into his inner life, such a man presents challenges for the biographer which Meic Stephens accepts with alacrity. Drawing on hitherto unavailable sources, including many conversations with the writer's brother, he describes the early years of the Blaenclydach grocer's son, his bohemian years in Fitzrovia and visit to the Lawrences in the south of France, his love-hate relationship with the Rhondda, and above all, the dissembling that went into *Print of a Hare's Foot* (1969), 'an autobiographical beginning', which he shows to be a most unreliable book from start to finish...

BIOGRAPHY

www.parthianbooks.com

Coming soon in 2015

Encounters with Osi
Edited by Iwan Bala and Hilary Osmond

Osi Rhys Osmond is one of the finest Welsh painters of his generation. He has been fascinated with colour throughout his life. 'Colour is the basis of my craft – I talk through colour, I speak through colour, I use colour to express myself and convey my ideas', he told the *Western Mail* in 2009.

Encounters with Osi will feature essays by members of his family, Ex-students, Fellow students, academics, poets and performers who engaged with his work. Among the contributors; Che, Luke and Sara Rhys Osmond, Sian Lewis, Karl Francis, Mererid Hopwood, Ben Dressel, Lynne Crompton, Menna Elfyn, M. Wynn Thomas, Bella Kerr, Ann Oosthuizen, Ivor Davies and Simon Thrisk.

It is as if...
Edited by Iwan Bala

It is as if... will feature essays by Dr Anne Price Owen, Osi Rhys Osmond and Iwan Bala. You will see colour images of Bala's drawings for PROsiect hAIcw, made in collaboration with musician Angharad Jenkins, celebrating the poetry of her late father, Nigel Jenkins. Other works featured will use text and poetry by Iwan Bala using text and poetry he has incorporated over the last three years. The book will include a CD/DVD of music and recitations of poetry with a film of the performance.

Iwan Bala is a senior Lecturer at the School of Creative Arts and Humanities at the University of Wales, Trinity Saint David, Carmarthen. He is an award-winning Welsh artist, creates his art-work using memorised and imagined maps and landscapes, commenting on Welsh culture.